M000208053

LEGALIZING LGBT FAMILIES

Legalizing LGBT Families

How the Law Shapes Parenthood

Amanda K. Baumle and D'Lane R. Compton

NEW YORK UNIVERSITY PRESS

New York and London

NEW YORK UNIVERSITY PRESS
New York and London
www.nyupress.org

First published in paperback in 2018

© 2015 by New York University
All rights reserved

References to Internet websites (URLs) were accurate at the time of writing. Neither the author nor New York University Press is responsible for URLs that may have expired or changed since the manuscript was prepared.

Library of Congress Cataloging-in-Publication Data
Baumle, Amanda K.
Legalizing LGBT families : how the law shapes parenthood / Amanda K. Baumle and D'Lane R. Compton.
pages cm   Includes bibliographical references and index.
ISBN 978-1-4798-5764-7 (cloth : alk. paper)
1. Same-sex marriage—United States. 2. Same-sex marriage—Law and legislation—United States. 3. Children of gay parents—United States. 4. Gay parents—United States. 5. Sexual minorities' families—United States. I. Compton, D'Lane R. (D'Lane Rebecca), 1977– II. Title.
HQ1034.U5B38   2015
306.84'80973—dc23   2015024531

New York University Press books are printed on acid-free paper, and their binding materials are chosen for strength and durability. We strive to use environmentally responsible suppliers and materials to the greatest extent possible in publishing our books.

Manufactured in the United States of America

10 9 8 7 6 5 4 3 2 1

Also available as an ebook

For our children

CONTENTS

PREFACE

We began work on this project in 2010, when only four states and Washington, DC, had legalized same-sex marriage. Florida's ban on gay adoption was still good law, and the media was rife with stories about lesbian, gay, bisexual, and transgender (LGBT) parents being denied recognition of their parental rights. As we complete the writing of our manuscript, overt bans on gay adoption in the United States are absent, same-sex marriages are legal in thirty-seven states and Washington, DC, and we stand on the precipice of a Supreme Court decision on the constitutionality of denying marriage to same-sex couples.

Children in LGBT families have been at the center of much of these debates over marriage. Opponents of same-sex marriage have argued that the marriage institution is supported by the state because it is the optimal environment for raising children, and contend that the same could not be expected to hold for a same-sex household. Proponents have emphasized that children are already being raised in same-sex households and that denying their families access to the rights and privileges of marriage results in harm to these children.

The crux of the recent LGBT movement, then, has been focused on family and, in particular, on children. This emphasis on the stories of children has been an effective framing for a public discussion about the law's role in generating equal opportunity and outcomes for LGBT individuals and their families. In turn, there has been increased recognition of the ways in which the law has a very strong presence in family life in general, raising questions as to what its role is or should be with respect to generating identities and rights related to the family.

Our hope is that the stories and analyses presented in this book will add to the overall public discourse about the meaning of the law with respect to families, and how we as individuals are active participants in generating the laws to which we are subject. Our findings support the notion that legal context affects the available options for LGBT parents and shapes their responses to the law. We also observe the manner in which individuals reinforce heteronormativity within the law, or engage in processes to manipulate, work around, resist, or defy the presence of the law in their family lives. These activities make apparent the ways in which the construction of legality is an interactive process, and one in which the characteristics of individuals and the environments in which they are nested play an important role.

ACKNOWLEDGMENTS

We are indebted to many individuals, organizations, and institutions for their contributions toward the completion of this project. Most notably, we would like to thank the 137 men and women who agreed to participate in our study. This book could not have been written without their willingness to share the very personal stories about their families and their experiences with the law, including all of the joy, humor, frustration, and anger that were a part of navigating the legal landscape with their families.

We would like to recognize the research assistants and transcribers whose hard work in assisting with organizing and transcribing our interviews was invaluable: Nathalie Delise, Nicole Farris, Moumita Mukherjee, Jenny Savely, Ragini Sengupta, and Brandi Woodell. We would also like to give special thanks to Alison Kuemmel for her geographic information system (GIS) skills and to Heather Horton and Isabelle Notter for their help with the demographic coding and their service in the final stages of this manuscript.

Funding and support for this project proved essential to the feasibility of completing in-person interviews with a large sample of geographically diverse participants. In particular, we received funding and support from the University of Houston Division of Research; the Joseph S. and Rosella H. Werlin Memorial Fund; and the University of New Orleans Sociology Department, College of Liberal Arts, and Office of Research and Sponsored Programs. In addition, countless individuals provided assistance in locating participants, spreading the word about our study, and housing us during our trips to interview sites.

Throughout the process of writing the manuscript, we received direct and indirect feedback from many individuals whose ideas and suggestions were important in shaping the final book. In this regard, we would like to thank our NYU Press editor, Ilene Kalish, for her support and commitment to our project. We would also like to acknowledge the thoughtful feedback provided by the reviewers of our manuscript. We appreciate the time and thought that went into their reviews, and believe their comments resulted in greater clarity and strengthened the final manuscript.

Both of us received support and guidance throughout this project from colleagues at our respective universities, including the faculty of the Department of Sociology at the University of Houston and the Department of Sociology at the University of New Orleans. In addition, we value the support and insights provided by Dana Berkowitz, Renia Ehrenfeucht, Michael Kimmel, Susan Mann, C. J. Pascoe, Dudley L. Poston Jr., Brian Powell, and Kristen Schilt.

Finally, we would like to thank our families for the support they provided throughout our work on this project. Through the many interview trips, the nights spent reviewing and coding transcripts, and the months of writing, our partners and children have been patient, tolerant, and essential to the completion of our project.

Introduction

Our child was very aware that we were not married, that we
were not allowed to get married. When she was really little,
like kindergarten, . . . Bush was president. She would say,
"Okay, pretend George Bush is dead," and she would . . . have
us exchange these plastic rings and she would say, "Now
you're married. You can keep your kids forever." So for children I think, especially for . . . older adopted children who
understand that the state can help form or destroy families,
I just think that children like her really understand that it
does matter what the state says about your family.
—Sandra

Given that the law typically coincides with social norms, conflict is rarely
felt between formal law and one's familial desires. Tension between the
law and one's family life seems to be particularly absent when it comes
to issues surrounding family formation and having children, which are
often viewed as private matters that are external to legality. It is when we
find ourselves in conflict with the normative structure, however, that the
coercive nature of the system is powerfully felt (Rousseau [1762] 1997).
We rarely recognize the importance of the law for our family life *unless*
we cannot have a child biologically, *unless* we are unable to get married,
unless we want access to resources, *unless* we break up and cannot agree
on custody issues, *unless* we cannot share our wealth with those with
whom we identify as family, *unless* something undermines our desires
and, in turn, renders the law salient.

Lesbian, gay, bisexual, and transgender (LGBT) individuals encounter conflicts with the normative sociolegal structure more frequently,
which has the potential to make the law more tangibly felt within family decisions. For Sandra, quoted at the beginning of this chapter, legal
same-sex marriage did not affect whether or how she became a parent.

Nor did it provide her any additional rights over her child, given that she lived in a state in which she had a registered domestic partnership that she understood to confer the same rights as legal marriage. However, the law and marriage became very significant for this woman, her child, and her family. It was evident, even to her child in kindergarten, that the state and those who govern us can "help form or destroy" families. To this child, as with many adults and much of society, legal marriage represents legitimation and permanence. Marriage means a "real" family. In this respect, the law becomes significant beyond actual rights, as well as on a symbolic, social, and emotional level. It can be understood as having the power to create or transform relationships, as well as to bestow benefits and obligations.

The effect of the law on the family might be felt even more for LGBT parents without access to rights, particularly when they live in a place that does not recognize them as legal parents. As relayed by one of our participants, Sarah, the absence of formal legal rights is powerfully felt when a relationship dissolves:

> [My partner] completely walked away. And, there was nothing that I could do. I had no child support, nothing. . . . But at this point I think it's—not that it's a stupid decision, but it's a very risky decision for two women to have a child in a state that doesn't protect you. It's very risky, from my experience. You know, today's relationships. . . . You fall in love and you want them to work out, but a lot of relationships today don't work out and then you have these children that are in limbo and it all depends on how compliant the ex-partners are. It's scary.

In Sarah's state, there are few legal protections for same-sex couples. The state has no legal marriage, civil union, or state-level domestic partnership. Nor does the state provide access to second-parent adoption for a nonadoptive or nonbiological parent. In situations such as these, then, formal law is experienced not just through the social or emotional recognition that it is able to bring to the family, but also in the very tangible absence of legal rights and control over one's family and future.

In this book, we examine how the law becomes salient in the lives of same-sex families, how individuals navigate the law as part of their family decision-making, and how these practices and interpretations of the law vary across legal contexts. Through in-depth interviews with 137 LGBT parents from throughout the United States, we explore the ways in which the law affects—or fails to affect—decisions to become a parent, the method of becoming a parent, and everyday parenting. The varied ways that LGBT parents grapple with legality shed light on the manner in which the law can be, at times, embraced, manipulated, modified, or rejected by those seeking to create and protect families within a heteronormative legal system.

LGBT Families and the Law

The family as an institution is heavily entangled in most of our other social institutions—including our legal system—and is often taken for granted as universal, innate, and essential (Powell et al. 2010). It is in the family that we typically spend the most time and where we are largely socialized. Further, it is often believed that our strongest social and emotional attachments are to our families, and without those ties we are considered to be at a disadvantage. In particular, various privileges, social acceptance, and rewards are associated with the family (Baca Zinn and Eitzen 2008). Consider the resources that are available based on marital status, and whether one is an "immediate family member"—from gym memberships and cell phone plans, to work-related social invites and health insurance access, to issues related to state and federal taxes. Because of the effects of family on access to social and material benefits, the family has a profound effect on our life outcomes, including our health and well-being, financial standing, and even life expectancies (Stolzenberg and Waite 2005; Waite 2005).

The parent-child relationship is a fundamental component of the ways in which family operates to affect life outcomes, including the effects of being a "parent" as a social identity and the manner in which parenting can affect the well-being of both parents and children. Accordingly, many of the earliest studies concerning LGBT families centered on questions related to the health and well-being of children growing up with LGBT parents. These studies largely focused on the social and emotional effects of these household types, in addition to the effects of household structure on child behavior (Stacey and Biblarz 2001; Biblarz and Savci 2010). More recently, researchers have advocated shifting the focus away from examining whether children raised in LGBT families have equivalent outcomes to heterosexual families and toward understanding the manner in which social and institutional structures produce constraints or inequalities for LGBT families (Baumle and Compton 2014; Meadow 2013; Moore 2011; Richman 2008, 2013; Badgett 2010).

As with other family types, LGBT families are influenced by institutional and contextual factors—such as urbanization, market economies, education structures, and the law. Legally, LGBT families face a number of issues that are not relevant to, and are even taken for granted by, heterosexual families. For example, since most jurisdictions deny same-sex couples the right to legally marry and same-sex marriage is not recognized consistently across states, LGBT couples and their children typically do not share the same legal rights and protections as experienced by married heterosexual couples and their children (Demo, Allen, and Fine 2000; Cahill, Ellen, and Tobias 2002). Moreover, there are many laws, policies, and practices in the United States and internationally concerning the regulation of adoption, foster care, child custody, and visitation rights which are biased in favor of heterosexual people, their relationships, and their families (Cahill, Ellen, and Tobias 2002). These factors influence the organization and health of families and relationships, in addition to how they are viewed socially.

Faced with legal animus or outright legal prohibitions on adoption, fostering, or surrogacy, one might expect that LGBT individuals would be deterred from family formation. Indeed, this deterrence is the motivation for the proposal and enactment of many of these laws. Conversely, those living in states with family laws that prohibit discrimination on the basis of sexual orientation might be expected to form families more readily and to parent with fewer legal conflicts. According to US census data, however, a greater proportion of children are living in same-sex households in states considered legally and socially hostile to LGBT individuals—particularly, in the southern United States (Gates 2011). These data raise important questions regarding the manner in which LGBT couples form families, and whether unfriendly family laws actually deter or inhibit childrearing.

As exemplified by the comments from Sandra and Sarah, some of our participants believe that the law primarily serves to convey social recognition of their family; other participants believe the law can or should play a role in decisions regarding family formation or dissolution. And yet still other participants believe that the law is entirely irrelevant, both in their decision to have a child and in regulating their everyday parenting. In this book, we examine these, and other, understandings about LGBT families and the law, paying particular attention to whether and how conceptions of the law in family life differ across legal contexts.

Our Framework: Examining LGBT Legal Consciousness

Our focus in this research is on examining the legal consciousness of LGBT parents. When we talk about legal consciousness, we are referring to the meanings given to the law by individuals, including the way in which these meanings are used, reproduced, or contested by individuals (Silbey 2005; Marshall and Barclay 2003; Nielsen 2000; Ewick and Silbey 1998). Throughout many everyday tasks, we encounter legality—whether in adhering to traffic signals, paying our bills, or completing administrative forms. In these mundane practices, as well as in more direct interactions with formal law, our understandings and our behaviors are guided by shared meanings about the law. These shared meanings reflect our legal consciousness—a consciousness that is communally experienced and communally constructed (Silbey 2005; Marshall 2005; Ewick and Silbey 1998).

In one of the seminal works on legal consciousness, Ewick and Silbey (1998) sought to identify some of these shared meanings about the law that comprise our legal consciousness. They described three schemas— before the law, with the law, and against the law—that reflect common understandings of, and interactions with, the law in the United States. In the case of the "before the law" schema, the law is understood as being derived from a legitimate moral authority. Having this understanding of the law results in individuals feeling very little agency over legal outcomes; instead, they view the law as a force external to individuals, which cannot be manipulated. When individuals rely upon this understanding of the law in their interactions with legality, they typically serve to reinforce the status quo of legal structures because they are more likely to both adhere to, and to believe in, the power of the law on the books.

In the case of the "with the law" schema, the law is understood as contingent and malleable. Individuals view legal outcomes as dependent on individual circumstances, context, and resources. Accordingly, people believe that they can marshal their resources in order to work within the existing system and achieve favorable outcomes. Having this understanding of the law can render differences in social networks, social class, and other assets as particularly important for how an individual understands his or her legal prospects.

In the "against the law" schema, the legitimacy of the law is rejected, the relationship between individuals and the legal system is understood to be adversarial, and individuals engage in acts of resistance. Some of these acts of resistance are the more traditional approaches of challenging the legitimacy of the laws themselves through the judicial system, or challenging the moral authority of legal actors. Others are everyday actions that serve to subvert the intent of the law, such as technical compliance with the law as written but in a manner that was clearly unintended by lawmakers. Viewing the law as oppressive and adversarial, and engaging in resistance to the law, has the potential to expose weaknesses in power structures and perhaps modify legality. The ways in which individuals' understandings and use of the law vary from the formal law can serve as a powerful shaper of the law in action, thereby transforming what we understand to be the law.

These three schemas do not necessarily operate independently from one another or consistently over time (Ewick and Silbey 1998). A person might be "before the law" in one aspect of his or her life and "against the law" in another. Further, it is possible that individuals demonstrate conflicting understandings of the law and actions even on the same issue.

Through the lens of legal consciousness, the law can be understood as an interactive process, with persons receiving circulating discourses about law, and accepting, modifying, or rejecting these meanings. Preexisting legality is then either reinforced or new meanings might become institutionalized, rendering individuals active participants in constructing the law. This means that LGBT parents are not simply passive recipients of legality. Instead, they are participants in the process of shaping their legal options, including both those that further or that restrict their family goals.

Contributions of Our Research

Although research on LGBT families and the so-called same-sex marriage debate has increased, the majority of this work has sought to portray gay family life and family diversity, or to confirm or challenge myths and stereotypes (Weston 1991; Stacey 2011; Risman 2009; Garner 2005; Lareau 2003; Powell et al. 2010; Moore 2011; Lewin 2009). Further, some consideration of legal forces has been paid to LGBT families within the sociolegal literature. For example, some works have focused on explaining the manner in which understandings of what constitutes a family are shaped by legal and other cultural forces (Hull 2003, 2006; Richman 2013), and others have examined the manner in which legal definitions of family are too constraining for nontraditional families, including LGBT families (Polikoff 2008; Richman 2008). These works have not involved a close examination of the manner in which legality is understood, utilized, or challenged as part of the process of LGBT parenthood.

Our research, then, builds upon and extends prior work on both legal consciousness and LGBT families. First, we are focused on a broader analysis of LGBT individuals' interactions with the law than what has often been analyzed in studies of LGBT families. Rather than concentrating on what happens as LGBT individuals attempt to access the legal system via marriage licenses or pursue adoption through the courts (see, e.g., Richman 2008; Hull 2003, 2006; Connolly 2002), we examined both direct interactions with formal law and less direct, everyday interactions with laws, rules, and policies. In doing so, we sought to gain a comprehensive picture of the manner in which LGBT parents' understandings of and interactions with the law are shaped by formal law, institutions, social networks, and individual desire. Our hope was to shift the focus from describing the thoughts and behaviors of individuals who are interacting with formal law, and to examine instead the manner in which human agency and structure interact in the production of legality.

In addition, our research expands upon prior studies of legal consciousness that examine how disadvantaged groups understand or use the law (Connolly 2002; Hull 2003, 2006; Nielsen 2000; Marshall 2005; Sarat 1990) by paying particular attention to how variations in legal understandings occur *within* the group. The heterogeneity in legal consciousness across legal contexts is particularly notable for LGBT parents, given the inconsistency of state and local laws across the United States. Few groups encounter as much variation in access to everyday legal rights as they pertain to the family. This variation in legal environments within and across states for LGBT families provides a rather unique opportunity to examine ways in which legal context affects understandings of legality. Prior research has often examined how legal consciousness is shaped by a particular social identity (see, e.g., welfare status [Sarat 1990], working class [Merry 1990], or race and gender [Nielsen 2000]) or by an organizational location or organizational structure (see, e.g., Larson 2004; Hoffman 2003; Marshall 2005; Dellinger and Williams 2002), but our research examines the manner in which geographic location affects cultural messages about the law and interactions with the law for individuals of a particular social identity. In this respect, we seek to integrate these bodies of literature by highlighting the manner in which the construction of legality is multidimensional, operating across individual, group, and structural levels.

Drawing upon these concepts, we develop a multifaceted theory toward understanding how LGBT parents participate in the construction of legality, and how legal context can serve to shape their understandings and uses of the law. As detailed in the conclusion, we observe that LGBT parents are active recipients of cultural schemas about legality, including those of being *before*, *with*, and *against* the law. Which schema prevails for an LGBT parent at a particular moment in time is determined in part by their legal context; mediating factors such as social networks, interactions with legal actors, and the media; and individual factors, including familial desires and demographic and socioeconomic characteristics.

Our findings illustrate that LGBT parents' interactions across these levels operate both to reflect and to create legality. Whether LGBT parents accept, modify, or challenge the law is dependent on how interactions occur across these three levels. For example, an individual without economic means who is located in a legally and politically conservative city, will often have little access to other LGBT parents or local organizations for assistance in becoming parents or navigating legal issues related to parenthood. Their economic, social, and geographic embeddedness can produce acquiescence to the law, as they might feel they do not have the information or resources to manipulate the system or the support to challenge a hostile legal environment. Accordingly, throughout this work we trace sources of the law and the ways in which individual factors, mediating factors, and legal context interact to produce legality for LGBT parents.

About This Project

Prior to initiating this study, we were engaged in more quantitative examinations of US Bureau of the Census data on same-sex unmarried partners. We were particularly interested in exploring what these data could reveal about the ways in which demographic outcomes differed for individuals in same-sex relationships as compared to different-sex relationships, including variations in family structure. Our analyses typically incorporated a consideration of both individual and contextual factors in studying family structure, given that contextual factors such as legal environment can serve to shape structural forces that act upon individual desires and characteristics. In some respects we were surprised with our results, which suggested that restrictive laws limiting or prohibiting certain routes to parenthood might have little effect on parenting outcomes for same-sex couples (Baumle and Compton 2011; Baumle, Compton, and Poston 2009). This runs contrary to the expectations of many in terms of how prohibitive laws work for LGBT individuals (see chapter 2). These findings raised questions regarding the degree to which LGBT individuals consider the law when forming families and, more broadly, the ways in which they understand and use the law as parents. These questions pushed us toward taking a more in-depth, qualitative look at the manner in which legal consciousness is constructed for LGBT parents.

Accordingly, in this research we examine how and when the law becomes salient in the lives of LGBT families, and how individuals then choose to navigate the law in their family decisions. While our book focuses primarily on the results from our qualitative interviews, our ability to situate and inform our analysis with data from the national population lends added validity and context to our findings. Our interviews provide a fuller description of American LGBT family life and reveal the manner in which LGBT parents work with, around, or against the law in making very personal decisions about family formation and parenting.

Defining Legality

For this research, we define *legality* as a process in which organized patterns of beliefs and behaviors (i.e., cultural schemas) about rules and law are utilized in everyday interactions as well as in more formal legal settings (Silbey 2005; Marshall and Barclay 2003; Nielsen 2000; Ewick and Silbey 1998). This notion of "doing law" recognizes the role of human agency and structural constraints as interactive and reflexive in producing legality. Law is not something that is solely experienced as a force external to individuals, but is something that is at times grappled with, selectively invoked, or ignored.

This process of engaging with the law plays an important role in constructing legality. Current laws and legal structure are reflected or reified when individuals accept and act upon them. On the other hand, new legal meaning can be constructed when legal authority is resisted or rejected. When we examine the way in which law affects outcomes for LGBT parents, we are examining the manner in which interactions with the law take place in both unexpected, as well as expected, times and places and how these interactions affirm or modify legality.

Defining LGBT Families

Historically, definitions of *family* have frequently relied upon the existence of relationships established by blood or law (Weston 1991; Seidman 1993; Brown and Manning 2009; Powell et al. 2010). Families are also typically portrayed as being responsible for the bearing and the raising of children, for comprising the structure within which individuals reside, and for being the means by which property is shared and passed down (Waite 2005; Baca Zinn and Eitzen 2008). Upon closer inspection, these sorts of definitions are often based on legal or structural terms housed within heteronormativity. This becomes quite problematic for families that fall outside of the ideal nuclear heterosexual family type—as is the case with LGBT families.

For the purpose of our work, and in line with social and academic discourse, *LGBT families* refer to families that consist of at least one gay male, lesbian, bisexual, or transgender parent with one child or more, or to a gay or lesbian couple irrespective of whether children are present (Cahill, Ellen, and Tobias 2002). The term *LGBT families* has been criticized because families do not have a sexual orientation, rather it is the individuals who make up families that have sexual orientations (Baca Zinn and Eitzen 2008). Nonetheless, this term persists in family literature and its usage is common practice. Based more on household form, it allows for a different and broader conceptualization of family irrespective of legal and blood ties. Further, it most appropriately fits our population of interest and recognizes the diversity of our participants' gender and sexuality.

Our definition of families was specifically inclusive of lesbian, gay, bisexual, transgender, and queer parents in order to examine any differences in the experiences and challenges faced by parents across gender and sexuality. To some degree, individuals in all of these categories experience similar restrictions on parenting, due to challenges in biological reproduction, access to legal marriage, or access to adoption. Further, individuals who identify as lesbian, gay, bisexual, transgender, or queer encounter similar stigmas due to their transgression from sexuality and gender norms. Nonetheless, individuals across these groups may have different experiences when navigating the heteronormative legal system, and a more inclusive definition of LGBT families allows for nuanced insights into the construction of legality. For example, speaking to a bisexual single parent illuminated the difference in legal concerns based on sex of partner and access to marriage. Similarly, some of our families with a transgender parent were able to fly more under the radar legally and access greater resources due to legal sex changes. At the same time, these individuals were highly cognizant of their privilege and expressed concerns about how their situation might change if they were "outed" as a nonheterosexual family. Given that these factors can play a role in experiences with the law, we elected a broad definition of LGBT families for our study.

Throughout this book, we refer to our participants as LGBT parents or LGBT families when referencing the sample as a whole; individual participants are referenced based on how they self-identified during the interview. Due to the variety of academic and nonacademic viewpoints on terminology for this population, we also include in the appendix a more detailed discussion regarding our election of the term *LGBT* to describe our participants (see "A Note on Terminology" in the appendix).

Locating Our Participants

To address our questions, it was important for us to gather a diverse set of parents across a range of legal contexts. To begin with, individuals must have been parents or in the process of becoming parents, and identified either as LGBT, that is, as being in a same-sex or LGBT partnership, or previously parented within an LGBT partnership to be considered for the study. Since we were dealing with a "hidden" or "invisible" population, we recruited our sample via multiple referral chains, using affinity or social groups, formal organization leaders, individuals, and contact lists including social media such as Facebook and Twitter. Because LGBT parents are often subjected to scrutiny from researchers and the public, referrals were an important mechanism for gaining trust and rapport with participants. We then employed a purposeful and theoretical sampling design, stratified by sex and nested within particular legal contexts—that is, a state's legal position on LGBT family issues. Based on legislation and case law on LGBT parenting and marriage issues (see chapter 2 and the appendix for details), we categorized states as legally positive, legally negative, or legally neutral (having no relevant legislation or case law on the books, but typically negative leaning sociopolitically). Additional details about our theoretical approach and methodology are contained in the appendix.

Our approach resulted in a sample that was stratified across legal contexts, as well as fairly representative of the sociodemographic characteristics of same-sex parents (tables I.1 and I.2). The participants in our study represent seventeen states across the United States—33 percent from legally positive states, 34 percent from legally neutral (but negative-leaning) states, and 34 percent from legally negative states. Our participants were parents to 114 children (see table A.3 in the appendix for the demographics of their children). Children came to be in our participants' lives via a number of routes, including heterosexual intercourse (17 percent), insemination (45 percent), adoption (25 percent), fostering (5 percent), surrogacy (3 percent), and other ways (5 percent; most often as stepchildren or siblings).

Throughout the sampling process, we were highly cognizant of the academic criticisms of studying LGBT populations and hidden populations as a whole—particularly the concern regarding homogeneity of participants drawn from convenience samples and the lack of racial and socioeconomic diversity. As such, we drew on data from nationally rep-

TABLE I.1. Descriptive statistics of participants (N = 137)

Demographic characteristics	Average	Std. dev.	Min.	Max.
Mean age	39	8.03	23	70
Median household income ($)	100,000	91,600	9,000	800,000
Number of children	1.5	0.74	On the way	4
Mean child's age	8.5	8.5	On the way	44

TABLE I.2. Descriptive statistics of participants (N = 137)

	No. of participants	Percentage of N (%)
Gender identity		
Female	107	78.10
Male	23	16.79
Transgender	7	5.11
Sexual identity		
Gay/Lesbian	110	80.29
Bisexual	6	4.38
Queer	21	15.33
Race and ethnicity		
Non-Hispanic	124	90.51
White	115	83.94
Black	4	2.92
Other	3	2.19
Multiracial	2	1.46
Hispanic	13	9.49
White	2	1.46
Nonwhite	7	5.11
Multiracial/-ethnic	4	2.92
Marital status		
Married	59	43.07
Partnered	59	43.07
Single	19	13.87
Legal context		
Positive state	45	32.85
Neutral state	46	33.58
Negative state	46	33.58

resentative surveys, such as the US Census Bureau's American Community Survey (ACS), to guide our recruitment of participants to ideally create the greatest applicability of our work. Our sample characteristics were relatively comparable to those of same-sex partners captured by the ACS, with the exception of racial and ethnic composition (see the appendix for a detailed discussion regarding how our sample characteristics compare with the ACS data). Although our participants are mostly non-Hispanic white (84 percent), their households are fairly diverse with 37 percent living in transracial households. Thus, while we wished for greater racial and ethnic diversity in our sample than we were able to achieve, we do offer a wide range of experiences at the individual level and a greater racial and ethnic representation at the household level.

Overall, our participants represent relatively diverse households and exemplified a wide array of backgrounds, circumstances, and experiences with respect to family formation, parenting, and the law. Our multifaceted approach to locating participants, as well as our larger sample size, generated a sample that is varied and able to speak to a range of LGBT parenting experiences across the United States.

The Interviews

In this book, we examine how LGBT individuals understand and use the law through the analysis of 97 in-depth interviews with 137 LGBT parents (some interviews were conducted with couples) or would-be parents (some parents were expecting, awaiting adoption, or no longer had custody of their foster children) from across the United States. Our interviews were semistructured and included topics and questions related to family, parental decision-making, social networks, and the manner in which laws affected family formation and parenting.

Both authors were present for 75 percent of the interviews, while we individually conducted the other 25 percent. We are both Caucasian females, with one of us identifying as heterosexual and one identifying as nonheterosexual, and one of us being a parent and the other a nonparent at the time of the interviews. Our insider status in each of these areas garnered trust with participants, leading to a reflexive dialogue. Further, our differing standpoints and academic interests (one of us identifies more as a legal scholar and the other as a family scholar) led us to ask our participants probing questions that might not have been addressed by a single researcher. We believe this to be a notable strength to our data collection process and study. Additional details regarding our interview process and data analysis are included in the appendix.

Our interviews took place within states located in every region of the country, and in very diverse settings, including urban, rural, and suburban areas. We met participants at the days and times of their convenience, meaning that we interviewed on Saturdays through Sundays, and from very early in the morning to late at night once the children had gone to bed. We also interviewed at the locations selected by participants, including at their offices, at university campuses, in public libraries, and at restaurants. The majority of our interviews, however, took place in the homes of our participants. Our participants lived in single-family, multifamily, and communal households. Their homes varied from low-income apartments to manufactured homes, row houses, suburban pop-ups, brownstones, and mansions with paid staff. Some of our participants had tenants or friends living in attached apartments, rooms, or spaces, including one individual who lived in a tent in a garage.

During the at-home interviews in particular, we were able to see firsthand many of the legal effects of access, or lack of access, to resources on households. Additionally, participants' preferences regarding locations (private or public, quiet or loud, with children or without) provided indications of their level of comfort or concerns regarding their families, as well as how they felt their families were viewed socially and legally.

Book Overview

In this book we develop our theory of the legal consciousness of LGBT parents by examining family laws for LGBT parents, exploring the routes by which our participants came to be parents, discussing the various sources of legal information for LGBT parents, and then examining the ways in which human agency and structure interact to produce legality for LGBT parents. In chapter 1 we describe the legal environment for LGBT parents in the United States. Law and legal discourse play a role in LGBT families in ways well beyond the law on the books, but the formal laws within a state are one of the more visible forces in shaping access to parenthood and parenting rights. The ways in which these laws vary across state lines are important, not just in terms of how the law can affect access but also in the manner in which variation in laws convey different cultural messages about whether and how the law can be used. Next, we examine differences in family laws across states and present statistical analyses that explore the manner in which formal laws appear to affect the presence of children in same-sex households and particular routes to parenthood. These analyses illustrate the ways in which formal law, at times, appears to have surprisingly little effect on the family outcomes of LGBT parents. Accordingly, these findings raise questions regarding how formal law might be ignored, modified, or rejected by LGBT individuals who are engaged in family formation, and whether legal context plays a role in shaping these outcomes. We conclude by discussing the manner in which we measure legal context for our study, including examining the challenges inherent in measuring a broad, dynamic concept such as the law. In the remainder of the book, we explore the conditions that produce legal understandings and interactions with the law for LGBT parents, paying particular attention to legal context.

In chapter 2 we focus on describing the particular paths to parenthood undertaken by our participants. We primarily examine the demographics of our participants as they pertain to the method of becoming a parent (e.g., insemination, prior heterosexual relationships, adoption, marriage, fostering) in order to begin to explore the ways in which individual factors produce family outcomes. We further examine some of the rationales offered for selecting a particular route to parenthood, and how legal context plays a role in producing choices and access for routes to parenthood. Our findings illustrate that factors such as income prove important in the route to parenthood, including the role that economic differences play in access to surrogacy for gay men. In addition, we find that legal context shapes the particular path to parenthood and participants' security regarding their parenthood status. Those living in legally positive states and who are nonbiological parents of their children, for example, indicated that they were able to acquire parenthood rights via second-parent adoption or marriage. Regardless of whether they actually elected to pursue these legal protections or whether they were correct in their belief that they were afforded parental rights via marriage, they nonetheless felt additional security over their parenthood status as compared to those in less friendly states. The findings in this chapter indicate the manner in which individual factors and legal context interact to affect choices in paths to parenthood for LGBT parents.

In chapter 3 we highlight sources for legal understandings in order to examine more closely the process of constructing legality for LGBT parents. An important aspect to understanding LGBT parents' legal consciousness involves examining the sources from which they receive cultural messages about the law as it pertains to their families. Some participants described gaining legal knowledge through traditional venues, such as attorneys or consulting legislation, whereas others relied upon social networks, media, movies, books, or the Internet. We explore the manner in which learning about the law varies for LGBT parents across individual characteristics, as well as legal context. Legal context can affect whether individuals even pursue information about the law; some participants living in legally positive states articulated an assumption that they had legal rights, and some living in legally negative states an assumption that rights were absent. For LGBT parents, whether and how they gain information about the law plays an important role in how they then choose to interact with formal and informal law in their lives.

In chapters 4, 5, and 6 we examine more directly the ways in which LGBT individuals understand and use the law in becoming parents or in parenting. We organize our discussion across the *before, with,* and *against* the law schemas (Ewick and Silbey 1998), illustrating the manner in which LGBT parents navigate and construct legality. In chapter 4 we look at how our participants' interactions with the law indicated a belief in the legitimacy and permanence of the law. Our participants were more likely to embrace this sentiment in legally positive or neutral states, including articulating ways in which they understood the law to play an important role in "making families," legitimating relationships, or forming commitments between adults or adults and children. By voicing these understandings of the law, participants suggested that the law has a unique power in formulating identities and commitments, and that human agency is relatively absent from dealings with the law.

In chapter 5 we focus on the manner in which our participants' interactions with the law reflected an understanding of the law as contingent and malleable. We found that, across all legal contexts, our participants often viewed the law as a game, where they could utilize resources such as income, education, or social networks to achieve desired ends. In addition, they engaged in forum shopping for favorable judges or favorable laws, which broadened their family formation options. Although participants in all legal contexts manipulated or worked around the law, we found that this practice was particularly important for those located in legally neutral states given the uncertainty of legal outcomes. When participants employed a "with the law" understanding, they signaled an acknowledgement of the manner in which the law is subject to human agency and, accordingly, they indicated an awareness of the role that they might play in modifying legality.

In chapter 6 we examine the ways in which participants resist the law, eschewing its moral authority and enacting everyday resistance. Few participants engaged in collective action or overt legal challenges, despite their expression of resentment with formal law or administrative procedures. Nonetheless, through acts of everyday resistance, such as masquerading as single or heterosexual, or modifying documents, our participants reflected the manner in which they rejected legal authority over their parenting. These acts were particularly important for those residing in legally neutral or legally negative states, where participants were embedded in a negative sociolegal climate that produced greater hostility and defiance. This defiance, however, was tempered by the desire to achieve their family goals and to protect their children from retaliation, resulting in few overt legal challenges. Participants who expressed this understanding of the law indicated not only their rejection of the moral authority of the law, but an oftentimes gleeful resistance to power structures operating within their state.

In the conclusion we examine our emergent theory and our contributions to studies of legal consciousness and to social and legal policy. Our research reveals how LGBT individuals frame their access to the creation and maintenance of families; the legal, social, and geographic obstacles to those goals; and their responses and reactions to those obstacles. We find that individual factors such as demographics and familial desires; mediating factors such as social networks, legal actors, and organizations; and legal context all interact with cultural discourses about the law in order to shape LGBT parents' legal consciousness. Our findings thus illustrate that there is no single experience of LGBT parents with regard to legality. Their legal consciousness as part of the parenting process is as varied and contextual as the legal and sociopolitical environments in which they reside.

1

The State of the Law for LGBT Parents

It really doesn't matter what [the laws] say. It is not going to
keep people from having children. If it was a straight situation, the law isn't going to keep people from having sex, they
are still going to get married, they are still going to live together even if they don't get married. If it was a racial issue,
back in the day, interracial couples still got together, they
still had children, whether other people saw it as legal or not.
I mean, life is going to go on. Whether they say we can do it
or not.
—Traci

When proposing and enacting formal laws and regulations, there is an
assumption that the law matters—that the law will, ultimately, affect
our decisions and behaviors. But, as many of our participants noted,
the law does not "matter" in the same way across all aspects of our
lives. As pointed out by Traci, a married, Native American lesbian in
her forties who lives in a legally neutral state, "life is going to go on,"
and many LGBT individuals will find a way to have children despite
legal constraints on family formation. For others, however, legal restrictions might play a more powerful role when making decisions about
parenthood. This is the case both in terms of actual obstacles to forming a family (e.g., adoption or insemination restrictions), as well as laws
limiting the rights that one or both parents might have over any child
that enters the family. Given the degree of variation that exists in formal
laws across states, the question of whether law matters does not have a
singular answer for LGBT parents.

Throughout this book, we argue that a fundamental aspect of one's
legal consciousness is derived from contextual factors, including the
legal and sociopolitical climate in which one resides. This makes for a
complex and dynamic landscape to be navigated for LGBT parents, who

are nested within a variety of legal, social, and political environments across the United States. Our research is focused on examining this rather unique variation in legal context for LGBT parents to explore how context, and its interactions with group and individual goals and characteristics, plays a role in the construction of legality. Given our interest in legal context, we focus in this chapter on providing a framework for our project by introducing a few key topics related to state-level family laws. We begin by describing the legal obstacles that existed at the time of this study for LGBT parents or would-be parents and by discussing the manner in which these obstacles vary across legal contexts in the United States, as well as how these variations might be expected to affect the parenting experiences of LGBT individuals.

We then provide a brief overview of key findings from two of our prior quantitative studies that analyzed whether state-level laws affected the presence of children in same-sex households or the type of parent-child relationship in same-sex households. These quantitative analyses, which utilized large, nationally representative datasets on same-sex partners, provide indications that legal context matters for LGBT parents—but not always in the ways in which one might expect. Our quantitative findings raise additional questions regarding the mechanisms by which LGBT parents come to learn about, interpret, and utilize the law.

In the following chapters we build upon these analyses by drawing on our interviews with LGBT parents to more directly examine the manner in which legal context plays a role in shaping legal consciousness. Accordingly, we conclude this chapter by discussing how we classified states by legal context for our study, including the challenges posed by measuring legal environments and their effects during a time of fluctuating laws and public opinion on LGBT parenting.

LGBT Families and Legality

Traditionally, law and society scholars have often focused on the ways in which formal law (e.g., legislation and judicial decisions) affects outcomes for individuals, including considerations of how formal law might be interpreted by various actors within the legal system. In describing how formal law plays a role in the construction of legal consciousness for LGBT parents, we reiterate that formal law is but one facet of legality;

as discussed in the introduction, individuals encounter the law in every-day interactions, as well as through more direct dealings with formal law. Accordingly, our focus on formal law in this discussion is intended to provide an overview of variation in legal climates, rather than to sum-marize the entirety of LGBT parents' possible interactions with the law.

Formal law has the potential to affect family formation and parenting for both heterosexual and LGBT families in that these laws provide a set of terms for marriage, adoption, fostering, and surrogacy. Although for-mal law, as well as informal legalities, regulate many familial interactions and outcomes, individuals are often less cognizant of the role of the law in their family lives. Rather, the family is viewed as a private endeavor, often understood to be sheltered from external legality (Mather, McE-wen, and Maiman 2001; Jacob 1992; Ellickson 1991). LGBT individuals, however, confront formal law more regularly than do heterosexual indi-viduals as a part of their family formation and parenting, and are more likely to experience conflicts between their desired outcomes and the law.

In most states, what constitutes a family differs for LGBT persons as compared to heterosexual persons (Powell et al. 2010), affected by restrictions on same-sex marriage and adoption. As Badgett (2001, 163) observed, since laws "determine who is considered a parent in allocat-ing legal parental rights and obligations," then "the legal institution of parenthood seems likely to influence lesbian, gay, and bisexual people's decisions about becoming a parent." At the time of this writing, nine-teen states and the District of Columbia grant marriage to same-sex couples.[1] For those not residing in one of these states, the lack of access to relationship recognition would be expected to color the experiences of couples who are seeking to have children together. Legal marriage, rather than simply legal recognition, appears to be important for same-sex couples, with prior research indicating that same-sex couples largely preferred marriage to civil unions or domestic partnerships (Badgett 2013). Marriage is sought after not just for specific legal rights conferred but also for the social and emotional recognition that accompanies the institution. For couples considering having children, these social and emotional benefits could prove just as, if not more, important for their parenting experience as are the legal rights granted (Cahill, Ellen, and Tobias 2002; Demo, Allen, and Fine 2000).

In addition to marriage, laws in many states directly regulate whether LGBT individuals are permitted to adopt, foster, or enter into surrogacy agreements. Much as with marriage, these laws do more than define a set of rights, such as the ability to engage in adoption. Parenting laws also carry social and emotional implications, including serving as guidance as to which individuals are defined as a "real" parent. For example, Yngvesson (1997) described the manner in which adoption renders the adoptive party the parent and leaves the biological parent without legal nomenclature, even in the case of open adoptions. The implications of these definitions for the individuals' own understandings of their relationships, as well as for how they are perceived by others, indicate the powerful role that laws can play for LGBT parents in defining their familial relationships (see also Baumle and Compton 2014).

In some instances, state laws have prohibited gay men and lesbians from adopting children jointly or individually, even the children of their partners. This is done both directly, when the law prohibits gay individuals from adopting (see, e.g., Florida Adoption Act 2003, but also *Florida Department of Children and Families v. In re: Matter of Adoption of X.X.G. and N.R.G.* [2010] for decision ruling the Florida Adoption Act unconstitutional), or indirectly, when unmarried or cohabiting individuals are barred from adopting (e.g., Michigan). In other cases, states have outlawed surrogacy agreements entirely (e.g., North Dakota) or for unmarried individuals (e.g., Nebraska), or have provided limitations on insemination (e.g., Louisiana). Such measures provide additional obstacles for LGBT individuals who wish to use assisted reproduction in order to have a child.

Even in the absence of restrictive laws, uncertainty about the legal system—including legal rights, definitions, and processes—affects parenting outcomes for LGBT individuals (Badgett 2001). There are many states where neither the legislature nor the courts have made determinations regarding the status of parental rights for LGBT individuals. For example, in Louisiana "a single person, eighteen years or older" is permitted to petition to adopt (Louisiana Adoption Act 2004). As of the time of writing, there has been no indication from the legislature or the courts in Louisiana as to whether sexual orientation would bar an individual from adopting.

In states like Louisiana where the law is uncertain, LGBT individuals might be hesitant to interact with formal law as part of the parenthood process due to its perceived unpredictability. A rocky legal history of battling for legal rights and recognition for LGBT persons contributes toward a sense that, at any moment, presumed legal rights might be ruled unavailable. Such was the case for adoption law in Michigan. Like Louisiana, the adoption statute simply permitted any "person" to adopt (Michigan Adoption Act 1998). Michigan courts, however, had previously issued custody-related rulings suggesting the state might oppose adoption by same-sex couples (see *Boot v. Boot* [2001], ruling that sexual orientation could be a factor in a custody decision, and *Irish v. Irish* [1980], ruling permitting visitation to a lesbian mother only if her partner was not in the house). These rulings were followed by decisions in 2002 and 2004 regarding same-sex adoption and second-parent adoption that resulted in same-sex couples in Michigan being unable to adopt, and effectively curtailed all petitions for second-parent adoptions by LGBT individuals.[2] Legal ambiguity, thus, can have a chilling effect on parenthood decisions because of the implications of what "silence" in a negative sociopolitical climate might mean for future legal rights over children.

Up to this point, we have focused on formal law that suggests a negative or unsettled stance with regard to LGBT family rights. Some states, however, have taken affirmative steps toward providing legal rights to LGBT families. As of June 2014, twenty-four states and the District of Colombia permitted second-parent adoptions wherein individuals were able to adopt the biological or adopted child of their partner (Human Rights Campaign 2014).[3] For example, Vermont's statute provides: "If a family unit consists of a parent and the parent's partner, and adoption is in the best interest of the child, the partner of a parent may adopt a child of the parent" (Vermont Adoption Act 2003). Although "partner" is not necessarily equivalent with same-sex partner, the Vermont Supreme Court has ruled that this statute expressly authorizes second-parent adoption by LGBT partners (*Baker v. State of Vermont* 1999).

As in the case of negative laws, the creation of affirmative legal rights for LGBT individuals can influence family outcomes. In states where the legislature or the courts have provided positive familial rights for same-sex partners, the way LGBT individuals understand their legal obstacles and the means of overcoming those barriers likely differ from those in other states. Their unique contextual situation, therefore, can shape the manner in which they form their families and the ways in which they parent.

Given these variations in legal climate for LGBT parents, it is clear that legal context has the potential to affect interactions with the law, through both direct limitations on available paths to parenthood, as well as through shaping individuals' understandings of the law and its uses. For example, living in a state with negative LGBT family laws can generate obstacles to becoming a legal parent, and can also affect whether LGBT individuals in those states will approach formal or informal law as something antagonistic or helpful for their families. To further examine this issue, the next section provides an overview of findings from our prior quantitative studies which laid the groundwork for gaining an understanding of how legal context might shape the parenting experiences of LGBT individuals.

Legal Context and Family Formation

While our book draws upon interviews from a nonrandom sample of LGBT parents in the United States, our inquiries were guided by findings from quantitative analyses of large-scale, nationally representative data from the US Census Bureau. Through these studies, we sought to provide an initial glimpse into the manner in which legal context might influence family formation for LGBT individuals. Although the Census Bureau data cannot reveal complexities regarding how legal consciousness affects paths to parenthood for same-sex couples, we were able to assess whether variation appears in the presence of children in same-sex households across legal contexts, as well as in the types of parent-child relationships that are identified across legal contexts. The Census Bureau data produce a complicated picture of the ways in which laws sometimes appear to affect, and sometimes appear to fail to affect, the parenting outcomes for same-sex couples.

The Law and Children in Same-Sex Households

Drawing on the US census data of 2000, we first examined the manner in which variations in legal restrictions or protections might modify whether members of same-sex unmarried partners became parents.

We employed multilevel modeling to examine the effect of positive and negative state-level family laws on the presence of children in same-sex unmarried partner households (Baumle and Compton 2011).[4] The full details of our methodology and the full results from these analyses are presented in a prior publication (Baumle and Compton 2011). We focus in this chapter on identifying the ways in which these analyses suggest that state-level laws are related to the presence of children in same-sex households.

In terms of prohibitive laws, we found that laws involved with bringing children into a household—including fostering, adoption, and surrogacy—did not have a statistically significant effect on the presence of children in the household (i.e., whether any child eighteen or under was in the household).[5] However, we found that laws limiting second-parent adoption *did* have a statistically significant, negative effect on the presence of children in the household. Specifically, the odds of children being present in same-sex households decreased by 12 percent in states that prohibited second-parent adoption, compared to those that did not do so. These findings suggest that individuals might pay more attention to restrictive formal laws when considering establishing a flow of legal rights between parent and child, such as with second-parent adoption, but less so as part of family formation, such as with laws related to surrogacy, insemination, or adoption. Thus, our results provided little support for the notion that prohibitive laws regarding LGBT individuals adopting or fostering children actually reduce the likelihood of children being present in same-sex unmarried partner households. In other words, these laws appear to be largely ineffective.

We also examined whether laws that prohibited discrimination based on sexual orientation (i.e., positive laws) for gay and lesbian parents had an effect on whether children were in same-sex households.[6] We considered a consolidated measure of positive family laws that included laws that prohibited discrimination in adoption and in second-parent adoption; the same set of states had laws that prohibited discrimination on these two practices as of the census of 2000.[7] We found that these positive family laws had a statistically significant, positive effect on the presence of children in the household. Our results indicated that the odds of children being present in same-sex households increased by 15 percent in states with positive family laws compared to states without these protective laws. Given that the same states had protective laws related to adoption and to second-parent adoption, we were unable to disentangle their effects to determine which played a greater role in increasing the likelihood of children being present in the household. Based upon our findings from the negative law models, we suggested that it is possible that the pro–second-parent adoption laws could be generating the greatest contribution to this statistically significant effect. Such an interpretation would be compatible with literature suggesting that individuals become informed about the law, and are more likely to rely on formal law, for family outcomes involving property transference or gaining legal rights (Mather, McEwen, and Maiman 2001; Jacob 1992; Ellickson 1991; Merry 1990). In addition, a desire for formal legal recognition of the family via second-parent adoption could motivate a reliance on formal law. Decisions regarding pathways to becoming parents, however, might be more likely to be viewed as individualized, personal family matters that are less influenced by either positive or negative family laws.

Although we were able to suggest several possible explanations for why certain types of family law might play little role in family formation outcomes (Baumle and Compton 2011), the census data permit only an examination of outcomes rather than the decision-making processes. As a result, our findings could not reflect whether same-sex partners are consciously opting out of formal law when forming their families or whether they are unaware of state laws regarding family formation. State laws might also have little effect on family formation if many of the children in same-sex households are children from prior heterosexual marriages. Census data indicate that the odds of having a child in a same-sex household are almost 2.5 times higher for individuals who identify their marital status as divorced, separated, or widowed (Baumle and Compton 2011; Baumle et al. 2009). This phenomenon, however, might change over time as LGBT individuals continue to come out at increasingly early ages and are less likely to enter into heterosexual marriages that produce children.

Overall, our findings from the 2000 census analyses suggest that negative family laws have a limited effect on whether or not individuals become parents, but that positive laws could play a more important role in family formation for LGBT individuals. Further, these results indicate that second-parent adoption laws might prove particularly important for LGBT parents as part of the path to parenthood, including establishing a parental identity and legal rights over children.

The Law and Parent-Child Relationships

Although our analyses of the 2000 US census data suggested that negative laws might have little effect on whether children are in same-sex unmarried partner households, we considered whether the particular route to parenthood might be more directly affected by formal law. Drawing on Census Bureau data from the 2009–2011 American Community Surveys (ACS), we examined the manner in which legal context might play a role in determining whether same-sex couples have biological, adopted, or stepchildren (Baumle and Compton 2013). We once again employed multilevel modeling to examine the manner in which individual- and state-level characteristics affected the odds of a particular parent-child relationship being identified on the ACS.

We conducted two separate analyses. The first focused on households where the householder (i.e., the first person listed on the census form for a household) has identified children as his or her "own children," defined as *biological, adopted,* or *stepchildren* by the US Census Bureau. As reflected in table 1.1, the majority of children in same-sex households are categorized as "own children," and approximately 59 percent of children in female households and 66 percent of children in male households were identified as having a biological relationship with the householder (see also Gates 2013). Due to biological and legal constraints, however, pathways to parenting an "own child" (biological, adopted, or stepchild) likely differ for same-sex couples versus different-sex couples. Accordingly, we were particularly interested in exploring whether state-level family laws had an effect on the odds of a householder in a same-sex household identifying a biological child, as opposed to an adopted or stepchild.

The second set of analyses examined children who come to be in same-sex households through other mechanisms, such as other relatives or nonrelatives. For some individuals in same-sex households, the lack of a clear legal or biological relationship to a child can lead to uncertainty in how to identify relationships. Indeed, prior research suggests

TABLE 1.1. Parent-child relationships of householders, by sex

Type of relationship	Women (%)(n = 2,236)	Men (%)(n = 928)
Biological child	59.0	66.2
Adopted child	12.1	13.3
Stepchild	6.8	3.8
Other child	22.1	16.7
Total	100.0	100.0

Source: 2009–2011 American Community Surveys

that same-sex households are more likely than different-sex households to experience boundary ambiguity in which the categorization of a child along a biological or legal relationship is uncertain (Baumle and Compton 2014; Henehan et al. 2007; Krivickas and Lofquist 2011). This ambiguity can result in many same-sex households identifying parent-child relationships using categories outside of the "own child" options. As reflected in table 1.1, approximately 22 percent of children in female households and 17 percent of those in male households were identified as related in ways other than the "own child" categories. These categories include: child-in-law, sibling, sibling-in-law, grandchild, other relatives, foster children, and other nonrelatives. In our analyses, we were particularly interested in exploring whether state-level family laws affected the odds of a child in a same-sex household being identified with a parent-child relationship other than one of the "own child" (biological, adopted, or step child) categories.

The full methodological details and the results from these analyses are presented in a separate paper (Baumle and Compton 2013). Given the potentially strong implications for how legal context influences LGBT parents and families, we discuss in this chapter the results that are directly related to the manner in which family laws affected the odds of identifying specific parent-child relationships. Our analyses incorporated variables related to state-level family laws, including the presence of laws on adoption, second-parent adoption, and same-sex marriage as of April 1, 2009 (given that we draw upon ACS data from 2009–2011).[8]

Overall, we found that state-level laws appeared to have a limited effect on the odds of a householder identifying a particular parent-child relationship. Neither positive nor negative adoption laws proved statistically significant in predicting either the odds of an "own child" being biological (as opposed to adopted or a stepchild), or the odds of a child being identified in one of the categories other than "own child." This finding supports assertions like Traci's at the outset of this chapter, that LGBT parents will find a way to have a child even when faced with presumed legal barriers. The predominance of biological children for same-sex households likely renders adoption laws less relevant in family formation for these households.

Laws pertaining to second-parent adoption, however, do appear to play some role in predicting the odds of identifying a particular parent-child relationship. These results echo our previously discussed findings that second-parent adoption laws affected the odds of children being identified as present in same-sex households. Men who reside in a state that prohibited gay individuals from engaging in second-parent adoption were approximately 3.8 times more likely to identify a biological versus an adopted or stepchild, than men who reside in states without such laws. We believe this finding reveals more about the identification process for a relationship on a survey than about how men come to have families across states. For example, a couple with one partner as the biological parent and residing in a state without second-parent adoption could (a) strategically select the biological parent as the householder (so that the child would not be identified as a "nonrelative" to the non-biological parent), or (b) the nonbiological parent might opt to identify the child as "biological" on the survey if he felt that it was the category that best reflected his relationship to the child (and he lacked the legal relationship provided through second-parent adoption). Indeed, our participants in the interview-based portion of our study indicated that similar types of identification processes are engaged in by LGBT parents who lack second-parent adoption (Baumle and Compton 2014). By contrast, those men living in states that permit second-parent adoption might identify the parent-child relationship via the legal relationship established by their adoption.

For women, both laws that enable second-parent adoption and those that permit same-sex marriage decreased the odds of identifying a child as one of the categories other than "own child." First, the odds of reporting a relationship other than "own child" decreased by approximately

40 percent for women living in states with laws that permit second-parent adoption, as compared to women in states without such laws. In addition, the odds of reporting a relationship other than "own child" decreased by about 40 percent for women living in states that permit same-sex marriage, as compared to women who are not living in such states. Given that both adopted and stepchild are "own child" categories, it seems likely that the availability of second-parent adoption results in more identification of a child as adopted and marriage results in the identification of a child as stepchild. In states without these protective laws, parents without a biological or legal relationship to a child might be more likely to select a category such as "other nonrelative" to describe their relationship to the child. Prior research suggests that same-sex couples are more likely to have "other nonrelative" children in their households, and that these children are often the children of the householder's partner (Baumle and Compton 2014; Krivickas and Lofquist 2011; Henehan et al. 2007). In this respect, laws likely both generate the actual relationship between parent and child (thus increasing the numbers of adopted and stepchildren within these states), and affect the identification process on the survey for parents conforming to legal parent-child definitions.

The results from these two census-based studies suggest that LGBT parents might be able to avoid direct interaction with formal law during family formation, but are perhaps more driven to engage with the law as part of acquiring additional rights through second-parent adoption or marriage. In addition, findings from the ACS data suggest that legal context can play a role in shaping the ways in which LGBT parents identify their relationships to their children, which has implications for both social identity and legal rights over children. Given the geographic variation in family laws, our findings suggest that legal context can make a difference in the degree to which individuals use the law and the manner in which their relationship identities can be situationally determined. These studies provide support for the notion that context matters for the relationship between LGBT parents and the law. The remainder of this book draws on our interviews with LGBT parents to further unwrap the findings and questions raised by the census data regarding the role of legal context in forming the legal consciousness of LGBT parents.

Measuring Legal Context

LGBT individuals who are nested in varying legal contexts might be expected to approach the moment of family formation and parenting with different cultural expectations of what the law is or how it can be used. In this respect, the question of whether and how law matters for LGBT individuals who are having children and parenting is ultimately a question about constructing legality. Specifically, how are cultural schemas about rules and law integrated into the process of becoming parents or parenting for LGBT individuals, and to what degree does the act of "doing law" in this facet of their lives involve acquiescence, manipulation, or resistance?

In the following chapters, we address this question through our interviews with LGBT parents located throughout the United States. In order to assess the role of legal context in the construction of legality, it was important to sample participants located in legally and geographically diverse states. Our first challenge, then, was to formulate and operationalize our definition of legal context in order to construct our sampling framework.

Measuring something as multifaceted as a legal environment is complex in the best of situations. The law functions at multiple levels, including through legislation, case law, administrative guidelines, institutional rules, and abstract everyday conceptions of right and wrong. These aspects of law are not always complementary within a particular localized context; legislation could suggest a positive legal environment for LGBT parents but institutional rules or practices could produce insurmountable barriers. Further, legal environments that appear to be protective of LGBT families can, at times, create additional hurdles for accessing parenting rights. For example, if marriage and/or second-parent adoption are legally available, must an LGBT parent who resides in such a state go through these legal procedures in order to be recognized as a parent? Thus, the conceptualization of what constitutes a friendly or unfriendly legal environment for LGBT parents is certainly not simple.

This process of defining and measuring legal context for LGBT families was made even more challenging given the dynamic and fluctuating legal landscape regarding LGBT rights. Legislation, case law, and public opinion regarding LGBT families have dramatically shifted over the past five years (see, e.g., Dorf and Tarrow 2013). This meant that some of our participants were interviewed during a time of flux in the legal dynamic within their state. As we discuss throughout the book, these legal changes opened new doors for some participants, such as providing access to adoption or marriage to which they had been previously barred. For other participants, the changing legal landscape served primarily to emphasize that their grasp on legal rights or parental identities was tenuous—a shift in the legal winds, or a crossing of jurisdictional boundaries, could render their legal situation unstable.

Given the challenges that all of these factors produced for measuring legal context, we opted to focus on what is arguably the most objective measure of legal environment: the law on the books. Specifically, a state's legal position on LGBT family issues was measured by a review of legislation and case law (as measured by court of appeals decisions or higher) as of the start of our project in 2010. In general, state statutes and decisions by state courts are the guiding authorities for the status of LGBT families. It is possible that state agencies fail to adhere to statutes or case law, acting in a manner that is more or less permissive than indicated by the law. Further, it is possible that state legislatures or state supreme courts will choose to override legal decisions of courts of appeals, rendering defunct what appears to be established case law.

In choosing the best manner to categorize states, however, we felt that it was preferable to concentrate on state statutes and their judicial interpretations for two principal reasons. First, we focus in part on the manner in which formal law affects family formation and parenting for LGBT parents. The law itself, as set forth by statutes and case law, seems to be the best means to assess the effects of such policies. Second, we did not wish to make assumptions about the perceptions that LGBT parents living in particular states might have about the law in the absence of a clear statute or legal decision.

Accordingly, states were identified as *legally positive* or *legally negative* in terms of their LGBT family laws (adoption, second-parent adoption, fostering, and marriage) dependent on whether the state had a clear (positive or negative) statute on the issue, or the state had a court of appeals or higher judicial decision (positive or negative) regarding a family law issue that was still good precedent (i.e., that had not been overturned by a higher court).[9] If a state did not have a clear statute or legal prec-

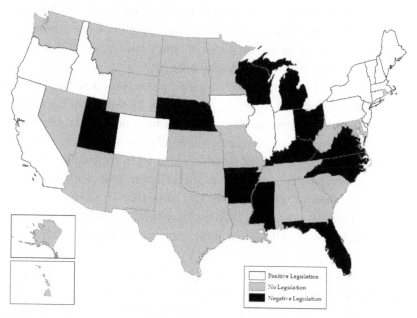

Figure 1.1. Legal context, by state

edent, the state was coded as *legally neutral,* meaning that the law was neutral on its face. In practice, however, states could have judicial decisions in related areas that would suggest the state to be either positive- or negative-leaning toward LGBT families. Thus, neutrality corresponds only to the particular laws in question, as well as only to formal law (i.e., state statutes or decisions from courts of appeals or higher). Some states might be legally neutral but have laws or environments that are more positive or negative toward LGBT families. These situations differ from states with clear positive or negative legal environments in that those LGBT persons who reside within the states must deal with legal ambiguity regarding their potential parenting choices. This could provide legal flexibility in some situations, or constraints due to uncertainties of outcomes. For these reasons, we wished to sample from neutral states in addition to positive and negative legal environments.

Figure 1.1 illustrates how each state, as well as Washington, DC, was coded based upon the legal status as of the start of our project in 2010.[10] We coded a state as positive if it had one or more protective or positive laws, negative for one or more prohibitive laws, and neutral if there were no relevant laws in place. Table A.1 in the appendix depicts how each state was coded across the categories of family laws, as well as the resulting coding as legally positive, negative, or neutral.

Out of ethical concerns regarding legal procedures that are in flux in some of the states from which we sampled, we do not report the specific states in which we interviewed. It was our goal, however, to capture contextual and within-group variations in legal consciousness by sampling participants evenly across all three legal contexts. In selecting our particular interview sites, we focused primarily on states with more than one positive law for positive states, and more than one negative law for negative states so as to strengthen the likelihood that our categorization of the legal context matched with the experiences of LGBT individuals located within those states.

Employing these three categories of legal context, the remainder of our book draws upon our interviews with LGBT parents to examine the ways in which legal context plays a role in shaping how LGBT parents engage in the process of constructing legality with respect to their family lives. In addition to the legal context, we also examine how much agency LGBT parents employ regarding their families and the law, including exploring interactions between individuals and institutions as part of constructing legality. Unlike our analyses of census data, our interviews provide the opportunity to engage directly with LGBT parents regarding the modes by which the law enters into their family life and decision-making.

In the next chapter, we begin to discuss the findings from our interviews by first addressing our participants' routes to parenthood and the ways in which they described individual-level factors and legal context as affecting their options or choices.

2

Routes to Parenthood

I had just found the queer bookstore and I would go there and I was so excited and it was so amazing. . . . And I remember there [were] the queer buttons that you would put on your bag when you were being out, and one of them was: "Sorry mom, no grandkids." And I remember reading that button and thinking, "Oh, I guess I never thought of that; I guess I won't have kids." At the time I was coming out, even though it wasn't even all that long ago, that was still part of the culture. . . . And then later, . . . my landlord . . . and her partner were trying for a kid. . . . That was the first time I was aware of queer people going through machinations in order to have kids and structuring families in different ways. . . . I remember that probably being the time that it was sort of on my radar, like I guess I can do this.

—Dana

Definitions of "family" often rely upon the existence of relationships established by blood or law (Weston 1991; Seidman 1993; Brown and Manning 2009; Powell et al. 2010). Given biological limitations on reproduction for LGBT individuals who are not in heterosexual relationships, establishing blood ties between parent and child necessarily involves greater challenges. Further, the absence of legal recognition of same-sex relationships in most of the United States results in unclear relationships between nonbiological parents and their children (Baumle and Compton 2014). Legal barriers to adoption, joint adoption, and fostering can also render it difficult to establish legal ties between parents and children. As such, the route by which LGBT individuals become parents has implications not only for the success of family formation but also for family identity. LGBT individuals have various options for their routes to parenthood—some of them biological, some of them through legal mechanisms, and some informal. As Dana, quoted at the beginning of this chapter, observed, both the notion that parenthood is a possibility for LGBT individuals and the availability of different routes to parenthood vary across time, context, and individual characteristics.

Given the implications of the selected parenthood route for both individual and public family identities, the factors affecting the many routes to parenthood are important in understanding the ways LGBT individuals navigate legality. In this chapter we examine routes to parenthood by first providing an overview of the routes selected by our participants and the manner in which these routes varied across individual characteristics and legal context. We then take a closer look at the various routes to parenthood, discussing the significance of each route, the common characteristics defining each route, and the rationales offered by participants for electing one route over another.

Overview of Routes to Parenthood

Table 2.1 reflects a breakdown of the total number of routes to parenthood reported by our participants; given that some participants reported multiple routes, the total number of routes exceeds our sample size. As reflected in table 2.1, participants in our study primarily reported five routes to parenthood: heterosexual intercourse (typically stemming from a prior relationship), insemination, adoption, fostering, and surrogacy. In addition, some participants reported other routes to parenthood such as stepchildren or informal adoption of relatives or nonrelatives. Overall, the most popular path to parenthood was via insemination, with approximately 45 percent of our participants choosing this route. Adoption was the next most popular route, at 25 percent of our sample, and approximately 17 percent reported becoming a parent via heterosexual intercourse. The remaining paths to parenthood were identified by small subsets of our participants, with 5 percent reporting fostering, 3 percent reporting surrogacy, and 5 percent reporting other routes to parenthood (such as stepchildren or parenting other relatives).

Sociodemographic characteristics—including age, income, sex, and marital status—appeared to play a role in affecting which route was selected by participants. Across the various paths to parenthood, parents were quite similar on age, although parents in the "other" category were

Table 2.1. Routes to parenthood for participants

N = 150	Heterosexual intercourse		Insemination		Adoption		Foster		Surrogacy		Other	
	n	%	n	%	n	%	n	%	n	%	n	%
	25	16.7	68	45.3	37	24.7	7	4.7	5	3.3	8	5.3
Mean Age	41		39		41		38		40		44	
Median household income ($)	77,000		106,150		110,000		86,000		250,000		110,000	
Female	19	84.0	62	91.2	23	62.2	3	42.9	2	40.0	6	75.0
Race and ethnicity												
Non-Hispanic	23	92.0	61	89.7	34	91.9	6	85.7	5	100.0	7	87.5
White	21	84.0	56	82.4	32	86.5	6	85.7	5	100.0	6	75.0
Black	2	8.0	0	0.0	2	5.4	0	0.0	0	0.0	0	0.0
Other	0	0.0	3	4.4	0	0.0	0	0.0	0	0.0	1	12.5
Multiracial	0	0.0	2	2.9	0	0.0	0	0.0	0	0.0	0	0.0
Hispanic	2	8.0	7	10.3	3	8.1	1	14.3	0	0.0	1	12.5
White	0	0.0	0	0.0	1	2.7	0	0.0	0	0.0	0	0.0
Nonwhite	1	4.0	3	4.4	2	5.4	1	14.3	0	0.0	0	0.0
Multiracial/multiethnic	1	4.0	4	5.9	0	0.0	0	0.0	0	0.0	1	12.5
Marital status												
Married	8	32.0	34	50.0	17	45.9	2	28.6	2	40.0	6	75.0
Partnered	7	28.0	28	41.2	17	45.9	3	42.9	3	60.0	2	25.0
Single	10	40.0	6	8.8	3	8.1	2	28.6	0	0.0	0	0.0
Legal context												
Positive state	4	16.0	25	36.8	12	32.4	2	28.6	1	20.0	2	25.0
Neutral state	11	44.0	17	25.0	17	45.9	5	71.4	3	60.0	3	37.5
Negative state	10	40.0	26	38.2	8	21.6	0	0.0	1	20.0	3	37.5

the eldest with an average age of forty-four years and foster parents were the youngest with an average age of thirty-eight. Parents who underwent the surrogacy route had the greatest median household income at $250,000, which was significantly higher than the other parent types. Parents whose children came from heterosexual intercourse had the lowest median household income at $77,000, followed by those that fostered at $86,000.

Out of the two paths to parenthood involving reproductive technologies, women dominated those who opted for the insemination route,[1] while the majority of those using surrogacy were men. Nonetheless, there were sex differences in the degree to which these paths were used. Only four men in our sample used surrogacy, while the majority of men chose adoption as their route to parenthood. By contrast, insemination was the most popular route for women. This sex difference in the use of reproductive technologies is unsurprising given that women have far easier access to sperm donors than men do to surrogates to carry a child, and considering the asymmetrical economic costs involved.

We are unable to ascertain any clear parent route trends related to race and ethnicity, largely due to the relatively smaller numbers of racial and ethnic minorities in our sample and the manner in which multiracial couples and households confound relationship patterns. Given the importance of intersections of class and race, however, one might expect that many of the patterns related to class would be intensified for racial and ethnic minorities due to their being concentrated at the lower ends of the income spectrum. For example, of our six participants who indicated household incomes of less than $30,000, 50 percent identified as racial or ethnic minorities and the rate increases to 60 percent for those under $20,000. Controlling for sex and partner status, participants who identified as white typically indicate household incomes of approximately $45,000 more than parents who identified as a racial or ethnic minority.

The partner status of our participants also reflected differences across routes to parenthood. Within some routes (such as surrogacy, fostering, and other), our sample size is too small to draw conclusions about how partnership status might play a role in determining route to parenthood. Nonetheless, we do see that those who indicated an "other" path to parenthood had the greatest proportion reporting being married, at 75 percent. This is largely due to the fact that many within this group reported parenthood via a stepchild relationship—a designation most likely to be claimed when a couple is married. Those utilizing insemination and adoption were the next most likely to be legally married. Meanwhile, parents who have children via heterosexual intercourse were by far the most likely to indicate being currently single at 40 percent.

In legally positive states, approximately 54 percent of the routes were classified as insemination, making this the most common path to parenthood for participants in these states, followed by 27 percent classified as adoption. The remaining routes were much less common for participants in legally positive states, with heterosexual intercourse at 9 percent, fostering and other routes each at 4 percent, and surrogacy at 2 percent. In legally neutral states, the paths to parenthood for participants were more varied. However, insemination remained one of the most frequently taken paths to parenthood at 30 percent, tied with adoption (also at 30 percent). Approximately 20 percent of the routes in legally neutral states involved heterosexual intercourse. The remaining routes were less popular, with approximately 10 percent involving fostering, and surrogacy and other routes each at 5 percent. The trend of insemination being one of the most frequently taken paths continued in legally negative states, with approximately 54 percent of the routes being classified as insemination. Unlike the other two state types, however, heterosexual intercourse (rather than adoption) was the next most commonly cited route, at 21 percent. Nonetheless, approximately 17 percent of the routes to parenthood in legally negative states did involve adoption. Approximately 6 percent of the routes in these states were classified as other, 2 percent as surrogacy, and 0 percent involved fostering. As detailed in our section on adoption and fostering later in this chapter, we also see fewer state adoptions, unsurprisingly, taking place in the legally negative states compared to participants who live in states with other legal environments.

In the following sections, we take a closer look at each of these routes to parenthood, including the characteristics of our sample across these couple types and some of the rationales offered for selecting one route over another.

The Old-Fashioned Way

The majority of LGBT parenting literature is focused on what can be referred to as "intentional" parenthood and largely avoids the subject of having a child as the product of a heterosexual relationship, intentional or otherwise (e.g., Moore 2011; Goldberg 2012). Very little work has really delved into the experiences of those who have become parents outside of a same-sex relationship or, as one of our participants deemed it, "the old-fashioned way," meaning heterosexually. Nonetheless, many children within same-sex households appear to come from previous heterosexual relationships or experiences. As noted in chapter 1, census data suggest that the largest predictor of children being present in a same-sex household is whether a partner indicated a previous, presumably heterosexual, marital relationship on the census (Baumle et al. 2009; see also Baumle and Compton 2011). This route to parenthood carries different implications regarding the effectiveness of negative LGBT family laws, given that such laws do not directly affect different-sex partners having children. It is also within this route that parents and partners have the least difficulty in responding to our identity and identification questions. For example, in many cases a third parent may be present (i.e., the other biological parent), and the partners of the biological parent thus draw on the stepparent identification rather than a biological or adoptive parent identity. The presence of a third parent also creates different dynamics for legal considerations, such as the ability to access second-parent adoptions and precautions taken in navigating LGBT parenting when another biological parent might sue for custody.

Approximately 17 percent of our participants, twenty-five in total, indicated their children came from previous heterosexual relationships or experiences—this includes parents who cited prior marriages or dating relationships with an opposite-sex partner, and one-night or other heterosexual encounters, including rape. Contrary to some popular media stories, we had no participants who engaged in heterosexual intercourse in order to get pregnant while in a same-sex relationship. Of the participants who had children via heterosexual intercourse, 84 percent identified as female and 84 percent were white. Approximately 32 percent were now legally married to their same-sex partner, while 28 percent indicated a partnered status, and 40 percent were currently single. Compared to the other parenting routes, these parents had the lowest median household income of around $77,000 (related, in part, to the greater number of single individuals), and were least likely to live in a legally positive state.

For our participants who reported this path to parenthood, the children were primarily intentional within heterosexual relationships, particularly within more lengthy relationships. This group of parents indicated a romantic or ongoing relationship with their significant others at the time of conception, and most of the parents cited issues other than sexual orientation as leading to the relationship dissolution. By contrast, two parents indicated their children were the product of a one-time, consensual heterosexual encounter. For example, Lynette, a single, black lesbian in her twenties living in a negative-leaning legally neutral state, explained: "Basically when I was working in [the city], I was working at a bar as well as [here], and that's where I met his dad. And at the time I was going through a break up with my live-in girlfriend, so she was like not there at all, and he was always there, so that's basically how that came about. . . . There was really no, you know, 'I like you; we should be in a relationship' type conversation that took place. [It] just kinda happened." When asked if she planned to have a child, Lynette responded: "Not with him, no. Not at that time. I always planned on having . . . like I wanted to have kids, but I always wanted to do it, you know, with my partner. But it didn't play out that way."

LGBT individuals could also become parents via heterosexual relationships as the result of planned decisions to have biological children with opposite-sex partners, outside of a romantic relationship—a practice that seems more prevalent in popular culture media than in current practice. This approach could be particularly considered when laws or finances restrict the availability of adoption or insemination and surrogacy approaches to parenthood. While none of our participants chose this route to parenthood, a significant number had considered such an approach or knew individuals who had used this approach. For example, Lynette described two of her friends who considered this option:

> One of my older lesbian couple [friends], they were trying to have a baby. . . . The guy that she was trying to have the baby with, [he] started causing all kind of issues because he was like, basically if it was a boy, he

wanted to be there, but if it was a girl he didn't. And she was like: "That's not fair, like you can't really have a say so. This is, you know, me and my partner trying to raise this child, not with you." So, they wind up just, the stud had the baby, so it was kind of interesting to me.

This example highlights some of the concerns of our participants when they did consider parenting outside of a romantic relationship. Most of these considerations involved parental vulnerabilities and fears regarding their ideal family construct. This was particularly the case in less legally positive states or when individuals had access to fewer economic or informational resources. These fears regarding legal vulnerability and parent-child identities make it unsurprising that this was a less attractive route to parenthood for our participants, resulting in most of those who considered this option ultimately selecting insemination. Penny, a married, white gay woman in her fifties who lives in a legally negative state, maintained that she would have "screwed to have [her] own baby," but only if it had been the only way to have children—and it was not her only option. Overwhelmingly, then, our participants indicated that children from heterosexual intercourse came from "romantic" interactions rather than as the result of a planned route to parenthood while in a same-sex relationship.

While approximately a fifth of our participants reported having children as a result of heterosexual relationships, many noted the ways in which this route to parenthood is likely to continue to decline in popularity. As LGBT individuals continue to come out at increasingly early ages, they may be less likely to enter into heterosexual relationships or marriages that produce children. Indeed, a number of our participants made statements that support Weston's (1991) findings regarding the ways in which coming out inferred not only singleness but also childlessness. For example, when we asked Penny whether she had ever considered becoming a parent prior to her current relationship, she responded that she "didn't know [parenthood] was an option" for her due to her sexual orientation. In fact, she had never really thought about parenthood until she had a "ready-made" family through her relationship with her stepchild. Quite a few parents across the age spectrum echoed the sentiment that at one point they believed it was an either/or option to being queer or being a parent. For example, Dana, who is quoted at the beginning of this chapter, is in her thirties; and yet she originally understood coming out to exclude the possibility of parenthood. By contrast, many of the younger parents in our study indicated that they always expected to have children. These ideas expressed by more of our younger participants suggest that there is a cultural lag and that more LGBT individuals now expect to have access to parenthood options that go beyond heterosexual intercourse.

Insemination

Children in LGBT households are also biological children that were conceived via reproductive technologies. Previous studies find that women are more likely than men to turn to insemination using known or unknown donor sperm (Appell 2001). This approach is often economical, with the ability to perform at-home insemination resulting in a low-cost and more intimate approach to parenthood—something our participants echoed frequently. If medical assistance is warranted, however, then insemination becomes a more costly route. Among our participants, 45 percent used insemination, making it the most popular route to parenthood. Approximately 91 percent of parents in this category identify as female, although our sample of those using insemination also includes five transmen and one gay male who coparents with a lesbian couple. The median household income of this group of parents was approximately $106,000, and there was strong representation across all income ranges and legal environments.

A number of our participants spoke of insemination as the obvious or "natural" choice. Particularly for women participants, insemination was cited as a well-known parenthood option that was most popular among their social networks. As Vivian—a married (in multiple states and countries), white lesbian in her thirties residing in a neutral state—put it, "Everybody's doing it!" Perhaps because of the seeming naturalness of insemination, most of our participants who did insemination at home or in a clinic did not contemplate legal restrictions. For example, it did not even occur to Jean and Anna, a married couple in their thirties who live in a legally negative state, that there may be legal restrictions related to insemination with a known donor until they met with a midwife. As Jean explained:

So we talked to her and she told us . . . [that] we couldn't use known donor sperm and actually have it go to a bank. Like, we couldn't just show up with a paper bag at a doctor's office. . . . That wasn't legal. . . . So we knew that if we were going to use a known donor, the only option was to do it at home. So, I think that maybe there are some other ways you can go about it, maybe by shipping it out of state. I don't know, some other maybe not technically legal ways, but other ways. But it just seemed easier to place a phone call, and have him knock on the door in thirty minutes.

Much like Jean and Anna, very few of our participants seemed to consider whether there were restrictions related to insemination, especially if the process occurred at home. A number of our participants discovered legal restrictions related to insemination after they had already completed the process. In some cases, this meant that participants learned that they technically broke the law by inseminating at home; in other cases, participants learned that they had fortuitously adhered to the law despite being unaware of its existence. Heather, a married, white woman who identifies as queer and is in her thirties, lives in a legally positive state with her family. She indicated that she and her partner later discovered that their insemination choices were perhaps the best ones they could have made from a legal standpoint, stating: "Actually, it turned out well because in [this state] surrogacy is illegal, or something like that. . . . That's what our lawyer told us. . . . So it's good that we had a doctor doing the inseminations so we have a paper trail so we could be sure of it. To show that the donor didn't have a legal claim on our child, basically. That we had the proof from the sperm bank that it was anonymous, the proof that the doctor was using . . . anonymous sperm to generate this child." For Heather, legal concerns did not act as primary determinants in the decision to pursue insemination with an anonymous donor. Afterward, however, she and her partner appreciated the relative legal protection that they believed they were provided by pursuing insemination using an anonymous donor.

Compared to some of the other routes to parenthood such as adoption, fostering, and surrogacy, insemination is sometimes perceived as being less restricted either by the state or through its procedure; this results in many parents feeling they have greater control over the process. This was the case for Sam and Brenda, a married, white couple in their forties who live in a legally negative state. Sam explained: "We have a friend of a friend who runs an adoption agency. So, it was a realistic option for us, but in doing the investigation research we decided we had most control over an insemination process." Insemination provided relative independence from the potential influence of other actors when pursuing family goals. Rather than relying on adoption agencies or judges to process an adoption in their favor, parents often preferred being able to take control over the situation. Along these lines, Sam and Brenda further added that they were specifically told by adoption attorneys that a biological route was the best choice and that it would be "the ideal situation."

Similarly, Natasha, a partnered, white lesbian in her forties living in a legally neutral state, noted that she did research online and "ruled out adoption pretty quickly just based on finances, and, ah . . . our own personal issues" related to feelings of vulnerability and family security. Natasha's concern was echoed by a number of other participants who opted for the insemination route over adoption or surrogacy. Many participants assumed the adoptive or surrogacy processes would be not only expensive but also lengthy and intrusive. In some ways, insemination thus comes across as the route that has it all—or at least offers the most to parents regarding lower costs, control, family security, and legal protection.

Although insemination was an attractive option for many women participants, its perceived accessibility as compared to alternate methods played a role in pushing or pulling participants toward this route. For example, Marlene's primary concern with insemination was related to whether she would be able to locate a provider who would agree to inseminate. Marlene is a partnered, white lesbian in her forties residing in a negative-leaning neutral state where insemination was not commonplace or easily accessible. In weighing the choices of public adoption or insemination, Marlene considered both overt legal barriers (e.g., whether adoption was accessible due to sexual orientation) and barriers related to access to insemination services:

> Well, I would see same-sex couples that would always have to be single parent[s to adopt] if you lived in [this state]. Then I knew some other people that were adopting in [the Northeast] and that they do same-sex

adoptions [there]. . . . But around the time that we were doing it, that is when the insemination thing was coming and private practitioners would not do it [here]. You had to go to fertility institutes. My private OB/GYN did mine. She was also a friend. A lot of practitioners at that time . . . wouldn't inseminate lesbians. Right around the time I was doing it was around the time it started changing. [Another of my friends] did it with a turkey baster because they couldn't find [a practitioner to inseminate]. . . . Her son is eleven, so he is significantly older than our kids. She couldn't find anyone to do it, so they did it [themselves].

Marlene's story is striking in the way that it emphasizes the roles that the law, social location and networks, and accessibility to resources play in becoming a parent. Whether a route to parenthood is legal is not the sole question for LGBT parents considering their options; rather, whether the route is actually available within their locale becomes of practical import.

Overall, participants cited comfort with the insemination process, family security, and the greater financial costs of other parenthood routes as their largest motivators in picking this path to parenthood. These rationales dominated discussions of selecting this route to parenthood, rather than articulated preferences for a biological relationship with a child. A small minority, however, did indicate that a biological relationship to their child would be an ideal starting place; these comments, however, were almost exclusively framed in emotional terms of biological kinship rather than out of consideration of any legal implications.

Surrogacy

In addition to heterosexual sex or insemination, surrogacy also provides an option for LGBT individuals to have biological children. For men especially, surrogacy is an option to have a biological child through utilizing either donor eggs or the egg of the surrogate (Davis 2011; Goldberg 2012). Surrogacy, however, is very costly and thus not a viable option for many individuals irrespective of sex (Goldberg 2012). It also presents itself with more potential legal hurdles than do other routes to parenthood. Given these barriers, it is unsurprising that this would be a less frequented approach to becoming a parent for our participants.

Only 4 percent of our participants underwent the surrogacy route, two-thirds of which were male. For our six participants who used surrogacy, the median household income was $250,000, the greatest of all parent types. They were also most likely to be male, least likely to be single, and least likely to live in a legally negative state compared to those using other paths to parenthood.

The thing that stands out the most about parents drawing on surrogacy is their available resources. Surrogacy offers many of the same advantages as insemination related to biology and, by association, rights to a child and added family security from a legal perspective. For gay male couples, this is the only option for a biological child without shared custody or coparenting. While economic costs played a role in deterring participants from the surrogacy route to parenthood, our participants that did use surrogacy cited rationales related to the ideal family construction, the preference for a biological child, and legal family security. Alongside these considerations, individuals who used surrogacy noted that a primary determinant was that it was a financial *possibility* for them to do so. This did not necessarily mean, however, that all individuals using surrogacy were able to do so without feeling the financial impact. Two couples emphasized that they felt they made financial sacrifices in undergoing this route, but ultimately indicated that it was worth it.

In addition to financial costs, participants using surrogacy also made note of the intensive labor that went into locating surrogates, agencies, and lawyers in order to complete the process. As Devin, a partnered, white gay man in his forties residing in a legally positive state, explained: "[I] stumbled across surrogacy moms online, this kind of website bulletin board for people looking for a donor, people looking for surrogates, looking to be surrogates, looking to donate. And that became the vehicle through which [we] launched our surrogacy. We found, maybe through [an organization], an ideal doctor in [another state] who was gay and positive and we decided to work with him, but that we'd find a surrogate on our own." Devin's discussion of navigating surrogacy suggested that the process was intensive, especially as compared to the tone from those who undertook insemination. It is clear that insemination is a path much more commonly traveled, which results in producing greater resources including sperm donors or information related to the process. In addition, the presence of the law in the surrogacy process was much more pervasive than in insemination and required greater navigation. In fact, all of the parents we interviewed that used surrogacy drew on attorneys at some point during their process to parenthood, indicating the additional barriers and legal considerations that are a part of surrogacy. Thus, unlike insemination, which allowed individuals to bypass some of the intrusiveness of the law, surrogacy involves extensive and complicated navigations of legal processes.

In addition to legal complexities, other participants emphasized the importance of making contact with the right person and networking as part of the surrogacy process. This is particularly the case if they were trying to circumvent having to interact with the law or were concerned about the economic expenses. As a parent who was initially open to various routes to parenthood, Clara, a single, Hispanic queer woman in her thirties who lives in a legally positive state, described the manner in which she understood some gay men attempted to network to locate surrogates:

> So my partner and I went to [this prospective parents' group offered by one organization], and there were a bunch of people talking about legal issues around [parenting] and there were a few people from sperm banks. . . . There were at least some people I could tell for sure that were kind of wanting it to be a networking experience, especially, as they were talking about surrogacy situations. There was a gay male couple that was there and they were kind of like, "That's a lot of money. Like, wouldn't it be cool if there were just a networking experience, you know, lesbians who don't need $100,000 to have our baby that want to share in the experience."

Locating surrogates, then, raised additional concerns and complications, including the costs associated with paying a more traditional surrogate.

Despite the desirability of surrogacy as a means for having one's biological child, surrogacy appeared less popular and practical among our participants because of the complexity of the process and the costs involved, including more direct interactions with the law and with attorneys. Much like insemination for women, for some participants surrogacy implied the best of all worlds if one has the resources to negotiate the process, including finding and securing a surrogate. Unlike insemination, however, the overwhelming costs created a financial barrier for most of our male participants, resulting in the more commonplace use of adoption or fostering.

Adoption and Fostering

Outside of biological means of having children, LGBT individuals also turn to adoption and fostering in order to become parents. This route to parenthood has received some of the greatest amount of academic attention, due in part to the more direct legal and structural barriers in place for LGBT individuals (see, e.g., Goldberg 2012; Gates and Badgett 2007). According to the National Survey of Family Growth (NSFG), 46 percent of lesbian or bisexual women report having considered adoption as a route to parenthood; this contrasts with only 32 percent of heterosexual women who considered adoption (Gates and Badgett 2007).[2] Although adoption appears to be a commonly considered approach to having children, the proportion of gay men and lesbians who actually have an adopted child remains fairly low. Based on data from the census of 2000, Gates and Badgett (2007) estimated that approximately 1.6 percent of same-sex households contain an adopted child under the age of eighteen. Data on the exact number of children adopted by gay or lesbian parents are unavailable, however, Gates and Badgett used census and NSFG data to generate an estimate of 65,500 adopted children that are being raised in the United States by gay men or lesbians (either single or in couples); this accounts for approximately 4 percent of all adopted children in the United States. Based on data from the US census and the Adoption and Foster Care Reporting System, Gates and Badgett concluded that approximately 14,000 children are being fostered by gay men or lesbians, representing 6 percent of all foster children.

About one quarter of our participants indicated that they were adoptive parents, and 4 percent were foster parents. A number of our adoptive parents' children came to them via foster-to-adopt programs, and all of our six foster parents were fostering with the intent to adopt. About half of the parents that fostered in our study had cared for one or two children before being able to adopt. They implied one had to pay dues within the foster system before being able to adopt, which produced financial and emotional costs involving the wait time and the potential for separation from a child who had been a member of the family. Marlene, a partnered, white lesbian in her forties who lives in a legally neutral state, had fostered nineteen infants at the time of our interview, and had never been allowed to adopt due to adoption regulations and practices. She was later able to adopt via private adoption, but articulated frustration with a system that trusted an LGBT individual enough for fostering but not for adoption. This frustration was echoed by three other participants who resided in legally negative states or legally neutral states that were negative-leaning.

Approximately half of our foster parent households and 62 percent of our adoptive households were female-headed. Overall, however, fostering and adoption were more common routes to parenthood for men as compared to women. Of the men in our sample, 48 percent cited adoption or fostering as their path to parenthood compared to 20 percent of the women in our sample. The median household income for the foster parents was $86,000 (with household incomes ranging from $55,000 to the $170,000s); for the adoptive parents it was $110,000 (ranging from $24,000 to over $250,000). Compared to other parent types, adoptive and foster parents were least likely to live in legally negative states.. None of our foster parents lived in legally negative states as would be expected, particularly in states with antigay adoption bans.

As noted above, we had a wide range of incomes represented among our participants who adopted. This is explained in part by the fact that there are a number of forms of adoption, some of which require greater financial resources than others. These range from state and public adoption programs, which require the least resources, to interstate and international adoption programs and private adoptions, which are more costly. Table 2.2 presents a breakdown of the types of adoption used by participants in our study.

Thirty-seven (27 percent) of our 137 participants indicated drawing on legal adoption. As indicated in table 2.2, adoption varies across legal contexts—with the majority of adoptions taking place in legally neutral states (43 percent), followed by positive states (35 percent) and then negative states (22 percent). However, there was little variation in the type of adoption reported by participants across the three legal contexts. Given that we have relatively small sample sizes across the categories of

TABLE 2.2. Adoption, by legal context

	Total		Positive state		Neutral state		Negative state	
	n	%	*n*	%	*n*	%	*n*	%
Adoption	37	100	13	35	16	43	8	22
State	22	59	7	58	10	59	5	63
Private	7	19	3	25	3	18	1	13
International	8	22	3	25	3	18	2	25

adoption type, we are unable to conclude whether legal context affects the particular type of adoption selected.

Qualitatively, however, some participants' stories suggest legal context did have an influence on their selection of a particular route. For example, Dianna, a partnered, white lesbian in her forties, felt it was unlikely she would be able to adopt in her legally neutral state of residence. Drawing on a small inheritance, she decided to look into international adoption. Although she was partnered at the time, she presented herself as a single parent and explained: "[This one African country] was my only option and then I kind of went on the state department website and read more about it, about [the country] and adoptions and that they did adopt to single people. . . . I mean, it's not open, it's kind of still hush. I mean, if you ask them it's one of the most homophobic countries." As discussed in chapter 6, presenting as single and drawing on heteronormative assumptions is one way in which parents are able to "fly under the radar," avoid biases related to sexual orientation, and ultimately foster or adopt. Taking this approach enabled Dianna to adopt while living in a legal environment that she perceived as unfriendly toward LGBT adoptive parents. She initially adopted one daughter from an African country, and jokingly blames Angelina Jolie for making her second daughter's adoption more difficult and expensive. Jolie's adoption of her first daughter from Ethiopia occurred between Dianna's adoptions and greatly increased the awareness surrounding the potential of international adoptions for single individuals. Stories such as Dianna's reflect the manner in which some participants perceived legal context to shape the particular type of adoption that they elected to pursue.

For some participants, adoption in general was a more affordable route to parenthood than insemination or surrogacy. In fact, it was the more prevalent route for gay men in large part because they cannot afford or do not have access to surrogacy. For example, Keith, a single, white gay man in his thirties who makes in the mid-$80,000s and lives in a legally neutral state, explained the manner in which finances affected his route to parenthood:

> Oh, I really would have loved to have done surrogacy, but once again it was cost prohibitive. I mean, you know, . . . I didn't want to . . . have that much debt, cause it would [had] to have been debt to make it happen. . . . I thought, you know, a child is going to be enough cost, I didn't want to add to it. . . . But yes, I really did look at surrogacy, you know, I just surfed the Internet and looked at different options . . . and decided that it's just such a risky thing in my opinion at the time. And then, you know, I knew there were so many children out there who needed homes through the C[hild] P[rotection] S[ervices] system.

Adoption was a desirable option, then, for many parents due to the fact that it was less costly than an option like surrogacy or insemination if extensive medical interventions were involved; accordingly adoption became one of the only options for some participants due to concerns over costs.

In addition, individuals who chose fostering or adoption, like Keith, often articulated the notion that they wished to adopt in order to help children who were already in need. For example, Hannah, a partnered, white lesbian in her forties who lives in a legally neutral state, indicated that adoption was her preferred route to parenthood due to her desire to assist children without families. Her interest, she explained, was a very personal one: "I'm adopted. So, adoption has always been, you know, a good option. An important option, I mean." Although other considerations ultimately pushed her and her partner toward insemination, Hannah's expression of the important contribution of adoption to assisting children in need was echoed by many participants. In some respects, it was the counterweight to the articulated preferences for biological children. If biological children were not practical or desired, the notion of assisting children was often voiced as a rationale for selecting adoption as a route to parenthood.

As detailed in chapters 5 and 6, legal considerations also affected whether individuals pursued fostering or adoption as their route to parenthood. Some individuals represented themselves as single in order to bypass issues of sexuality, and others were able to navigate sexuality through carefully worded home studies. In the majority of cases handled in legally neutral and legally negative states, parents indicated that sexuality was not mentioned in their home study, but partners were mentioned as being part of the household (e.g., as roommates). Additionally, none of our participants who engaged in in-state adoption in legally neutral states indicated that they deliberately hid their partner or sexuality from the system. This strongly suggests that the process was more broadly focused on whether a home was suitable for a child rather than on the sexuality of the applicants. Prior research further supports this notion, indicating that informal adoption agency practices that seek primarily to place children in good homes can provide a manner for LGBT individuals to circumvent unfriendly laws (see, e.g., Hastings and Bissett 2002; Riggs 1999).

Several of our participants commented that there had been a shift across time in the ways that administrative practices affected the accessibility of adoption and fostering for LGBT individuals. For example, Anthony, a single, white gay man in his thirties who lives in a legally neutral state, explained that his foster-to-adopt process may have been a different experience compared to just a couple of years earlier: "I know that my friends who adopted the fourteen-year-old, they started the process much earlier than I did, years before I did, and they encountered some problems with CPS workers and people in the courts who were adamantly against gay people adopting . . . or just against single parents adopting. There has been bias in [this state], and probably still is, but I think it's getting better." As more parents undergo foster and adoption processes, participants suggested that this route to parenthood seems to open up and become smoother for those who follow. For example, in a number of states and across legal contexts there were go-to attorneys and social workers that participants knew about and drew on to assist in the adoption process. Largely, they found out about them via their social networks, parenting listservs, and online forums. In two states, participants described campaigns to build awareness about foster and adoption programs that were specifically marketed toward the LGBT community.

In two other states, both legally neutral, participants indicated less formal and public campaigns, but regarded adoption as marketed toward LGBT parents nevertheless.

Overall, we found that legal context does appear to matter in terms of whether adoption was used as a route to parenthood. Unsurprisingly, participants in legally negative states drew on it the least, as they were most often cut off from public or state adoption programs. In addition, qualitatively it appears that the particular type of adoption used by LGBT parents is sometimes shaped by legal context. The ways in which context drives particular adoption routes may be less apparent in our sample due to the smaller sample sizes across adoption categories, and the fact that we interviewed across so many states with varying legal terrains regarding adoption even within our three legal context types. For example, international adoption was actually less of an option for married participants who lived in some legally positive states, as these states would not represent them as single individuals. Their status as married to someone of the same sex then cut off their access to international adoption. Likewise, some legally neutral states were more open to permitting LGBT individuals to adopt children than other legally neutral states.

Adoption as a route to parenthood for LGBT individuals is quite complex in that there are numerous forms of adoption, each with its own technicalities, including limitations and loopholes, for LGBT individuals to navigate. However, we found no state in which all forms of adoption were completely cut off for LGBT parents. For example, individuals may be able to adopt as a single parent, with a heterosexual assumption or no discussion related to sexual orientation if they had the resources. This was the case for Esther, who resides in the same state as Dianna and privately adopted from an acquaintance. While public adoption seemed impossible to Dianna, private adoption and international adoption were technically available and were employed by participants within this state. In this respect, adoption appeared to be a viable path to parenthood for participants across legal contexts.

Finally, we also found that some of the most open routes for adoption, including second-parent adoption, are located in sociolegal locales that would be surprising to most mainstream culture, LGBT people, and even longtime residents of those places. This suggests that sexuality serves as less of a barrier to fostering and adoption than might be generally perceived. Although our focus on LGBT parents necessarily excluded some of those who were unsuccessful, nonetheless most of the parents we interviewed did not forego the adoption or fostering process for another route to parenthood due to legal obstacles.

Second-Parent Adoption

Of our 137 participants, 99 (72 percent) had access to second-parent adoption. Of those that had access, approximately half underwent second-parent adoption. As indicated in table 2.3, second-parent adoptions were equally popular in legally positive and neutral states, with 23 (46 percent) parents in each legal context reporting they had used second-parent adoption. Those in legally negative states were much less likely to indicate that they had undergone the process. In fact only 4 (8 percent) parents in legally negative states indicated they had undergone second-parent adoption. In three of these cases, individuals had moved from legally positive or neutral states. In the fourth case, their state had recently lifted a ban on gay and lesbian adoptions including second-parent adoptions. Another couple in a legally negative state was planning on applying for a second-parent adoption in the near future as a heterosexual couple since one of them had had a legal sex change. In all but one of these cases, second-parent adoption was not available within their legally negative state. In addition, second-parent adoption was not available in one of the legally neutral states in which we interviewed, and was unavailable in a number of the jurisdictions in other legally neutral states (which resulted in forum-shopping for friendly jurisdictions, as described in chapters 5 and 6).

Second-parent adoption provided unique legal considerations for participants regarding parental identities and identification, particularly for parents who are partners with a biological parent. Second-parent adoption was not typically voiced as a route to parenthood for our participants. Rather, most participants who reported second parent adoptions instead indicated that they became parents via insemination or prior heterosexual relationships. Nonetheless, second-parent adoption did affect how parent-child relationships were identified and how secure couples felt regarding their parental ties legally. Those with second-parent adoption were less likely to identify their child as a stepchild, other relative, or

TABLE 2.3. Second-parent adoption, by legal context

	Total		Positive state		Neutral state		Negative state	
	n	%	n	%	n	%	n	%
Second parent	50	100	23	46	23	46	4	8

other nonrelative on administrative documents like the census (Baumle and Compton 2014). Rather, they were more likely to describe a child as their "own child" or—drawing upon the legal identity provided through adoption—as an adopted child. Nonbiological parents to partners that underwent insemination demonstrated the greatest uneasiness and incompatibility with their parent-child relationship, given the tension between what they perceived to be a "biological" relationship with the child and the legal relationship afforded by second-parent adoption.

Other Routes to Parenthood

A small percentage of our participants, 5.3 percent, indicated that they became parents via informal adoptions of relatives or nonrelatives and through stepparenting, among other routes. The primary distinguishing characteristic for this category of individuals involves their partnership status, with 75 percent of them identifying as married. This is to be expected, given that those who became parents due to stepchildren are also those who are likely to be married. Although the "stepchild" label can be, and is, utilized by those who are not married, it is more commonly employed by legally married individuals (Baumle and Compton 2014). In addition, some of our participants in this category became parents out of other step relationships, such as when their spouse's younger sibling lived in the home. Given the small sample size of those identifying one of these other routes to parenthood, we cannot discern any patterns regarding legal context or other individual characteristics that typify this group of parents.

Multimethod Routes to Parenthood

As reflected in table 2.4, about 15 percent of our participants indicated undergoing more than a single route to parenthood. Most commonly,

TABLE 2.4. Multimethod routes to parenthood

	n		%
Participants	22		14.7
Mean Age		39	
Median household income ($)		140,000	
Female	17		77.3
Race			
White	19		86.4
Black	1		4.5
Other	1		4.5
Multiracial	1		4.5
Hispanic	0		0.0
Marital status			
Married	14		63.6
Partnered	8		36.4
Single	0		0.0
Legal context			
Positive state	8		36.4
Neutral state	8		36.4
Negative state	6		27.3

this was the case if one of the children came from a previous hetero-sexual relationship, and then a same-sex couple pursued having a child within their subsequent relationship. The median household income of parents who underwent multiple routes to parenthood was $140,000, with about 77 percent of them being female-headed households. None of these parents identified as single, while approximately 64 percent were legally married to their same-sex partner and 36 percent indicated a partnered status. A multimethod approach to becoming parents was fairly equally prevalent across all legal contexts.

Conclusion

In stepping back and considering how parenthood decisions were made for our participants as a whole, we found that individual demographic characteristics and legal contexts affected particular paths to parenthood. Unsurprisingly, class and access to resources contribute greatly to the parents' choices —including what routes LGBT individuals consider, what they fail to consider, and what the overall outcomes are. For men, class factors become particularly notable in influencing decisions across biological (i.e., surrogacy) or nonbiological (i.e., adoption or fostering) routes to parenthood (see Goldberg 2012 for similar findings). For women, class differences are most prevalent for the category of individuals who became parents via heterosexual sex, with their greater single status resulting in lower household incomes. Class seems to operate as a lesser barrier toward biological children for women, given that women participants across many income ranges were able to access insemination through known or unknown donors. As we discuss throughout the book, these differences produce interesting distinctions in terms of the type of legal concerns expressed by male and female parents given that at least one female partner is more likely to have a biological tie with children in the household.

Overall, the majority of our participants expected to form families despite variations in legal environments. Although most were ultimately successful in forming families (largely due to the numerous routes to parenthood), this did not mean that legal context did not affect individual choices. Most participants living in legally positive states said living in a state without legal protections would affect their route to parenthood. For example, Sandra, a married, white lesbian in her forties who was living in a legally positive state, explained that having a child via insemination was primarily an option for her and her partner due to the ability to acquire legal rights for the nonbiological parent. Sandra observed: "We were very aware of all those horrible, horrible cases where lesbian couples break up and the bio mom says, 'I'm a fundamentalist Christian now, we're not a family, I never was gay. You're not a parent.' My partner had had a terrible breakup, no religious overtones, but she is very aware that people just behave a lot worse than you ever would think. And she would not have had a kid unless we had legal . . . rights."

These fears regarding who is the "real" parent in terms of the biological or legal relationship affected the route to parenthood for many individuals. These concerns guided decisions involving choosing (a) between known or unknown donors for insemination, (b) the biological parent for insemination or surrogacy, and (c) the individual who would adopt in situations where coadoption was not permitted. Although such fears existed across legal contexts, nonetheless those living in positive states were often less fearful due to the option of other available legal protections (e.g., second-parent adoption, coadoption, or marriage). Even when parents were unsure as to whether these options existed, or chose not to exercise them, residing in a positive state provided more security regarding the likely outcome if there was a dispute over legal rights. This, in turn, made some routes to parenthood appear less legally tenuous for those in legally positive states than those in legally neutral or negative states.

Insemination was the most common route to parenthood across all legal contexts, although it was a more dominant route in legally positive and legally negative states. Legally neutral states, by contrast, reflected a more varied approach to parenthood, which resulted in insemination and adoption being equally common routes.

Heterosexual intercourse also was a less common route among our participants located in legally positive states as compared to legally negative or neutral states. This could suggest that a friendly legal and sociopolitical environment might result in coming out at an earlier age and a lower tendency to enter heterosexual relationships. Becoming a parent through prior heterosexual relationships also meant that many laws restricting LGBT parenting and family formation were less applicable, enabling greater access to parenthood via this route for those in legally negative states.

Our participants in legally neutral states had greater variation across routes of parenthood. This could suggest that, without laws in support or against LGBT families, parents have less well-traveled paths or streams to parenthood than we would expect if (a) laws supporting access to parenthood were creating more efficient and utilizable paths for parents, such as in legally positive states, or (b) laws hindering access to parenthood were blocking specific paths to parenthood, in which case our participants became more restricted in their paths, such as in legally negative states.

Certainly laws regarding adoption, fostering, and surrogacy can be particularly important for LGBT individuals considering parenthood. Our interviews also yielded the effects of other laws and practices on parenthood routes. For example, in some states the most difficult step in undergoing insemination was finding someone to do the insemination or learning on your own, while in other states it was securing the instruments for the process such as a syringe or catheter (some states have laws regulating the selling of syringes and various medical equipment). Likewise, in some states, the availability of same-sex marriage actually cut off some parenthood routes—most predominantly international adoption, as married individuals were unable to depict themselves as single in order to adopt from countries that were unwilling to adopt to same-sex couples (see chapter 6).

The routes to parenthood for our participants, thus, illustrate the manner in which legal context can both directly affect available options, as well as have more indirect implications for the manner in which individuals are able to access a desired parenthood route. Accordingly, it becomes important to examine how LGBT individuals gain an understanding of what is legally possible in terms of family formation and the ways in which to pursue their family goals. In the following chapter, we take a closer look at the sources of legality for LGBT individuals who are pursuing family formation or who are parenting.

3

Locating Legality

We did not [consult a lawyer]. It didn't seem like, to be honest, that we needed to. It seemed like it was all pretty much out there, that you could find some authorities on the matter. . . . You know, you have to watch what you read and not take it as gospel like, ohh I read it on the internet, must be true. But when you start reading the same things over and over again and it's not this circular reference, . . . they aren't all referencing each other. . . . You are like, okay. Then you start talking to other parents. This is how it worked for us.
—Curt

The law is a multifaceted construct, incorporating lay notions of rules and procedures as well as more formal law on the books. Conceiving of legality in this broad fashion renders individuals active participants in its interpretation and construction. As such, the law is often considered a living or evolving entity that saturates most aspects of our lives. If the law is a part of everyday life, then it can be encountered when interacting with store managers, bosses, schoolteachers, or organizations. Further, information about the law can be transmitted via a number of sources, including movies, television, the Internet, books, or social networks. Law is everywhere; accordingly, understandings of the law and willingness to use the law are shaped from our everyday interactions and the information received from a variety of extralegal sources. In this respect, the law is not the sole domain of formal legal actors, such as judges or attorneys, and extends beyond the law on the books, stated regulations, and precedents set by judges and officers of the court.

The ways in which LGBT parents obtain information about the law reflect that legality can be found in both expected and unexpected places. As observed by Curt at the beginning of this chapter, the Internet and other parents can serve as legitimate sources of information about rules and laws that govern family matters, sometimes enabling individuals to bypass attorneys. Which sources of information become most salient for an individual serve to shape their understanding of the role of the law within their families. In this respect, their assumption about what is possible for their families is affected by their understanding of what is legal or permissible, and vice versa. We wish to emphasize that their understandings of the law are not always correct, or might not translate across jurisdictions. In this respect, their sources of legal information shape their understandings and beliefs about what the law might be, but do not necessarily reflect the actual state of the law.

Although most people do not directly consult attorneys or the law on the books when making family decisions (Mather, McEwen, and Maiman 2001; Jacob 1992; Ellickson 1991), they do tend to have a perception of whether their actions align with the law. These perceptions are influenced by cultural factors, including sources of legality. It is through culture that we frame and understand the law and our relationship with it.

Drawing on Attorneys

Overwhelmingly, it is expected that attorneys will know how to navigate the legal process. The notion that drawing on attorneys will keep LGBT parents and their families safe is a strong reoccurring theme in our interviews. Despite this presumption of attorneys as important legal resources, a large proportion of our participants never consulted an attorney about their family. While over half (60 percent) of our participants did consult an attorney about their family at some point, very few did so as one of their first steps toward becoming a parent. Those that did were primarily individuals who used known donors and wished to ensure that the rights of all parties were protected prior to beginning insemination. For example, Michelle, a married, white queer-identified woman in her thirties who lives in a legally neutral state, indicated: "We did talk to a lawyer before we started. We got a donor insemination agreement, we laid out all of our intentions and his intentions and we all signed it with a notary and everything." Others who consulted with attorneys prior to beginning the process were individuals who were uncertain about adoption possibilities within their state due to the unsettled nature of the law. Thus, it was more difficult for them to look up information online because the state of the law was in flux.

Overall, only about 5 percent of our participants consulted an attorney prior to a pregnancy. Most often, however, parents consulted with attorneys, or planned to do so, once children were already present or were on the way. In these cases, attorneys were primarily utilized for purposes of deciphering legal language in laws or forms, arbitrating or drafting protective documents in times of direct conflict with a partner or family member, establishing lineage or passing on property, or obtaining security.

Attorneys as Decoders of Legality

Most commonly, attorneys were consulted to assist in deciphering legal information. Participants frequently needed clarification regarding existing laws or procedures, or assistance in completing procedural paperwork or processes. This was the case for approximately 42 percent of our participants. Margo, a married, white bisexual woman in her thirties who lives in a legally neutral state, explained the desire to have an attorney complete second-parent adoption paperwork due to the complexities of navigating legality: "Our friends had talked about all the ways you can . . . do all that paperwork on your own. And we sort of looked into that a little bit but I didn't want to get it wrong." Thus, for most of our participants, attorneys' legal expertise was primarily needed to decipher legal language and procedures. But they also more subtly implied that attorneys were needed due to the concern and desire to protect their family and to be "legal"—they didn't want to get it wrong.

Maggie, a married, white lesbian in her thirties who lives in a legally positive state, exemplifies this notion of needing legal expertise in order to decipher complicated legal information. Maggie has a stepdaughter from a previous relationship and was planning on having a second child. She was uncertain as to what legal hoops she needed to jump through in order to protect her family properly:

Like on websites, some people say that you should still do the second-parent adoption in case you're in a state that doesn't recognize your marriage and the birth certificate, which has [both] names on it. Which doesn't make sense to me. And I was talking to a woman recently who . . . both [she and her partner] are on the birth certificate and . . . she was saying she . . . didn't have to do the second-parent adoption piece because of the birth certificate. But I'm seeing stuff that says yes. So definitely, we just need to meet with the lawyer once we get there.

For Maggie and her partner, an attorney was needed in order to assist in deciphering conflicting information that they were receiving from the Internet and from friends. Without this conflict, it is unclear whether Maggie would have understood an attorney to be a welcomed source of legal information or whether the attorney would simply have been needed to complete the more procedural aspects of adoption. However, given the discrepancies in the information she was receiving from other sources, an attorney's expertise seemed to be viewed as an essential part of engaging with the law.

This sentiment of needing an attorney primarily to decipher legal information and navigate complicated legal procedures seems applicable to most of our participants who consulted attorneys. Krystal, a married, white bisexual woman in her thirties who resides in a legally positive state, echoed this idea of needing an attorney in order to decipher legalese or nuances in the law: "It's hard to disentangle what the policy is and what the law is. . . . I mean, you hire a lawyer and then you kind of go with what they say is the best way to do things. I mean the one reason you hire a lawyer is because they make you sign these things that have tons of information and wording that you don't quite understand."

Similarly, Marlon a partnered, white gay man in his fifties who works as a legal professional within a legally neutral state, sought out an attorney for a specific task related to an out-of-state surrogacy agreement. He explained: "The laws in [my state] . . . didn't at the time really permit this type of business arrangement and in [this other state] it was established as a commercial contract business venture. That's at least how it was explained to me." Marlon's need to consult with an expert in order to decipher the law highlights the legal complexities for parents and the lack of intuitiveness of the law even for a trained legal professional.

Our participants frequently demonstrated that it is presumed that attorneys will be able to decipher the information and navigate the process more efficiently and effectively than laypersons. However, we also found a hint of vulnerability among our participants as they were largely dependent on their particular attorney's knowledge and resources. In some cases, participants found that attorneys' knowledge surrounding LGBT family matters was less sophisticated than they anticipated. For example, Kendra, a married white, gay woman in her forties who lives in a legally positive state, found she often knew more than her attorney and had to give her attorney instruction:

> [The attorney has] been doing this for thirty years, and that's one of the reasons we picked her too because we knew we had a creaky case. We had to do this interstate [process] and [our state] is just a pain in the ass when it comes to doing procedural things, and I know that. But I think that she was surprised at how much she didn't know, and she never really admitted that, and that was a problem with me. Like, I would follow up and say, "You need to do X, Y, and Z," because I was working with [an adoption organization] and sometimes I knew more than she did. And that really bothered me. I'm not paying you all this money for me to know more than you. You know what I mean? But anyway, it's done now.

In stark contrast to Maggie's experience, Kendra found that her extra-legal resources were providing her with what she perceived to be *better* information than what she received from her attorney. This led to frustration for Kendra, whose comments suggest a critique of the power dynamics at play in her relationship with the attorney. She was paying for expertise, and yet she felt that her so-called expert did not convey the degree of authority on legal matters that was expected.

Similarly, other participants voiced dissatisfaction with their attorneys' depth of legal knowledge because the attorneys they selected were not well versed in family matters, LGBT matters, or both. For example, Esther, a partnered, Hispanic lesbian in her forties who lives in a legally neutral state, found an attorney for her adoption listed in the phone book under "adoption." The attorney was not familiar with legal issues related to LGBT individuals adopting, leading Esther to good-naturedly observe: "She was pretty lame and she learned a lot. . . . Yeah, . . . you could tell the whole thing was just really blowing her mind. She was like, 'Wow, I don't know, I'm gonna have to look this up.' And we were like, ok!" For Esther, an attorney seemed to serve less as an expert on the particular legal issue at hand, and more as a resource for navigating legal procedures. She seemed comfortable with the notion that the attorney needed to, and could, learn enough about this area of the law in order to navigate the adoption process successfully. The fact that she resides in a more negative sociopolitical environment likely contributed to her lack of expectation of finding an attorney who was particularly competent in this area of the law. Her experience thus contrasts with that of Kendra, who perhaps was more frustrated by her attorney as a result of expectations generated by her location in a legally positive state, using an attorney who had extensive experience in this area of the law.

On the other hand, for Colin, a partnered, white Hispanic gay man in his thirties who resides in a legally negative state, locating an attorney who was an expert in LGBT family issues was viewed as incredibly important. Colin was in the process of adopting a child as a single parent, along with his partner who was not permitted to coadopt. Colin explained that, in looking for an attorney, finding an expert was essential: "I wanted somebody who specialized in what we were looking for. . . . Because I don't want to screw it up. It has to be done right. Our kid is the absolute most important thing to us, even more so than each other. And I didn't think that [was] possible. . . . I was a little afraid to tell [my partner] that when I realized it. And I told him and he was like, 'Oh, I feel the same way.'" Colin's concern that everything be done "right," juxtaposed with his comment that their child is the most important thing in their lives, suggests that he approached the selection of an attorney with a sense of fear that their claim over their child could be threatened. His location within a legally negative environment perhaps played a role in generating greater anxiety regarding the process, and pushing him toward a specialist.

Issues other than legal context, however, were sometimes articulated as driving participants toward attorneys who were *not* well versed in LGBT family law. For example, Maxine and Allison, a married, white queer-lesbian couple in their thirties who live in a legally positive state were in the process of going through second-parent adoption. They selected a family friend as their lawyer and, as Allison explained, the process was not smooth:

> We used a friend of ours and we were her second adoption and our other friends who had a baby, they were her first adoption. So she isn't a lawyer

who does this as part of her practice, but because she's our friend and she had never really done it before, she gave us a huge discount. . . . So . . . this was her first time in our city because the other [adoption] was in another town. So she originally filed the wrong paperwork, so it took longer to get a court date.

For Maxine and Allison, who both work in social work fields, cost appeared to be a driving factor in opting for an attorney who was not an expert on LGBT family matters. Thus, even though they lived in a legally positive state and had access to attorneys who would perhaps serve as better sources on the law, the discounted price played a role in their selection. Their story, along with those of Kendra, Esther, and Colin, highlight the manner in which our participants' push toward the use of attorneys as expert decoders was affected by legal context and socioeconomic factors.

Attorneys as Securers of Legal Protections

Attorneys were not only called upon for assistance in deciphering complicated legal information or attending to procedural aspects of family matters. About one quarter of the time, our participants also used attorneys as a source of legal information when they had concerns about protecting their family from opposing legal claims. Nine of our participants (6 percent) specifically sought attorneys in times of direct conflict with a partner or family members concerning custody or related issues. For example, Tina, a partnered, white lesbian in her thirties who now resides in a legally positive state, had her son while in college. She began raising him as a single mother with help from her family, while living in a legally negative state. She contacted an attorney due to a custody battle with her parents over her son:

> We wanted him to have [my parent's] healthcare coverage because he was on a state plan and they wouldn't approve all the things we wanted to have done for him to meet his special needs. And so I went to the attorney's office and signed over, basically, my custodial rights to my child, which looking back was not the brightest move ever. But I did. And then when I came out to my family and was going to move to take a job in

another state, . . . they threatened to have me arrested . . . because I didn't have guardianship of him. And so I moved and hired an attorney. She explained to me that the odds were stacked against me. One, because I was admitting in court that I . . . was a lesbian. And I had the legal two-prong test which was to not only prove that where he was wasn't okay for him, but the second part of that was that I could provide a better place for him. . . . And because I was living with my partner, and in what the law [in that state] deemed an illicit relationship, [it was difficult to meet the second prong].

Tina did not contact an attorney primarily to decipher legality or to complete procedural aspects of a legal process. Instead, she explained her motivation for consulting an attorney in terms of the desire to protect and gain custody of her child. Tina was never able to regain custody of her son until, at the age of eighteen, he was able to legally express a desire to move and live with her. Her experience in utilizing attorneys was, thus, a long and frustrating process. While Tina's initial experience began more than ten years ago when it could be easily argued that social tolerance rates were much lower, it is nevertheless important in framing how parents construct legality. Moreover, as she moved up in her career and gained access to more resources and wealth, she continually attempted to revisit the situation. In reflecting on her home state, she offered the opinion that it is still quite unfriendly to LGBT people and parents today and wondered why parents with resources would not leave for a safer location.

Several of our other participants described consulting an attorney in order to implement more proactive measures for protecting their family from perceived conflicts. For example, Kendra felt it was important to meet with an attorney while she was pregnant in order to secure guidance for drafting wills and powers of attorney. She explained that this was essential for her in order to safeguard her partner's claims over their child:

About three weeks before I delivered, we finally met with a lawyer and we spent two hours drafting everything that we needed to draft in terms of wills and power of attorney and all that kind of stuff. And that was really important to me. My mom and my brothers love and accept my partner . . . and it was never really an issue, but you never know, you know what I mean? And so, especially when a child was going to be born that was biologically my child. . . . So we did all these wills and everything, and that was important to have in place before. And I was actually starting to panic because it was only three weeks before and I was like, "I'm not going into labor without this, so if she doesn't do it, we're going to have to find another lawyer."

Although Kendra admitted that she contacted an attorney at the eleventh hour, she nonetheless emphasized how she understood an attorney's legal expertise to be necessary for obtaining an added sense of security in parental rights for her partner. Rather than turning to other potential sources for the law, such as online programs for generating wills, her concern about potential threats to her family pushed her to contact a legal expert.

Like Kendra, many parents referenced these more general "what if" concerns in connection with potential threats from family members. Those that mentioned more specific complications, however, typically indicated that an attorney was sought out to protect against an antigay family member or a side of the family. For example, Rhonda a partnered, Hispanic lesbian in her thirties who resides in a legally neutral state was concerned about her partner's brother potentially seeking custody should something happen to her partner, Joann. Rhonda stated: "Joann has a brother who is a complete A-double-S and is a pretty good attorney. And so I wanted to make sure we were as best protected against him in the event of her death." Rhonda's story exemplifies many of the more specific threats to the family that drove some of our participants to seek legal expertise rather than rely on more informal sources. In addition, her discussion about Joann's brother also highlights a common assumption among most of our participants related to attorneys, in which they believe that attorneys are uniquely skilled in manipulating the law for themselves or their clients. This notion of attorneys being able to use their specialized knowledge to "play the legal game" is further explored in chapter 5.

Perceived threats that required consulting an attorney came not only from family members. Participants also discussed the need to seek legal expertise from attorneys in connection with potential travel or moves out of state. These stories were more common among individuals in legally positive states, who felt secure within their current state but wanted to take proactive measures to safeguard themselves against unfriendly actors while visiting elsewhere. For example, Patti and Henrietta, a married white/Middle Eastern queer couple in their thirties live in a legally positive state but consulted an attorney in order to obtain a variety of safeguards for their family. One of these involved taking measures to protect them while traveling:

> HENRIETTA: And we were also seeing [the attorney] . . . because I travel so much. [I realized] that we should have some other protection documents in place, so . . . we drafted a power of attorney in the same meeting.
> PATTI: You drafted a whole series, like power of attorney . . .
> HENRIETTA: Power of attorney, declaration of representative, like a whole slew of [documents]. Just in case I died in Kansas, here's what we do.

For Patti, who laughingly identified herself as a type-A personality, there was an air of doing their due diligence that came from their conversation. Living in a legally positive state, the couple is perhaps more aware of the array of legal options that are available to them in order to protect their family and they wished to pursue them all, just in case.

Knowing an Attorney

About 25 percent of our participants cited knowing attorneys or legal officials who played a role in legitimating their decision-making processes. In these cases, attorneys were not formally employed or consulted. The perception of access to an attorney, however, gave participants an added sense of family security. Lynette, a single, black lesbian in her twenties who lives in a legally neutral state, described how her connection to an attorney provided her with access to legal information:

> My mother actually works for an attorney, and I have talked to her. Just basically, 'cause . . . I don't wanna live [here] for the rest of my life, and one of my concerns again is me trying to leave and his father trying to step in and saying, "Ok, well you can't take him," . . . but I talked to my mom about it and she . . . has let me know that if push comes to shove, she has no problem steppin' in and givin' me the legal advice that I need, and helpin' me if need be. I would hate for it to get there, because I don't

wanna be that whole, you know, "He's mine, I have him all the time, you barely do anything, . . . don't fight me on this." And at the same time, I don't wanna take his son from him. . . . . I'm hoping it doesn't get to that point, but I definitely . . . consulted with my mom about it cause now that he's here I wanna cover every single precaution that I need to make sure I'm not gonna lose him over anything petty.

Lynette lives in a culture of mistrust of the law in a neutral, but negative-leaning, state, yet she feels like she has many resources with a supportive family, access to an attorney, and being "the mom." Her story emphasizes the importance that participants sometimes placed on having identified an attorney as a starting point in case of a potential issue—feeling as if you have access to an attorney, knowing where one can be found, and feeling like you will be heard and supported from the start.

Knowing someone who works in the legal realm helped many participants feel more comfortable with their decisions, protected, and secure—at least, secure enough to not further pursue formal consultation with an attorney. Janis and Laura, a married, white couple in their late forties and early fifties who reside in a legally positive state, explained that they have a friend "who's a family law expert who actually works on these issues." In talking to her, just "a little bit," they became more comfortable in their legal decision-making. Similarly, Rebecca, a single, Hispanic queer woman in her thirties, did not formally contact an attorney in order to obtain initial information she needed regarding her pending divorce from her husband. Instead, she consulted with friends and family who worked in the legal field:

I mean, we've talked to friends who are lawyers. We've talked to other people who are divorced and asked them, like, how they did their process. . . . Oh, and his sister is a lawyer, so right when we first broke up she came to visit and we sat down with her and she kind of walked us through like some of the basic . . . broad brushstroke things that needed to happen. So, I mean, we haven't consulted a stranger who's a lawyer, but we've talked to lawyers who are close to us.

Stories like those of Janis, Laura, and Rebecca suggest that knowing an attorney can be utilized in order to obtain an informal overview of the state of the law on an issue. In this respect, knowing an attorney provides a source of legal information for individuals, in addition to just serving as security in the manner described by Lynette.

For some individuals, friends who were not attorneys but who were associated with the legal field served a similar function of translating the law. For example, Lou, a single, black lesbian in her thirties who lives in a legally neutral state, indicated that she had a friend who has a good understanding of legal issues: "She actually works for, um, the sheriff's office and I haven't had any questions for her, but like if something happens, she'll explain it to me." In this respect, knowing someone who works closely with the law within their profession enabled Lou to feel she had an additional resource to call upon in case she encountered legal obstacles. Other participants mentioned informally consulting with friends who were administrative workers, such as court clerks, in order to obtain information about the law. Although these individuals did not serve in the traditional role of an attorney, they functioned in much the same respect in terms of being a resource for legal information.

In a number of cases, participants mentioned knowing attorneys that had undergone various processes that they were interested in, particularly second-parent adoption or getting names added to birth certificates. This validated for them that things could be done, and done legally in their state. For example, Rhonda lives in a legally neutral state with a negative sociopolitical environment. In talking about legality associated with the insemination process, she explained: "I have some friends who had used [this IVF clinic], two women, and gotten pregnant. . . . And both of those women are attorneys, so I'm sure they knew more than I know about how to approach stuff." Rhonda's comment supports the notion that attorneys' specialized legal knowledge and insight into the legal system can confer legal legitimacy to an action. For those who were able to consult attorneys, formally or informally, using attorneys as a source of information can thus serve as a means to signify legality.

Waiting to Consult an Attorney

Typically, when participants drew on attorneys, they preferred to not have to make decisions on their own due to the degree of uncertainty and lack of clarity related to the law. While the perception of potential complications or conflict was a reason that some drew on attorneys, it also was a justification for not consulting with an attorney—the idea being that parents *could* contact an attorney if they wanted to or needed to at a later time.

For those who opted not to consult with attorneys during the family formation process, this idea of waiting until an attorney was absolutely necessary was commonly articulated. For example, Maggie, a married, white lesbian in her thirties who resides in a legally positive state, explained that they had not yet contacted an attorney to determine what steps they needed to take regarding legal documents or second-parent adoption because they had not reached the point when it was a necessity. She explained: "I think we were really just waiting [to see] if I could get pregnant before we did it, before we met the lawyer. We'd have nine months, you know." As with many of our participants, for Maggie there was little need to cross some bridges before others; rather, there is a progression to follow. She did not feel the need to look into obtaining second-parent adoption until a child was actually present.

In this respect, obtaining information regarding second-parent adoption was often undertaken by participants once a child was already on the way (either via insemination or adoption). Securing legal rights for the nonbiological parent, then, became secondary to navigating any challenges involved in bringing a child into the home. Many of the legal interactions that require an attorney's expertise, like second-parent adoption, were accordingly set aside until after parenthood was achieved.

For both parents with and without access to resources, this was a pragmatic approach. Parents with resources felt attorneys were capable and available should they need them, while others did not have the time or funds to deal with potential problems. Although nested in different legal or socioeconomic situations, both of these scenarios produced the same outcome of not drawing on attorneys as a source of legal information.

Other Sources of Legality

One reason why so few participants formally employed attorneys during the parenthood process was due to their perceived direct access to the law via the Internet, their social networks and friends, and various procedural guidelines already set in place, particularly for adoption. The sentiment among a majority of our participants was that attorneys are not necessary as long as you can understand the law and can find and follow the desired process for family formation or parenting. This was especially the case if participants felt comfortable in their communities, with a stronger support network and access to informational resources.

Kristen and Margarita, a married, white/Hispanic lesbian couple in their thirties, live in a legally positive state. When asked if they employed an attorney for their foster-to-adoption process, Margarita indicated that they understood the process of legally adopting their child and thus found an attorney unnecessary: "We did not [use an attorney]. No. We are not entitled to an attorney because we're not a party to the case before the adoption. And then once the adoption comes, we're certainly entitled to an attorney but there wasn't any good reason for us to have an attorney. So the only reason for us to have had an attorney was if we wanted someone to look at our open adoption agreement, which I don't think we had anybody look at." Much like many of our participants, this couple felt that there was no "good reason" to use an attorney if they felt comfortable with the adoption procedure and were able to access the process without legal representation.

Many of our participants had access to other legal resources that provided information that rendered an attorney unnecessary. Wyatt and Lauren's description of their process of navigating the law without an attorney highlights many of the resources that were articulated by our participants. Wyatt, a white transman in his twenties, and his wife Lauren indicated that they felt comfortable utilizing other resources in order to navigate a complicated adoption situation without an attorney in their legally negative state. The couple has four children, three of which came from Lauren's previous heterosexual marriage. The father is now absent from the children's lives, and Wyatt would like to adopt the children via second-parent adoption. While they live in a legally negative state that does not allow second-parent adoption for same-sex couples, as a transman who has had a legal sex change, Wyatt is technically legally able to operate as a male. As such, the couple is able to operate within heterosexual privilege. However, they are still wary of the legal system and historically have had difficulties working within it, most specifically related to Lauren's relatively recent divorce from her ex-husband. They also preferred to not have to draw on an attorney—largely due to the financial costs related to the divorce (from which they were still recovering), as well as due to the belief that it was not needed and would further complicate matters. For these reasons, Wyatt explained: "We're looking at the paperwork and trying to figure if we can do it without a lawyer. Like, if we can figure out how to do it by ourselves."

Initially, they seemed comfortable in their understanding of the procedure for adoptions because of Wyatt's membership in an organization that works on adoption issues, reading laws off a governmentally-run website, and the assistance provided by the court clerks. As Wyatt explained: "So I was [an officer in this organization]. So that's how I know about second-parent adoption. And then like adoption, we just printed the information off of the [website], [our area] has a really good website. It's a really well-resourced [place]. . . . So access, like to the courts, is really good. So, I feel like I could walk in and they would help me and explain everything. Like with a lot of the trans documents and stuff, I would go in and they would walk me through the paperwork." Lauren added: "[Our courthouse has] a resource for the do-it-yourself divorce, bankruptcy, all that. And so I went in there both times I tried to file by myself and they help you. They just walk you through the paperwork, tell you, you know."

Although Wyatt and Lauren seemed very confident in their knowledge and understanding of the law, this comfort and confidence seemed to be related primarily to their access to resources for helping them through the process. As Wyatt observed: "Yeah, so we'll probably have to [see the clerk] because I read through the paperwork of adoption and I was like, I have no idea what this is saying. It's like so much paperwork and so many pages." In this respect, Wyatt and Lauren seemed similarly bewildered by legal documents as were our participants who consulted attorneys. Nonetheless, they seemed more assured of their ability to avoid involving an attorney because of their access to other sources for legal information.

Wyatt and Lauren's story highlights the manner in which LGBT parents often draw upon many resources other than traditional legal counsel in order to arrive at an understanding of the law pertaining to their family: reading the law online, consulting with social networks and organizations, or using resources such as court clerks or social work-ers. For LGBT parents who deemed consulting an attorney unnecessary, several resources became important in establishing legality, including self-readings of the law (particularly off the Internet); social networks such as friends, work colleagues, or online groups; LGBT organizations; and the media. In the following sections we discuss the manner in which each of these sources served as important referents of legality for our participants.

Self-Readings of the Law

When law became relevant for accomplishing family goals, approxi-mately 30 percent of our participants used self-readings of the law or legal summaries as their first approach in constructing an understand-ing of the law. Of those that sought out their own self-readings, about 40 percent also went on to draw on attorneys. For most, the Internet proved an important resource for legal information, although some participants had specialized legal training that permitted them to more directly access legislation or case law. These readings of the law enabled individuals to self-educate and, in some cases, to sidestep more direct consultations with attorneys or with other resources, such as social networks.

Some of our participants had particular knowledge about the law, and thus were able to engage in self-readings/interpretations more readily. This was affected primarily by being employed within a legal field. For example, Anthony, a single, white gay man in his thirties is a legal pro-fessional who lives in a legally neutral state. He indicated: "I did Inter-net research quite a bit. When I was in law school I actually wrote a paper on adoption laws in [this state]. I've been researching this that long. Back in the late nineties was when I started looking into it . . . and the laws themselves have not changed. I think attitudes have changed which has made it easier for people to adopt. Technically, I could have done it in the nineties but it would have been next to impossible." Due to his legal training, Anthony seemed confident in his understanding of the law, and in his ability to access and interpret case law and statutes. While only a few of our participants are actual attorneys, being an at-torney or working in the legal field did not consistently yield the same thought patterns and behaviors with respect to seeking legal advice. In some cases, parents that were attorneys wanted to consult attorneys that specialized in families or in LGBT issues. In many of these cases, they themselves were unclear about how to interpret the law in application to their families.

Even those participants who were not attorneys often reported feeling empowered to read and understand the law due to its accessibility on several websites. For example, Curt, a partnered white gay man in his thirties who resides in a legally neutral state, described his Internet research on adoption laws regarding gay and lesbian families: "There were databases about adoption in every state, about gay people and single [people]. Like [whether] you have to be single or you cannot be single. Like I think Arkansas—I might be making this up at this point. Single people cannot adopt. I think that's actually true. In Arkansas, single people cannot adopt." Although Curt seemed uncertain about his recall regarding the legal procedures in other states, he nonetheless felt able to engage in self-education by retrieving relevant legal information from online databases. Maggie echoed that she also directly used the Internet to access and read state statutes. After reading the law, she concluded: "We can do second-parent adoption. I mean, I've looked at the [state] statutes on that, so I know that we can do that."

Undoubtedly, the Internet was one of the greatest tools for helping parents frame their understandings of what was legal and what was possible. This was especially the case if parents did not have a strong network or understanding of the law and what options were available for legally forming and protecting their families. Martin, a married, white gay man in his thirties lives in a legally positive state with his husband and son. He explained that he and his partner researched their adoption options online before making their first calls: "We did our research before I made the inquiry phone call. When I made the inquiry phone call it was, 'Oh, this is the way we want to do it.' We didn't have any gay friends who were parents. None; I still don't know if we do." By researching their options online, Martin was able to construct an understanding of what was permitted within their state in terms of adoption. Rather than calling and receiving information about the process from an administrator, their research empowered them to take control over the adoption process to a greater degree (i.e., "this is the way we want to do it"). He emphasized that his understanding of what was legal was primarily derived from what they researched online, in that they had no friends who were similarly situated and could serve as resources for legal information. In this respect, the Internet served as an important source of information particularly for individuals who were more isolated from other LGBT parents.

The ease and helpfulness of the Internet to directly look up and research laws, or to research the processes of what can be done and what other LGBT parents have done, cannot be overemphasized. The Internet greatly influenced perceptions of legality for our participants. Even if parents did not directly research legislation or case law online, their legality was framed through their research of the procedures and steps that need to be taken to accomplish family goals. For example, if the state adoption website indicates that an individual must follow certain steps to adopt, then parents accordingly assumed the legal component.

At some point, often initially, the vast majority of our participants drew on the Internet to research legal or procedural technicalities about parenthood. And over 40 percent of our participants cited being members of forums, listservs, or online communities that helped shape their understandings of the law and what was possible. Upon asking our participants how they found out about their legal options for parenthood, in a number of instances participants responded with such comments as "I typed X into Google;" "We just looked online;" "I googled it." As Johanna, a white, married lesbian in her forties put it: "Google. Man, you can find out a lot these days. . . . I usually, sometimes to the point of obsession, kind of read law and all sorts of stuff in a lot of excruciating detail."

Other common ways the Internet was utilized included verifying word-of-mouth information, finding contact information for attorneys and agencies, and drafting legal contracts such as wills, powers of attorney, and contracts between couples and sperm donors and custody agreements. Our participants also drew on the Internet to access state, local, and LGBT resources. Participants frequently mentioned state and county websites, adoption agency websites, legal sites such as Legal-Zoom.com, and LGBT informational sites like HRC.com, LambdaLegal.org and RainbowLaw.com as places that provided them insight into laws or procedures related to their family.

Although information and resources on the Internet allowed many of our participants to access the law more easily for their own readings and interpretations, many further sought to verify their understanding or to triangulate the information. As Ann, a partnered, white gay woman in her twenties who lives in a legally negative state, explained: "I've looked at [the state] law, but in terms of how it's going to shape down in practice. . . . Yeah, it's always been people that we knew [who explained things to us]." In the next section, we examine the role of social networks, including other LGBT parents, as a resource for legal information.

Social Networks

Attorneys and legislation have carved out various routes to parenthood for LGBT parents, but the path to achieving parenthood or parenting effectively often involves less direct interaction with attorneys or formal law. While most of our participants did not read actual laws or talk to an attorney, they did often look to common practices in their social networks in order to derive information about the law or as part of formulating assumptions about legality (e.g., my friend did X, so it must be legal).

Approximately 83 percent of our participants cited their social network as contributing to their legal understandings and decision-making processes. Participants' social networks greatly affected whether they were confident in their rights, the accuracy of their understandings of their rights, and their perception of the law as a whole toward their families. We overwhelmingly found that social networks drove informational access. In most cases, social networks streamlined processes and opened doors to resources for parents. In discussing their sources for information about the parenthood process, many parents did not address the law directly, but would mention a social network where they learned about how they could become parents or safeguard their families. In this respect, social networks were often essential in shaping legal interactions.

Prior research has found that our social networks play an important role in determining the best manner in which to address a problem or resolve a dispute. Social networks consisting of friends, family, coworkers, and members of organizations can influence whether an individual views a situation as legal and whether she or he chooses to use the law (Jacob 1992). If an individual interacts more with lawyers or has friends who used the law in a similar situation, they will likely receive more legalistic advice regarding their particular issue and might then pursue a legal solution to a problem. On the other hand, "the probability that social norms will be used increases when contacts in their network speak the language of relationships and stress social norms" (Jacob 1992, 571). Further, those who are members of LGBT organizations, such as the Human Rights Campaign, that provide readily available information regarding law and family matters, might be more likely to reference formal law when making parenting decisions. As described by Macaulay (1979), membership in organizations can influence whether individuals choose to utilize formal law or informal social norms as part of their decision making processes. We found that networks comprised of friends, coworkers, and organizations played a role in constructing legality for our participants.

TRUSTED INDIVIDUALS

Over one-third of our participants specifically cited friends or other LGBT parents who informed their legal understandings. In particular, participants referenced trusted individuals who provided information regarding options that were legally available and the process for accomplishing family goals. For example, Anthony told us that he knew there were not any prohibitions on fostering a child in his legally neutral state because he had gay friends who were currently fostering. Similarly, Lynn and Malcolm, a partnered, white queer couple in their thirties, knew they wanted to have children before moving to a legally neutral state. They were moving from a more socially liberal and legally positive state, but were able to ascertain their legal options from friends who lived in the state. As Lynn explained, "we knew [LGBT] people who had kids in [the state]," and they discovered second-parent adoptions could be done and that almost everyone used the same lawyer. Having been given a starting point, they then were able to contact the lawyer and examine the second-parent adoption process in more detail.

Much as experienced by Lynn and Malcolm, parents used trusted individuals to gather information about how to accomplish a parenting goal, as well as to gather information about what was legal. For example, Johanna indicated that she had never heard of second-parent adoption before some friends told her about it. These friends proved a vital resource to her throughout the parenthood process, as they also recommended the clinic she used for in vitro fertilization (IVF) treatments. Similarly, Curt's ex-partner told him about the process for second-parent adoption at a dinner. This first-hand knowledge from a trusted individual seemed to be worth more to Curt than the legal research he had conducted online, and gave him an advantage in moving forward by providing him with the more practical details about who to contact and what the process would entail.

Social networks, although a valuable resource, do not operate in isolation from other sources of information on the law. Many of our participants discussed the manner in which they combined information from various sources in order to construct an understanding of their options and the path forward. For example, Josie, a married, Hispanic lesbian in her thirties who lives in a legally positive state, indicated that she and her partner developed an understanding of their legal status as parents through their friends: "Basically, I have full legal standing in [this state], full equal legal standing as a parent. And I knew that I could be on [my son's] birth certificate when he was born and I knew that I could legally adopt him and that would hold out federally as well as locally and that was an option that did not exist in other states." In delving a little more into how she obtained all of this information, she responded:

> We have a couple of friends who are attorneys that do family law, so when we started thinking about it I think they told us. But also I think I looked online to see. I don't think I have a direct source. I think somebody [we knew] was talking to other attorneys in [our state]. And it is also the kind of information that just gets passed along in social networks, like people my age that are partnered and we have kids. We all just sort of share information. Like I have somebody that's going to talk to me. We went through the adoption paperwork process ourselves, so she is going to ask me how I did it in [this county]. So, there is definitely a network; people just share information with each other.

Josie combined information from friends who were attorneys, the Internet, and social networks of LGBT parents to develop information about her legal options.

Although all sources were valued by our participants, gaining information from trusted friends was oftentimes the most useful in terms of establishing what was possible and how to complete the process. Many participants were then able to follow what others had done before them. The common sentiment was that if it worked for their friends, then it would work for them too. In this way, a social network of friends or other LGBT parents is an efficient, effective, and powerful mechanism for accomplishing family goals and, concomitantly, constructing legality.

CONNECTIONS THROUGH WORK AND SCHOOL

Some of our participants' jobs and schools greatly contributed to their network ties and provided access to important contact persons or information. Approximately 20 percent were employed within social work fields or nonprofit organizations, some of which dealt directly with issues related to adoption. For example, Allison, a married, white lesbian in her thirties lives in a legally positive state and is employed in a position where she is required to work occasionally with an adoption agency. When she was gathering information on adoption, she initially went to the people she knew through work for her information. This connection garnered through her place of employment provided her with an advantage in arriving at information regarding her options; she did not have to call various agencies or search around for a trusted contact in order to begin a dialogue.

Similarly, Keith, a single, white gay man in his forties residing in a legally neutral state, also did not research the law separately because of the connections he established through his work in a nonprofit. In particular, Keith was able to gain valuable information from a previous coworker who now worked in the state adoption system: "She kind of talked me through a lot of those processes and assured me that, you know, there wasn't an issue with adoption. As I got into the [agency] system, it seemed like most of the people I met were gay, either gay couples or gay individuals. So, that made me feel comfortable—that I was at the right place." Keith's ability to obtain information about legal barriers and adoption procedures from someone he knew enabled him to move forward more readily with adopting his daughter. In addition, he had his information validated by working within the agency and seeing other gay individuals who were approaching adoption in the same fashion.

Some workplace or educational networks were particularly advantageous for LGBT parents. Universities or corporations that provided greater resources for LGBT individuals gave those who worked within them an added benefit. For example, Sam and her partner, Brenda, a white, married couple in their forties, are extremely well-connected and informed within their legally negative state due in part to their ties to a local university. Sam explained:

> We [are well-connected] essentially because of my connection with the university where I went to grad school, and political connections around the state. We know the people who litigated [an important LGBT family] case. . . . And they are connected to all of the statewide attorneys that are actually . . . making this stuff happen. We have a few friends who have preceded us with kids. So we are sort of an unfair measure because we actually know in deep detail, moment to moment, what is happening in state politics about something that's done.

Sam and Brenda have a wide variety of connections, spanning many different resources for information about legality. But her connection to individuals via her graduate school experience served as a starting point for establishing greater informational networks.

Sam's experience echoes that of other participants for whom connections to larger-scale businesses or service providers, such as corporations or universities, offer a different social climate from the state and additional resources to LGBT parents. Approximately 25 percent of our participants cited school or work-affiliated resources. This proved especially useful if they are living in a legally negative state. For example, both Wyatt and Mark have university connections in which they and their families have benefited from university resources, such as access to health benefits for their partners and children, in addition to legal counsel. In addition, the firm Anthony works for offers an LGBT network for its employees. These corporate and university connections often surpass what is required of the state for employers regarding their LGBT employees and were utilized by our participants as a source for legal information.

LOCAL ORGANIZATIONS AND CLINICS

The availability of local organizations and clinics, some of which exclusively served LGBT clients, also shaped parents' legality. The geographic variation in the availability of such services produced differing experiences across legal contexts. Having access to LGBT centers or local coalitions can give parents a starting point for access to other resources and a general idea of the social and legal climate for LGBT parents. Approximately 47 percent of our participants cited having access to such a resource. Ruby is a partnered, multiracial, and ethnic lesbian in her early thirties who lives in a legally positive state. She had access to a local center that offered drop-in hours with an attorney for their community. She began her process of understanding what was legal and possible by utilizing this resource: "So we went to that and talked to him, sort of when we started thinking more about adoption. And so we're like, 'How does it work? What about international adoption? Like, what are the rules and what have you seen be successful?' and stuff like that." While the resources offered at Ruby's center were not entirely focused on LGBT parenting, she was able to get the legal lay of the land regarding her parenting options.

Some centers, organizations, and clinics specialize in the LGBT population and offer classes and informational sessions that focus on helping form families. Maxine and Allison, a married, white queer/lesbian couple in their thirties who live in a legally positive state, discussed one such organization that offered an informational session once a month for a small payment: "[You can] go to this informational session and they teach you how to get pregnant on your own. . . . I mean, they explain to you everything, including how to do it at home, how to do it in the clinic, the process of looking for a sperm donor, the process of getting a lawyer, like that is what the informational meeting is about." It seemed most of the parents we interviewed in this geographic area knew about this particular resource, whether they had used it or not.

In a different legally positive state, Theresa, a single, white queer woman in her thirties attended an approximately two-month-long program of classes that her local clinic offered, saying: "So it was pretty comprehensive actually. And it is pretty striking when you think about what resources are probably available here. That we kind of walked into this ready-made system that was probably sort of nascent at the time."

Theresa's comment pinpoints the unique advantage offered to individuals who had access to local organizations or clinics in that they were provided with a "ready-made system" that had already completed the research on laws and procedures connected with family formation. Accordingly, parents with access to these services could bypass much of the search for answers that other LGBT parents experienced.

Overwhelmingly, the clinics that parents told us about which offered such comprehensive programs and services to the LGBT community were located in legally positive states and places associated with having a higher prevalence of the LGBT population. Parents living in legally neutral or negative states were much more likely to cite access to the more general informational sessions offered by adoption programs and agencies. Given the great deal of information that could be obtained within these clinics, the lack of access experienced by parents in nonlegally positive states tended to make their search for legality more complicated.

LISTSERVS, BLOGS, AND FORUMS

Parents with and without the luxury of local LGBT resources, such as the clinics or parenting classes mentioned in the previous section, were often able to gain a great deal of legal information via online networks such as listservs, forums, and blogs. Among our participants, we found that when they were speaking of picking up knowledge and knowing about the law from "just being in the community," they were often referencing online communities and networks.

As previously noted, over 40 percent of our participants cited being members of online communities via forums, blogs, and listservs. Kerry, a partnered, white gender queer woman in her thirties who resides in a legally positive state, indicated—only partially jokingly—that for parenting and legal issues she drew on her neighborhood listserv and forums: "For everything, [there's] like a yahoo groups sort of thing, it's [local] moms, gay families. So it's for gay families living in the [local] area. And then BabyCenter[.com forums], which I mentioned before. I've gotten tons of information from [there] about gay parenting issues."

Community listservs were developed for raising awareness and sharing information with their members—in these cases, LGBT parents. Additionally, we found that the most active listservs were typically in larger sprawling cities or from very specific gay enclaves or neighborhoods.

This was irrespective of the type of legal context in which individuals lived, and served to increase resources for individuals living in many locations that had fewer local offline resources. Listservs also varied in how comprehensive the information was that they provided, however some were extremely proficient regarding providing details of certain routes to parenthood and gaining legal rights.

Online forums and blogs were cited as useful tools as well, but were typically not as geographically focused. These had the benefit of creating an available network for individuals who were less likely to have a more organized listserv for their location, but ultimately offered less specific information regarding navigating legal processes within a state due to the geographic diversity of members. For example, Rhonda, a Hispanic, partnered lesbian in her thirties who lives in a legally neutral state, was an active member of an online forum and obtained a great deal of information about insemination procedures through the connections made there. She explained:

> There's this whole underworld of women who are trying to get pregnant. And one of the first cryobanks that we used had an online forum so women can talk about their issues . . . and multiple cryobanks have those forums. And people write in anonymously and they ask questions and it is a safe place where people can get their questions answered. And it is typically among other users who have been down that road. So it is a very informative environment. . . .
>
> The world of getting pregnant and these blogs and forums and theemotion, it is just incredible—such an eye-opening experience. How [people] helped each other and how they talked through these processes. I'm going to start tearing up here. How they would pray for each other and they would know when one was going to, the day they were going to be inseminated, and they had thousands of people thinking about them and praying for them. And they would share whether or not it took and it was just, whew.

For Rhonda, the online forum was very much a community, where individuals happily shared information about what had worked for them and supported one another through the parenting process. In these respects, the online community served many of the same functions as offline friends and networks. This emotional support was important for individuals going through the ups and downs of becoming a parent. Thus, forums were often important resources for gaining information about procedures and for support, but were less often mentioned in terms of providing specific information about local laws.

TRAILBLAZERS

In speaking with all of our participants, it was clear that social networks had a profound impact on their understandings of law, legal processes, and decision-making. Just knowing another LGBT parent, especially a trusted acquaintance, can allow individuals to bypass a great deal of work and speed up their process. This means that the implications of not having these networks can be great. Approximately 5 percent of our participants, however, were trailblazers on the parenthood front within their social networks—they were the first of their group to become parents or to use a particular method of becoming parents. This resulted in them navigating the law with far less certainty and resources than those who had a social support system or procedural avenue to follow.

For example, June and Ann, a partnered, white lesbian couple in their thirties, live in a legally negative state. While there are quality resources available in their area, at the time of their decision-making they were not very connected to these LGBT or parenting resources. Most of their friends were straight and they were the "odd ones" in their circle of LGBT friends when going through the insemination process. When they began looking into second-parent adoption, June ended up obtaining information about the process from a court clerk that dealt with adoptions: "She and I had personal e-mails going back and forth, so I mean, she was pretty much able to tell me everything. 'Hey, this is the judge you want, here's what he's been doing, he's just been bound from doing it, but as soon as he's able to slip back in I will let you know and you can get down here.' . . . We were lucky. She was a great person to work with." Given their lack of resources through their established social networks, June and Ann worked hard to gather details about the best practices for second-parent adoption. They were fortunate to locate an individual who was able to ease their way through the process, in much the same fashion that other networks provided to participants.

However, the lack of a network and its information also meant that parents could be in the dark or perhaps even have inaccurate perceptions about what is legally possible. Julia and Alyssa, a married, white lesbian couple in their twenties, live in a legally negative state with their two children. They believed that no one in their state was really clear with regard to the law and what could or could not be done, especially related to adoption. When asked whether and how they researched second-parent adoption, they explained:

> JULIA: Well, we didn't talk about it until after [the baby was born]. The hospital wouldn't let me put my name on the birth certificate, so then we started looking into what I needed to do to adopt. But no one [in this state] really knows. . . .
>
> ALYSSA: But recently we have contacted, like I have a friend whose brother is an attorney and he is gay, and he had no idea and he contacted every organization and all these other people and nobody could tell us what to do.
>
> JULIA: And we talked to [one progressive organization] ourselves.
>
> ALYSSA: Yeah, and they didn't know. So I found one other attorney who said we could start by getting the home study done because they are going to need it, but he doesn't know if anyone will ever approve it.

Julia and Alyssa managed to find and speak to a lawyer referred to them through the local ACLU chapter, but Julia frustratingly shared: "He's still not even really sure. But that answer right there took us awhile to get. That was at the beginning of July. I know we asked him when we were at [a gay function] which was the first weekend in June and we had asked even a couple months before that. So it has taken months just to get a, 'Maybe you can try this.'" Living in a legally negative state with an ambiguous situation on second-parent adoption, Julia and Alyssa's experience made them trailblazers in a very real sense. Unlike others who just had to look a little harder for information, their experience suggested that in some legally negative contexts, knowing the right individual was essential in order to be successful in parenting goals. At the time of our interview, they still had not been able to locate an individual with the right know-how, despite their seemingly thorough search.

Overall, we found that parents typically find a way to obtain necessary information about the law and process involved, even when they are trailblazers. For some, like June and Ann, they are initially disadvantaged due to their lack of social network ties, but ultimately this meant that accessing information was just much less efficient. Trailblazers on the whole spent much more time, energy, and in some cases money figuring out how to get their questions answered and goals accomplished. In some cases, like with Julia and Alyssa, they even may have missed out on opportunities or received misinformation.

On a positive note, our trailblazing parents were willing to help and share what they figured out and, in some cases, instigated social networking opportunities for other parents and future parents. For example, Devin, a partnered, white gay man in his forties residing in a legally positive state, was the first of anyone he knew who had looked into surrogacy. Given the challenges they faced to understand the process, they wanted to help smooth the path for others by sharing what they knew: "[There was a friend of ours] who did two simultaneous surrogacies, with a child in each surrogate. And they weren't born at the same time, so they're sort of twins, sort of not. And she did surrogacy because she was a friend of [ours] and sort of learned from us. So, *we* didn't know anybody, but we've sort of tried to spread the [word]."

Media

In addition to the Internet and online resources, 38 percent of our participants also mentioned a number of other forms of media that framed their expectations about the law and helped shape approaches to creating their families. These other forms of media included news stories, blogs, nonfiction books, and magazines that focused on LGBT or parenting issues (35 percent), in addition to fictional movies, books, and television (9 percent). In a less direct, but very memorable way, the media and popular culture helped shape how our participants viewed the law and their relationship with the law.

FICTIONAL MEDIA

For our participants, fictional media made a lasting impression on their understanding of when the law might become a problem for their families, as well as how to navigate obstacles. In particular, fictional films and books allowed for the dissemination of generalized information related to LGBT parenting, and activated participants to think about various scenarios that could happen to them and how they might work through these scenarios. While less than 10 percent of our participants cited fictional media as a primary or contributing force to the shaping of their legal understandings, these participants often referenced fictional accounts as being particularly powerful.

By far the most commonly cited fictional influence was found in movies. The movie most frequently mentioned by our participants that was related to legal issues was the Brooke Shields' film, *What Makes a Family*. For example, Jody, a single, white lesbian in her early forties, did not do research on adoption or the law prior to having her child in a legally negative state. Instead, she indicated that her perception of the hazards of adoption was derived from watching *What Makes a Family*:

> I think most of . . . our research on the law at that time had to do with . . . there was a Brooke Shields movie with the lupus. No, she's actually a nurse or she's some kind of healthcare provider and her partner has lupus, and they have a child, and they're in Florida. And the grandparents are just like, you know, takin' [the kid]. Yeah, they take the kid away once the partner died as a result of lupus. And so, that kind of actually—it was kind of like, oh shit, you know. We didn't actually look at laws in [this state].

Jody had not considered the impact that the state could have on her family, her rights, and issues related to custody prior to viewing this movie. After seeing the film, the notion that living in a legally negative state placed her family in a vulnerable position regarding custody battles was made tangible.

Josefina, a married, Hispanic lesbian in her thirties who lives in a legally negative state, also spoke about this movie and the emotions it raised for her. Referring to the movie as "emotionally tormenting," she explained: "I was devastated, just in fear of that because I watched that movie with Brooke Shields and thought, 'Why did I watch that movie?' And I was devastated and I was so scared." Josefina, like Jody, related to the situation depicted in the film given that she also lives in a legally negative state and was legally vulnerable as the nonbiological parent to her children. This movie, then, could be her situation. While other movies were mentioned as helping to frame legality, including films such as *If These Walls Could Talk* and *Two Mothers for Zachary*, *What Makes a Family* seemed to have had the strongest impact and be the most memorable for our participants, especially as regards parental legal rights.

Fictional books were mentioned less often than films, but a few participants mentioned specific novels that had an effect on how they later approached the law within their family. For Katie, a recently separated single mother in her fifties who resides in a legally negative state, it was a novel that made her begin to think about issues related to custody:

> It was a fiction book. It was called *Sing Me Home* . . . . That was really the first time I had ever thought about custody of something that is not even born, like an item, you know, something important to me that I might have put in a bank. But these are going to be like children one day. So she wanted her and her partner . . . to have the baby, and then he wanted his brother and his wife to have the baby. And then it became this whole big custody thing.

This book turned out to be quite pertinent to her situation, given both the custody-related issues as well as the fact that Katie had tried to have another child via a surrogate and an unknown donor. For Katie, like other participants who cited fictional books, the story made her consider potential legal issues that were not previously on her radar.

These fictional stories did not typically provide a specific path forward for participants in terms of how to navigate the law in their family lives; the stories were too fictionalized to offer this type of blueprint for participants. Nonetheless, they often spoke to the fears and concerns that LGBT parents had about the security of their family. Seeing these scenarios play out in a fictionalized world then served as motivation for some participants to seek out additional information or legal protection.

"WE READ BOOKS, LOTS OF BOOKS, AND BLOGS"

In addition to fictional books and films, many of our participants drew on how-to books that covered some legal issues and acted as guides to the routes to parenthood for LGBT individuals, especially for lesbians.

The books most commonly mentioned included lesbian conception books, such as *The Essential Guide to Lesbian Pregnancy and Birth*, *The Ultimate Guide to Pregnancy for Lesbians*, and *Mommies, Daddies, Donors, Surrogates*. In addition, three parents mentioned Dan Savage's *The Kid*, which tells the story of adopting a child.

Participants were most mixed in their reviews and critical toward the various lesbian pregnancy books. Seemingly established as "should read" literature for soon-to-be lesbian parents, these books were often referred to by the color of their jacket, most generally "the yellow one," or "the pink one," and so on. Although participants were often critical of these books, they were known, utilized, and influential even if just for offering one piece of useful information to parents. In many cases, the books contained suggested legal forms, such as parental rights agreements in donor situations. Parents who were unable or unwilling to consult with attorneys referred to these forms as guidelines for constructing their own understandings of the law pertaining to insemination or surrogacy.

Along with books, many of our participants also cited reading blogs of individuals or couples who had gone through or were going through various pathways to parenthood. Unlike the books, there was much less overlap in the blogs that our participants followed, with blogs enabling parents to be more selective in following family and legal issues that were most relevant to their situation.

NEWS

News stories about legislation or specific cases also were frequently mentioned as a source for information about legal issues concerning LGBT families. Our participants were very knowledgeable with respect to news items related to their local legal environments, as well as those across the nation or in other countries. We attribute a great deal of this to their connectedness via the Internet to various LGBT organizations and news outlets. Furthermore, issues related to LGBT legislation have recently been well covered by mainstream media. Over 35 percent cited news stories as important in constructing their understandings of what was feasible legally. For example, Nancy, a married, white lesbian in her thirties who lives in a legally negative state, explained that they were familiar with a lot of the legal landscape due to news stories: "Oh, I'm constantly reading the news. We're crazy. I subscribe to a whole bunch of LGBT type newsfeeds and such."

Nancy is not alone among our participants. Keith, a white, single father in his thirties who lives in a legally neutral state, shared that news articles and 20/20 special reports on surrogacy contributed to his path to parenthood via adoption rather than surrogacy: "Well, I mean, articles that you read about surrogacy, and you know. I mean, . . . there's a lot of, you know, 20/20 specials, things like that that you see, and then you hear about how much it [costs]. Or the 20/20 [report] that had the surrogate that kept the child, and fights, and battles, and all that kind of stuff."

Josefina, a married Hispanic lesbian who lives in a legally negative state, gave another example of the direct effect a news story can have on parents as they are considering potential legal hurdles connected with varying routes to parenthood. In contemplating fostering, adoption, or insemination, Josefina learned of a story that was brought to public attention by Rosie O'Donnell:

> You know, when Rosie [O'Donnell] came out and there was, she was an advocate for the gay couple in Miami. They were both registered nurses, two dads, and they took in HIV kids, foster kids, and one of the many reasons she came out was she was so heartbroken. She lives in Miami and she has a house up there and they were doing an injustice to one of the kids that they had had for twelve years, ten or twelve years. . . . So basically they were ready to now place him with a "real" family after he had known nothing but these two dads and he had siblings. Not biological siblings, but they had adopted other children out of state that were also HIV [positive]. So here he had this foundation of a home, siblings, and two parents. Now they were ready to remove him from the house and it was just horrible that they were even thinking of doing that. So Rosie was trying to bring this story out. And I thought, even back then, "Wow, that's just really not an option for me, I don't want to go through something like that."

The experience of this couple, who also resided in a legally negative state like Josefina, raised her awareness of the potential legal hurdles she would face if she chose the fostering or adoption routes to parenthood; accordingly, she and her partner decided to pursue insemination.

Julia, married to Alyssa, lives in a legally negative state and adopted her daughters internationally. In talking with her about how the news media affected her feelings about the law or access to rights or protections for her family, she stated: "Media in general terrifies me a little bit to see how some families are affected and some gay couples and what some politicians say and how venomous people can be. There are organizations here in [this state], like the one that passed the amendment to ban same-sex marriages. These are influential people . . . that all come together to make this happen and that feels horrible to think that people are so angry." As the adoptive parent, Julia can feel fairly confident regarding her legal position as a parent; however, her marriage is not recognized in her state of residence and this renders her wife, Alyssa, legally vulnerable in terms of her rights to the children in their state. Media accounts regarding antigay organizations or laws within her state, thus, raised fears for Julia regarding her family's security.

Julia and Josefina's stories demonstrate the role that politicians and celebrities had in framing legality for our participants. Media stories conveyed by, or about, influential individuals serve to generate an outlook on LGBT parenting rights that is then generalized by participants to a greater setting or context. Some notable people that our participants mentioned as affecting their perception of the sociolegal landscape for LGBT families were Anita Bryant, George Bush, and Angelina Jolie. Bryant and Bush are associated with traditional family values and antigay sentiments in addition to particular geographic locations (Florida for Bryant, and Texas and the United States for Bush), while Jolie was associated with international adoptions—increasing awareness of possibilities and access to adoption as a single person or as an LGBT person.

"THAT CASE"

A subset of news stories that were influential for our participants involved references to "that case" or "that one case." As cultural lore for LGBT people and parents, stories of popular legal cases covered by news and media outlets had a significant influence on our participants' view of legality. More specifically, these stories affected feelings of security and attitudes and behaviors toward various processes and legal actions taken. They become lessons and warnings that participants utilized as guidance for their future decision-making—whether to avoid or gain entry into certain systems, states, or legal actions. While some stories have happy endings, most came across as "horror stories" and drew attention to participants' greatest fears.

The greatest fear, by far, for our participants was to have their child taken away. While virtually none of our participants were concerned about the state coming in on its own initiative and removing their child based on issues of sexual orientation or caretaking, there was a great deal of concern related to issues of contestation of parental or custody rights. Examples of "that case" often accompanied their remarks, drove their interpretations, and justified their beliefs. In this way, "that case" was a very powerful source of information about the law, which brought parental vulnerability to the forefront and emphasized risks.

For example, Dianna, a partnered, white lesbian in her forties, lives in a legally negative state. In discussing her route to parenthood and why she elected international adoption, she drew on general adoption horror stories in recognizing her susceptibility: "I had heard quite a few horror stories about . . . foster kids or, um, even kids who were placed for adoption and then some family member shows up and they lose the kids, or it's just a very long process. And I think because of my age, I thought 'I cannot go through that,' you know? Just to have a whole bunch of disrupted adoptions because I was approaching, I think when I started I was approaching forty." Through previous instances in her state and national cases, Dianna came to believe that all adoptive parents are at risk legally, but that she would be less vulnerable emotionally and legally with international adoption.

Pamela, a married, white lesbian in her forties who lives in a legally positive state, reiterated the idea that she came to understand the emotion and risk involved with adoption as a result of hearing about "that case":

Yeah, if you think about it, at the time, in the late nineties, there were those cases where they were showing, you know, children being ripped away on national TV from adoptive parents because birth parents had changed their mind[s] but then the adoptive parents had tried to challenge it in court. It was . . . there was a famous case, what was that kid's name? . . . But, you know, there were cases where . . . you have that window of time where the birth mother could change her mind. But as I recall in that case it was the father that had never been notified, the birth father, and he came forward and wanted to challenge the adoption. And so the parents were challenging the adoption through the court, but that took, like, three years and then they eventually lost.

In trying to make sense of the threats presented by "that case," some participants like Pamela tried to tease out the ways in which things may have gone wrong that put other individuals in tenuous legal situations. By highlighting what steps were not taken, such as the father not being notified, it becomes apparent how legality is framed through lessons that are taught and learned through the cultural narratives. Some of these rationalizing processes, which sought to distinguish between their own experiences and those of individuals in cases, served as a means for parents to build security in their decision-making and families.

Kerry, a married, white gender queer person in her thirties described a similar story of learning about legal pitfalls through news stories about particular cases. Kerry and her partner were making decisions about insemination in their legally positive state, and considered legal issues related to choosing a sperm donor:

> I didn't know all the language and the jargon that goes with it, but I did understand the premise that, if you have a child with a friend, with somebody who does you a favor, and they, they can [claim the child.] . . . Because I know there were court cases, you know, in the nineties and early millennium about problems and that kind of thing, so I knew better than to . . . I knew that if anything was to happen, it should have gone through some sort of legal function before.

Kerry's story illustrates how these cases become a source of legality for parents. They become a lesson on the law and potentially its employment for individuals who are considering similar courses of action in their own families. In addition to donor contracts and issues surrounding adoption, parents also gave examples of how cases informed their understanding of partner and custody rights and the passing down of property.

Although participants typically discussed the manner in which certain cases became important because they seemed relevant to their situation, some described the way hearing about negative cases served more to generate a feeling of oppression or generalized vulnerability even when the case was not relevant to them. For example, Merle is a single, white gay man in his fifties who lives in a legally negative state. His child came from a previous heterosexual relationship. He described his general stance on legal issues within his state as often negative, due to the stories that he heard about other LGBT parents experiencing negative outcomes in court: "It's just always a scenario, you know, a gay couple fighting to keep a foster child that they've raised and the state won't let them do that or whatever. . . . Yeah, I can't point to any [case] names, I don't remember any of that. I just know that in recent years, in the last couple of years, there have been cases that have gone where people have battled it out and been unsuccessful because . . . it's pretty backward here." Merle's discussion of how these cases affected his perception of his situation as an LGBT parent within his state demonstrates the effect of "the case" to inform legality within LGBT culture as a whole.

One notable case in Florida was referred to multiple times by parents in many states in order to highlight the importance of partner rights. In this case, partner rights secured in Massachusetts were ignored in practice by a hospital in Florida. Interestingly, the take-away lesson communicated by participants was not that securing partner rights was ineffective, but that you should secure your rights and not go to Florida. For example, Pamela, a white, lesbian in her forties is legally married and lives in a legally positive state. In discussing this case, she noted: "Florida's famous for having medical cases where they're not allowing a partner to see somebody who's dying." Similarly, Johanna who is married and lives in a legally neutral state, mentioned, "There was one [case] in Florida where the partner was dying and the other partner was there and the doctor wouldn't tell her anything or wouldn't let her see her." Although these two women live in different parts of the country, they nonetheless both offered this case to emphasize the importance of having rights secured, if possible, and recognizing potential vulnerability.

Although "that case in Florida" was mentioned most frequently across varying legal contexts, our participants also cited to cases in other states (outside of their own location) as sources of information about legality. These cases serve to create realizations of legal boundaries and limitations across states. Furthermore, they set a tone for national understandings of the more complex interstate legal issues, including that the

Full Faith and Credit Clause that applies to most different-sex marriages does not apply to same-sex marriages. These cases also become the hints of doubt that even our most secure participants had—a potential possibility that something could happen, no matter how secure you believe yourself to be, because LGBT individuals are always legally vulnerable.

These stories about cases that are passed throughout the community can also serve as a benchmark for parents, contributing to parents feeling grateful and lucky about their families and situations in comparison to what is happening elsewhere. This seems to be particularly the case when participants felt their situation was not perfect, but recognized it could be much worse. While this initially may seem like a positive for parents, it appears to immobilize them occasionally from taking legal action available to them. In particular, the idea that their situation is better than that in other locations sometimes appeared to provide a base level of security for participants that resulted in complacency regarding legal rights.

"Of Course It's Legal": Assumptions of Legality

In some situations, our participants did not directly turn toward any of these sources for understanding the law. Rather, they assumed their family decisions and practices were legal because they were successful, because they had not contemplated the law playing a role in this aspect of their life, or based on prior experiences in other legal jurisdictions that generated false assumptions. Over one-fifth of our participants cited these types of assumptions of legality.

Many of our participants assumed legality because a process was available through a service or organization, or was a common practice among other LGBT parents. The availability or use of procedures for forming families, for example, legitimated the legality of these options for many of our participants. Accordingly, further exploration of the law was deemed unnecessary. Raymond, a partnered white gay man in his forties who lives in a legally positive state and adopted his son, exemplified this sentiment:

> What's funny is, I never actually thought about [the law], in any way, shape, or form, because to me, why shouldn't I be able to adopt him?

I'm single, I'm a guy, you know, I don't have a criminal record. Whether I'm gay or straight, it doesn't matter, I should be able to adopt. And if anybody, you know, if I hadn't known . . . [that gay people could adopt], [I would know that being gay] doesn't matter because other [gay] people have adopted. . . . So I knew I could adopt so I wasn't really worried about that. And then, once [my son] came into the picture and I told my social worker, she said, well, legally, here's the rules.

Although Raymond's understanding that he could legally adopt was affirmed by his social worker, he felt comfortable already in his understanding of the law based primarily on his assumption that a single male could adopt and his knowledge that other gay men had successfully adopted. Given this situation, he did not feel compelled to research much about the law, indicating that he never really even thought about it as a barrier.

Many of our participants voiced similar ideas indicating that the ability to do something was evidence of its legality, warranting no further research. Keith, a single, white gay man in his thirties who lives in a legally neutral state, indicated that he assumed a single gay man could adopt because he was, in fact, permitted to adopt:

I'm not sure what the specific laws in this state are. . . . I mean, obviously it can't be illegal or I wouldn't be able to adopt. . . . I guess I should have done more research on that, but I didn't. But I guess for me, . . . I personally didn't care about the law, as long as I knew I could do it. Then to me, once I knew that I could be a single parent, male parent, and adopt, it really didn't [matter]. You know, I wasn't going in it as, "I'm a gay parent, hear me roar, I'm going to show [you] that I'm going to get this child." I was just a single man that wanted a family, and went through the adoption process. And, I guess, according to [the adoption agency] that I talked to, it wasn't an issue with the law. So I said, "Ok." That's all I needed. I guess. [Laughs.] Why go to somebody else that I thought was an expert?

For Keith, much like Raymond, his only question about the law pertained to whether his family goals were possible. Once he confirmed that they were, he was relatively uninterested in whether LGBT individuals were otherwise foreclosed from adopting children if they were not single or if they disclosed their sexual orientation. The need to seek information about legality, thus, was very narrowly focused on a singular family goal.

Similarly, many of our female participants indicated that they assumed legality about in-home insemination primarily due to their success in completing the process. Clara, a recently separated, Mexican queer woman in her thirties who lives in a legally positive state, assumed home insemination was legal because she "could do it." She explained: "I didn't do any research but I mean, you know, the sperm. . . . Yeah, it is legal to do in the home because the sperm bank released it to us to do in the home. In fact, they'll even ship it to your home for a fee. . . . I was assuming it was legal because the sperm bank lets you do it and they are definitely very on top of all that legal stuff and there was like a ton of legal forms we had to fill out."

Tara, a married, white lesbian in her forties who lives in a legally negative state, echoed the same sentiment when asked whether she had examined the legality of insemination: "Well, not exactly. But I did talk with the sperm bank about whether or not they were willing to deliver to my home. And they were. So I didn't question whether or not I could use that in my home since they delivered it there." Keith, Clara, and Tara's mentality underscores how participants often assumed that if a service is available, then it must be legal. In coming to this conclusion, they seemed to suggest that various organizations and service providers have already done the legal research and, moreover, that this research is applicable to them as parents.

In addition to the assumption of legality due to the ability to complete a process, some individuals assumed legality because they did not really imagine that the law had a place to play in family formation. This was particularly the case concerning insemination practices. For example, it never occurred to Margo, a married, white bisexual woman in her early thirties to consider whether self-insemination was legal in their legally neutral state. Laughingly, she said: "I didn't look into that at all. I still don't know what the laws are around it for [our state]. I guess no one ever arrested us, so . . ."; as it turns out, home insemination is not illegal in their state. However, in an interesting twist the couple had traveled to a different state where home inseminations are regulated for the attempt that worked. Other participants also described crossing state lines for insemination, and such practices raise issues related to interstate variation in laws even for individuals who have researched the law in their own states.

Margo's story is not unique, in that most of our participants doing home insemination never thought to inquire whether it was legal; it did not even cross their minds. Whereas most participants had an idea of the law being associated with whether their state allows same-sex marriage or LGBT adoption, they were much less aware of the laws that regulate insemination (either at home or in a clinic). For some of our participants, the interview was the first time they had thought about the idea of the legality of insemination. Like Margo, participants often brought up questions of enforcement and how authorities would know about their practices. Moreover, among participants going this route, home insemination seemed to be a fairly common practice among their peers and in the greater queer culture, further legitimating it as a viable process (i.e., if it could be done, it must be legal). For many, the very notion that there could be laws regulating impregnating themselves within their home smacked of heteronormative biases and engendered hostility.

Finally, a few individuals assumed legality given that they were unaware of the great variation in legal rights across the country. They knew that something was legally permissible based on their experience in another state, for example, and made assumptions that it was also available to them elsewhere. For example, Mark a single, white queer-identified transman, and his partner were undergoing a second-parent adoption process when they moved for his job to a legally negative state that does not allow second-parent adoption. He was surprised to discover that second-parent adoption was unavailable, and explained: "I just thought second-parent adoption could happen anywhere. I just thought that was a universal thing." In this respect, expectations can be generated based on experiences within one legal environment that result in LGBT parents having an incorrect understanding of the state of the law within their new environment.

These assumptions of legality based on prior experiences can generate sizeable complications for LGBT parents. For example, Mark is in a legally tenuous situation with respect to the children that he and his former partner had together. He is not legally male and has neither second-parent adoption rights nor a formal custody agreement with his partner, who is the children's biological mother. He has managed to acquire a legal guardianship in his current state due to his partner not living with the children and leaving the state. His perceived vulnerability based on the lack of second-parent adoption is exemplified by the way in which he carries his guardianship papers with him at all times. He has not encountered any real problems in his daily interactions, but he is expectant. The inability to secure second-parent adoption as a result of its assumed widespread legality, thus, has resulted in a great deal of uncertainty for Mark.

Conclusion

Our review of participants' sources for legal information with respect to their families highlights the notion that information about the law permeates much of queer parenting culture. Information about relevant laws and procedures is everywhere, as observed by Ellis, a married, white queer transman in his thirties living in a legally negative state: "Oh God, [I learned about these things] just, like being in the queer community and hearing stories. It's all very anecdotal, I think. And documented as well." His comment reflects how complex, ubiquitous, and present legality is in practice—even for individuals with greater levels of education, access to resources, and insider knowledge, like Ellis. Understanding the law and how it is utilized, and knowing your rights, can greatly affect any person's experience and is particularly important for those who are members of a largely unprotected and disadvantaged group. This situation seems to generate within queer culture an expectation of due diligence—an obligation that LGBT individuals be aware of rights and context, and exercise caution throughout their daily actions and life affairs.

Parents' overall framing of legality often stems from multiple sources, with individuals producing an understanding of the law through the confluence of information with their particular legal context and resources in a nested and reflexive manner. Social networks played a large role in contributing to participants' access to information and resources. Their impact cannot be underestimated, given that over 83 percent of our participants cited their social network as contributing to their legal understandings. Indirectly, social networks—such as friends, employment connections, and access to queer or local resources—informed legality, especially via procedures and access to actual law or attorney referrals. Many people learned from others and the processes they underwent, and parents then inferred legality from established paths that worked for others before them. In fact, we had very few true trailblazers—only seven. Three were located in legally negative states, while two were located in legally neutral states and the other two in legally positive states. As such, they were fairly evenly spread across legal contexts.

The Internet and various media sources were most commonly cited by all our participants as contributing to accessing legal information, especially for informing initial notions about the law. Without a doubt, our interviews demonstrate that the Internet has played a huge role in framing legal understandings of what may be possible for LGBT parents via its connections with information, media, resources, and other LGBT parents. Additionally, knowing stories of conflict, disputes, and successes from media and social networks informed parental concerns, and affected estimates of risk related to the law and the actions taken to legally secure their families. For those without access to a resourceful social network, media became particularly essential as a source of information regarding avenues for securing families and their legal viability. Even fictional media, such as movies and books, shaped knowledge, concerns, and expectations with regard to what to look for, what can be done, and what to protect against. In fact media, in many cases greatly informed our participants of their potential vulnerabilities and framed their fears.

Most typically, our participants did not consult attorneys directly unless it was specifically related to garnering security or access to privileges. For many of our participants, their interaction with an attorney to accomplish their family goals was the first and only time in their lives that they had consulted an attorney. The majority of our participants that drew on attorneys did so after forming a family in order to address a potential or expected conflict related to their families or an outside source, such as the state. These fears related to legal claims over children reflect the manner in which family security is often tenuous within LGBT families; such security regarding parental rights is something heterosexual families often take for granted, yet LGBT parents recognize as privilege. In fact, all of our families who are able to operate legally as heterosexual families indicated an extreme awareness of this privilege and its advantages.

While some of our participants asserted that they did not directly consult the law, oftentimes due to an assumption of legality for actions related to their families, some individuals assumed legality because they were able to complete a process—thus, it must be legal. Others assumed legality due to an expectation that the law had no place regulating their conception activities. Assumptions of legality or a professed disregard of the law reflected a certain degree of privilege due to a legally positive context. For example, Dian, a partnered, white queer woman in her forties lives in a legally positive state and is surrounded by many protections for her family. When asked whether she did any research related to the law and parenting in her state, she responded: "No. And I think that's a reflection of how fortunate I am to not to have to be that vigilant. I mean, I felt about it like, I'm going to have my family, if anybody has a problem with that, fuck 'em. But I can say that because if anybody has a problem with it, they're kind of already obligated to keep their mouth[s] shut." For individuals like Dian, residing in a place that provides a level of security with respect to one's family serves in some respects to insulate LGBT parents from potential legal threats. Accordingly, some individuals felt they did not have to consciously research their rights because they assumed that they already had them.

Overall, we found that legal context played a role in determining which of these sources of legality prevailed for our participants. For example, participants in legally positive states were the least likely to draw on attorneys. Only one-third of participants that lived in legally positive states drew on attorneys, as compared to 55 percent in legally neutral states and 59 percent in legally negative states. This could reflect in part the lesser need to consult with an attorney to engage in workarounds to establish legal rights (see chapter 5).

Participants' reports of utilizing social networks were prevalent across all legal contexts, with approximately four out of five participants citing their utilization irrespective of the state in which they reside. Those in legally negative states cited social networks the most, with 86 percent of participants in these contexts drawing on a social network at some point to contribute toward parents' understandings of legalities; this was followed by 84 percent of participants in legally positive states, and 78 percent of our participants in legally neutral states. Moreover, our interviews reflected a high degree of access to informational resources across legal contexts and the way in which these resources became accessible via social networks. This was particularly striking within unlikely and unexpected places, such as rural areas located in legally negative states, where knowing the right person or gaining access to the right listserv made all the difference for a participant.

In addition, we found that those living in legally neutral states were the least likely to cite the media—including news stories and fictional and nonfictional LGBT family representations in movies, television, and books—as sources for information about the law. However, 52 percent of participants that lived in legally negative states and 44 percent in legally positive states indicated that media influenced their framing of legality.

Furthermore, participants who reside in legally neutral states were more likely to make assumptions about legality rather than to consult the law directly. In other words, these individuals were the least likely to draw on any legal resources or to firmly know their rights. Approximately 13 percent of participants in legally positive states and 16 percent in legally negative states indicated that they assumed their rights, compared to 37 percent of the participants in legally neutral states. In line with this finding, we also learned that participants in legally neutral states were less likely to have tackled self-readings of the law. In states where there are laws that specifically address issues of sexual orientation and LGBT families—whether they are protective or restrictive—individuals perhaps make fewer assumptions about the law than in a legally neutral setting due to the law seeming a more salient aspect (positively or negatively) in the family life.

Although reported sources of legal information differed across legal contexts, there was little difference in sources across individual characteristics such as sex, gender, race and ethnicity, class, or marital status. Rather, individual circumstances and legal context appeared to play a stronger role in determining which source of legal information (or combination of sources) was employed. We did find, however, that marital status played a role in the reported use of attorneys. Partnered and married participants were more likely than single parents to draw on attorneys. This finding, however, is driven by families that sought second-parent adoption; in single-parent families, there was less reported use of second-parent adoption and, accordingly, less consultation with attorneys for this purpose. After taking second-parent adoption into account, we do not continue to see a difference in the use of attorneys between those with partners and those without partners. Accordingly, this difference was primarily driven by the need for a particular attorney service rather than any other factor that rendered attorneys a more desired source of legal information for partnered individuals.

Although individual characteristics did not clearly emerge as shaping sources of legality for our participants, this does not mean that such characteristics are unimportant. Our lack of findings in this area could be attributed to several factors, including to the particular composition of our sample, which might render differences across characteristics like race and ethnicity or gender less salient. Further, the varied experiences of our participants in terms of their routes to parenthood and their particular legal contexts might overpower any patterns that could be discerned to occur across individual characteristics. Our participants overwhelmingly recognized the law and its potential impact on them. At the individual level, however, it varied as to how some sources were more influential than others when it came to the chosen path to parenthood and access to resources. For some parents, it may be about finding that one person or one bit of information that leads them to a process or toward learning about the law, while for others it may be more of an amalgamation of sources.

In the following three chapters, we turn toward analyzing how our participants take their particular understandings of the law—derived from the sources described above—to formulate their relationships between the law and their family. In particular, in these chapters we examine the way in which our participants play a role in the construction of legality through accepting, modifying, or resisting the presence of the law in their families.

4

Parenting before the Law

I feel like if the law was there, like if I were a man, and we were married, I feel like they would . . . look at me as a family member . . . with her. Like, we would be a family. But, the way the laws are now, it's like, I feel very much on the outside of everything. You know? I think a lot of times, I tell myself, "Oh, you're my baby, c'mere my baby." I think I say that so much because I don't actually feel it. So I have to keep telling myself, "Oh, she's my baby." Because . . . I don't feel like she's mine.

—Krissy

LGBT parents are often confronted by a legal system that does not incorporate, or outright excludes, their familial experiences. Nonetheless, they are not immune from the powerful cultural discourse conveying that the law is an objective definer of truths, transmitter of equality, and meaning-maker. Approximately 25 percent of our participants told stories about some aspect of the law in their family lives that supported these notions of legality. The idea of the law as "real" and immutable—something external to individuals that cannot be transformed or modified to fit individual circumstances (Ewick and Silbey 1998)—results in LGBT parents often performing legality in a manner that reproduces the status quo.

For our participants, the law was frequently referenced as the force that could define relationships and obligations to one another. As reflected in Krissy's quote, in the absence of legally defined relationships, people often feel insecure regarding their status within the family. For Krissy, like many of our participants, the law had the unique capacity to confer not just legal rights or commitments, but identities of parent or spouse. Along with establishing identities, participants indicated that the law legitimated their relationships to their partners or children in the eyes of others. Further, participants voiced that the law had the unique capacity to generate commitments to partners or to children. Other participants expressed a sentiment that the mere existence of friendly laws conveyed that those in positions of power viewed their families as valued or worthwhile. All of these framings suggest an understanding of the law as originating from a legitimate authority, with the ability to transform individuals and families in addition to just conferring rights.

Some participants also expressed a "before the law" mentality when it came to adherence to administrative or legal provisions. They explained that they followed these guidelines because they were the law, and a failure to do so would be ethically suspect. Although they might resent the present legal landscape for their families, they nonetheless expressed a respect for the law as legitimate and incontrovertible.

In this chapter we review these five key themes in which participants expressed being "before the law" in their family lives. Although approximately 25 percent of our participants articulated sentiments in the "before the law" category, many individuals conveyed ideas that fell into more than one of the five themes; this results in the percentages for the five themes adding up to more than 25 percent. We conclude the chapter by analyzing the relationship between this conception of legality and factors such as legal context, relationships with legal actors or social networks, and demographic characteristics. Our findings reflect, in particular, the importance of legal context in shaping a "before the law" mentality for LGBT parents.

Law Makes a Family

The law can make a family, defining familial relationships, rights, and obligations (Baumle and Compton 2014; Polikoff 2008; Yngvesson 1997). This cultural message regarding the role of the law in creating and sanctioning relationships through marriage or adoption is powerful. It serves as the basis for much of the debate regarding marital rights in the United States, where civil ceremonies or other representations of commitment between couples are viewed as less authentic than legal marriage (Badgett 2010; Hull 2003). When describing the process of becoming parents, approximately 15 percent of our participants drew upon cultural discourses about the power of law as a meaning-making system.

These individuals referenced the manner in which the law played a role in creating families or delineating relationships (between parents and children, or partners). Although participants typically viewed this as a positive force, recognizing how meaningful it felt to them to become parents or become a family, they also acknowledged that the law has the power to exclude groups from familial definitions. When legal recognition occurred, then, our participants frequently expressed emotions of relief, pride, and gratitude.

Participants who went through the process of adoption or second-parent adoption discussed this meaning-making process in the context of the law creating a parent-child relationship, or making them a parent. For example, Esther, a partnered, Hispanic lesbian in her forties residing in a legally neutral state, became a parent through private adoption. She described the manner in which the law essentially transformed her into a biological parent over her adopted child: "The way that the law is stated in [our state] is that once the birth mother gives up rights to the baby and the adoptive family assumes the baby, then that baby is as good as blood related to you. That's how the law reads, like that baby is then your blood. So I kind of like that." The notion that the law could, to some degree, remove the stigma of being the nonbiological parent and create a relationship "as good as" a biological relationship was significant for Esther. Her understanding of the way the law was written and its meaning for her family suggested a transformative power found within the law.

Individuals going through second-parent adoption often articulated a similar feeling of the law "making them a parent." For example, Laura is a married, white lesbian in her forties who resides in a legally positive state and is the biological parent of her child. She described her partner as feeling "much transformed" after the second-parent adoption process was completed in terms of her relationship with the child. Similarly, Dana, a married, white lesbian in her thirties who resides in a legally positive state, also conveyed the manner in which second-parent adoption was an important emotional process in generating a parent identity. She stated: "It felt really good to do. I would almost recommend it for people who could do it, even if you had marriage [which might give you similar rights]. It felt a little like that was more of my contract with him since I'm not biologically related to him. It felt like, between me and him, like, OK, we're square. It's not just that I happen to be your parent because I happen to be married to your real mom. Like, I'm your parent." Her encouragement for individuals to go through the process, even if they might not see a legal need due to their belief that marriage confers parental rights (a belief that is not necessarily upheld in all jurisdictions), speaks to the way in which the law is sometimes understood to be creating a parent in addition to allocating rights. The significance of second-parent adoption for identity formation was later reiterated by Dana, when she stated: "What I think would have happened if I hadn't had [second-parent adoption], . . . partially due to my insecurity and wondering who am I going to be to my kid, . . . is that I would have stayed home with the baby. . . . And I think part of the reason that felt attractive was that then I really am a mom." Her story particularly emphasizes that second-parent adoption was meaningful well beyond obtaining legal rights over her child; in effect, she felt that it made her a mom and removed the need to establish this identity in alternative ways.

Similarly, Marlene, a partnered, white lesbian in her forties, indicated that joint custody following a separation reinforced the notion that she was a real parent to her child by providing her with documented parental rights. Residing in a legally neutral state, she was unable to go through legal joint adoption. Accordingly, she felt that her status as a parent was more tenuous than that of her partner who had legally adopted their child. Joint custody, however, was important to her because it provided "the sense that he was really mine. . . . I always feel like I have to ask permission to see my child. He is my child too and I shouldn't have to ask permission." The idea of a joint custody agreement, formal or informal, provided her with perceived parental rights that she otherwise felt she was lacking due to her inability to adopt legally. In this respect, she seemed to view the law as a force that could establish or reaffirm a parent-child relationship, providing evidence that the child, in fact, belonged to her as well as to her partner.

A few of our participants also referenced the manner in which the law plays a more active role in defining who is and who is not a parent. Rather than establishing a parent-child relationship in conjunction with bestowing legal rights (as in the case of adoption), some participants understood the law to define more overtly who is and who is not a parent. For example, Marlon, a partnered, white gay man in his fifties and a resident of a legally neutral state, indicated: "So I didn't research the family code other than to the extent that I knew that a donor was not considered a father. . . . A donor is only someone whose sperm is used by a medical practitioner in a medical facility. A lot of people use donor sperm at home, and they aren't a donor anymore." Donors' parenting obligations and rights vary across state contexts, rendering Marlon's interpretation of the law correct in some jurisdictions. His discussion, however, signals his understanding of the law as a text that can directly delineate who is, and who is not, a father.

Participants who went through adoption or second-parent adoption frequently described the adoption procedure as being "celebratory" and "affirming." A common thread ran through most accounts regarding the role of the process in making families or establishing relationships. Participants described this idea as something that was communicated both by the judges to the participants, as well as a feeling that was experienced by the participants as a result of the process. For example, Beth, a partnered, white gay woman in her forties who lives in a legally neutral state, recalled that the judge at their second-parent adoption stated: "Look at all these cute babies, and wonderful families we're creating." In some cases, the judges indicated that they were creating sibling relationships as part of the adoption process. Pamela, a married, white lesbian in her forties and a resident of a legally positive state, described how her older child was present at the adoption of her second child, and "the judge asked [the first child] if she wanted a baby sister and did she want to make [the second child] her baby sister, and [the first child] said yes. And he had her sit up on his lap and she signed the adoption decree." The ceremony and the inclusiveness of the adoption procedures, thus, often communicated to the participants a feeling of making a family or becoming family.

Others described the manner in which the recognition of their family by an official figure created a strong sense of affirmation or validation. For example, Kendra, a married, white gay woman in her forties, was undergoing second-parent adoption in a legally positive state. She noted that she and her partner were initially resentful about the process, feeling like they should not have to go through this additional step to form their family when they believed that a married, heterosexual couple would not need second-parent adoption if donor sperm were used. Nonetheless, the actual experience was quite significant for her:

[The judge] said, "You come to me as a family . . ." I always get really emotional because it was so sweet. She said, "You come to me as a family and I'm here as an honored guest to recognize your family, as a representative of [this] state." And it was just a really, really sweet thing to do. And at this time, we hadn't been married, and . . . when we finally did marry, it was sort of the same feeling of that. I think as a lesbian couple you operate, you know, you operate without being validated . . . and I think it's easy to say, "Oh, it's just a piece of paper" or whatever it is, and that validation's not important, but it really was a pretty overwhelming process to have her [say that.] The way she just approached it was really kind and really nice.

Other couples described the adoption processes as validating in the sense that they felt they had been deemed "worthy" of being parents in the eyes of the law, or equal to heterosexual parents. Devin, a partnered, white gay man in his forties who lived in a legally positive state, described the hearing process for adoption as "very sweet; the judge was there and a social worker, evaluating us . . . and that was very affirming." Similarly, Margo, a married, bisexual woman in her thirties who is a resident of a legally neutral state, remembered the judge saying, "It sounds like you guys will do a great job." Joann, a partnered, white lesbian in her thirties who also lives in a legally neutral state, recalled the way in which the judge communicated to them that the second-parent adoption process meant they had responsibilities to one another "just like any other family." She concluded: "So it was really supportive . . . because we were going in there as a nontraditional family and he was like, 'This is it. [You] are just like any other family and you have the responsibility of these kids together.'" In this manner, the legal process acted as a legitimizing force for some participants, engendering feelings of normative parenthood.

Participants also identified administrative or procedural processes in becoming parents that were meaningful to them in terms of establishing or reaffirming their familial relationships. For example, Joann's partner, Rhonda, mentioned that when she underwent the IVF process, Joann was also asked to sign paperwork by the fertility clinic. As Rhonda, a Hispanic lesbian in her thirties, recounted:

Even though we are not legally married, Joann also had to sign. I had to sign paperwork and Joann had to sign paperwork that this effort was a together effort and that my embryos were effectively just as much hers as they would be mine. . . . So that was actually kind of cool. . . . For me, it was nice to know that we had people on our side, like we were truly supported as a couple. So there was an identity factor of "you count as the beginning of a family unit." But, you know, that is just kind of warm fuzzy subjective stuff.

While recognizing that this paperwork did not necessarily confer legal rights, the couple nonetheless viewed their joint signing as a meaning-laden act that recognized them both as parents and as a family.

Similarly, some couples described the way in which procedures related to birth certificates conveyed to them a sense that one or both partners were recognized as parents. Birth certificates, as administrative documents, provide less legal standing to individuals in some cases than many of our participants believed. Nonetheless, the process of completing the birth certificate paperwork was significant for some participants. For example, one couple found the birth certificate completion process to be "more moving than [their] wedding ceremony." Janis and Laura, a white lesbian couple residing in a legally positive state, were legally married at the time that Laura gave birth to their children. As a result of their marriage, both women were listed on the birth certificate which, as Laura noted, meant that Janis "counted immediately" as a parent. The completion of the birth certificate was, in their telling, a significant, ritualized process:

JANIS: Yeah, the hospital registrar came in.
LAURA: And she formally read out the birth certificate for each girl and it was really a little moment, it was nice.
JANIS: Which was really sort of celebratory and dignified. She was great.
LAURA: Yeah, that was nice.
JANIS: It was a really great moment. . . .
LAURA: It was the application she was going to be submitting to the town, but it was all the details and she read each line very solemnly and for each parent and for each child.
JANIS: So [our children] will be able to find these in town halls and everyone will know.

This reading of the birth certificate held significance for the couple due both to their perception that it recognized both women as parents, and for the manner in which the law recognized all four of them as a family unit. In their view, the document literally and figuratively made their family a matter of public record.

Kendra also related the manner in which hospital policy, a form of legality, was significant in terms of its recognition of the nonbiological partner as a parent. Describing the birth of their child, she stated: "My partner got an [identification] band, you know, so that we matched and we matched our kid when she was born. You have to have that band when you go into the NICU [neonatal intensive care unit]. . . . They give it to fathers . . . but they won't give it to a . . . grandmother, they won't give it to a sister. The only people who can have it are the parents. So [she] got a band, just like I did." She seemed to view the hospital policy regarding identification bands as both conferring legal parental rights to her partner (i.e., permitting the partner to gain access to NICU) and identifying the three of them as a family ("we matched our kid"). For Kendra, this administrative policy produced a sense of recognition and creation of a family unit.

Legal Marriage Legitimates a Family

Research on marriage has repeatedly noted that legal marriage not only confers rights but also creates social benefits including recognition as a family unit, a sense of legitimacy, and perceived moral superiority as compared to unwed families (Badgett 2010; Hull 2003). Marriage is often viewed as the gold standard for family units, despite the increasing rarity of the married family unit (Powell et al. 2012; Coontz 2000). For approximately 12 percent of our participants, legal marriage seemed to carry this power to authenticate relationships. For some of these participants, legal marriage altered their perception of their family as "real" or "legitimate." But, to an even greater degree, many of these participants discussed the manner in which legal marriage seemed to affect how their children, families, friends, or others understood them as an authentic family.

According to the ideal type, "first comes marriage" and then children can follow. Some part of this family sequencing is attributable to the way in which children are concrete evidence of sexual intercourse, and sex has often been legitimated through its association with marriage or love (see, e.g., Katz 1995). Vivian, a married, white lesbian in her thirties who lives in a legally neutral state, conveyed this notion. She became pregnant after a one-night sexual encounter with a man, and explained that she made the decision to marry due to her agreement with his sentiment that "we have to do this right." This heteronormative association between pregnancy and marriage was not isolated to our participants who had different-sex relationships; it was also a common thread through many of our interviews with participants having children within same-sex relationships.

Parents that used reproductive technologies and adoption to have children conveyed the idea that marriage was an important part of becoming a parent. This was particularly the case for our women participants. For example, Antonia, a partnered, white queer woman in her thirties living in a legally positive state, indicated that they first seriously started talking about having children "soon after" their commitment ceremony; her framing of the timing emphasizes the notion of marriage or commitment before children. Similarly, Ruby, a partnered, multiracial lesbian in her thirties who is a resident of a legally positive state, considered the reasons she and her partner decided to marry, and explained: "Well, we had been talking about it for a long time and, like, theoretically we were engaged for a long time, but we wanted to really move forward with those plans and make it . . . official and really do it. Mainly because we do want to have a family and we do want children and we do want our families to understand us as a family."

In addition to having other people understand that they "are a family," many individuals suggested that it was "natural" to marry prior to having children. Ruth, a married, white lesbian in her thirties who lives in a legally neutral state, conveyed this sentiment when telling the story of her relationship progression: "We got married . . . and then about two years into marriage, in the natural order of things, we thought—okay, time to start having children." Ruth reiterated this idea later, when describing how their friends went through a similar process: "We were all trying to get pregnant at the same time and, you know what I mean, the natural order was two to three years of marriage before having kids."

The decision to have children, for some, was one of the primary motivating factors in getting married. As Margarita, a married, Hispanic lesbian in her thirties who resides in a legally positive state, explained: "I had very mixed feelings about getting married and then didn't really want to get married, but the idea of having children, which I knew I wanted, sort of pushed me a little more in that direction because of the security of it." Allison, a married, white lesbian in her thirties who resides in a legally positive state, observed that this idea of marriage before baby was so prevalent among the same-sex couples that she knew, that they "were the first of [our] friends who didn't want to get married first and then have a baby." Dana recalled that she and her partner made very deliberate—and perhaps heteronormative—decisions about how they organized the steps in their relationship. She stated that: "We on purpose didn't live together until we were going to have what we thought would be our closest we could get to getting married [our commitment ceremony]."

The decision to marry was often made out of consideration for what having married parents might mean for the children's understanding of themselves as a family. This approach differed from the notion of marriage before children in that there was more of a focus on considering what the children might think about the marriage or lack thereof, as opposed to how those outside of the family might perceive the relationship. For example, Kendra indicated that she and her partner married not only for political reasons but also to show their children that they were married. She explained that they got married "because of the political statement and to be counted, but also because our older daughter at the time was asking, 'Did you get married? Are you married?' you know, and had a lot of questions and I felt like we needed to get married for her and for our younger daughter and to show that we were married." This couple was not opposed to the idea of marriage, as they also wanted to "be counted," but they were concerned about how their lack of marriage would be perceived by their children. They needed to "show" that they were married, to make an outward demonstration to their children that they were a family unit.

By contrast, Janis and Laura said that they were initially hesitant to marry due to their rejection of the meaning underlying the marital institution. Nonetheless, their perspective changed when they started to have children. Janis described their initial resistance as follows:

> We had done everything legally we could do to establish, essentially, a civil union. . . . We had powers of attorney and we own our house jointly

and bank accounts jointly, health care proxies. . . . And . . . we didn't encounter discrimination around those issues. Nobody balked whenever we said that we were partners. But we didn't go to [another state to] get married there or get a civil union established when that became legal. It wasn't really on our agenda, something we were worried about. But then when I got pregnant, we decided to do everything we could legally and also we . . . well, I should also say we didn't want to get married. I mean, when gay marriage became legal we felt that we didn't particularly want to participate in an institution that was normative and hegemonic. I mean, it was kind of a political resistance to getting married, although we were glad to have it happen.

Picking up on the discussion, Laura explained their transition from resistance to acquiescence:

We just didn't want to do it *ourselves*. Then once I was pregnant, we thought—these little girls are going to someday ask us if we're married and they're going to be pretty young when they do that and they're not going to understand our queer critique of the institution of marriage at that age. And what they're really going to be asking is, do you love each other, are you going to stay together? And we want to just be able to say yes, in a way that they would understand. When they're young, they want that reassurance.

This couple did not perceive any benefit to legal marriage for themselves; they believed they would gain no additional legal rights and, in fact, felt that legal marriage violated their belief system. Nonetheless, they felt that the security that was conferred through legal marriage for children was a worthwhile benefit. The law, to them, served as a signifier for family and stability.

Finally, some participants in this category articulated the power of the law in generating societal approval of their relationships following marriage. Ruby described the transformative process that seemed to occur following her engagement:

The minute we said we're really engaged and I started wearing an engagement ring that looks like an engagement ring, then everybody was like,

"Oh, now we understand who you are." And we're like, what? This doesn't make any sense. We've been together, like, seven years, or six years at that point, and lived together for almost all of that time. And always been as committed, nothing changed really. But for other people, including friends and parents who see us all the time and treat us very nicely, it still meant something different to them, so I'm very glad we made the decision. I'm very glad we made that decision.

Although marriage did not change the way they viewed their relationship, she described a process whereby the relationship became transformed in the eyes of others due to the label of marriage.

For Alexandra, a married, white lesbian woman in her thirties who resides in a legally positive state, the changes that came as a result of legal marriage were unexpectedly felt. Although she and her wife did not anticipate marriage would make much of a difference in their lives, she observed that: "It felt huge that we were able to be legally married. . . . The best perk was that it became really normal around here to refer to my wife and go to the social security office and change our names and it was, like, no big deal. It was the societal piece honestly more than the legal stuff that has been absolutely wonderful." Although she emphasized that it was the societal effects rather than the legal ones that she most appreciated, in many respects the societal and legal aspects of marriage are inextricably connected—with legal recognition providing the underlying legitimizing effect that results in greater social recognition. This is perhaps particularly the case when it comes to some of the administrative changes that she associated with the societal benefits of marriage, such as changing names at the social security office. As Laura observed, the legitimizing force of legal marriage might have both macro and micro effects on how same-sex relationships are perceived: "Tons more people in [the state] realized their neighbors were gay and in long-term relationships, and what they had gone through, and what marriage meant to them. And public opinion just shifted in that period of time."

Law Establishes Commitments

Contract law has historically served as one of the underpinnings of family formation, including marriage and adoption. One of the basic components of a contract is the notion of establishing an agreement between two parties that, if breached, results in penalties. Both the existence of a legal agreement undertaken jointly, as well as the threat of penalties, signal a commitment by the parties to perform. This expectation is a part of marriage and other family-related legalities, as well, and was often referenced by our participants as a rationale for seeking legal relationships. As described by approximately 10 percent of our participants, the law is perceived as generating or strengthening commitments between family members—which seemed particularly important given the lack of biological parent-child relationships for many of our participants.

For example, Marlon, a partnered, white gay man in his fifties who resides in a legally neutral state, adopted his children with his partner. He was the adoptive parent, but the couple was able to obtain second-parent adoption to establish a legal relationship between the children and the nonadoptive parent. Recounting the importance of second-parent adoption for him, as the sole adoptive parent, he stated:

> Well, it was always my intention that the children would be raised by [the two of us] and that is primarily for the children's benefit. . . . So we decided to formalize it, legalize it. And part of that is that if we didn't do that—and this was done on purpose by me—it is too easy to walk away from things if you're not legally bound by them. And [we] have had difficult times in our twelve years and, quite frankly, the fact that we are bound together in many ways, legally—even though we're not married, we've bought our houses together, we're both the parents of the kids together. Those types of things were kind of set up by me so that I just couldn't say, "You're done. These are my children, I'm leaving." Or he couldn't just say, "I'm leaving, I don't want anything to do with the kids." So it was intentionally done for some of the same reasons that people get married, and that is we want to put some roadblocks into just walking out the door.

His story suggests that he understands the law as providing a level of commitment, or at least a recognition of consequences, that is difficult to mimic through extralegal means. For two men having children, with only one able to establish an immediate legal claim to a child, the situation becomes quite different than in the case of many different-sex couples with access to biological or marital ties to create presumed obligations. In this particular context, the law is viewed as a powerful means to create ties and responsibilities that might not otherwise be present.

Johanna identifies as a married, white homosexual woman in her forties and resides in a legally neutral state. As a nonbiological parent, she described second-parent adoption as being significant for similar reasons—to establish commitment and ties, saying: "The primary reason we wanted second-parent adoption? The first thing that comes to mind is really taking this responsibility serious and wanting the responsibility forever, so I don't want an out. And, I think everybody sort of thinks that their relationship is strong—well, I don't know about everybody, but most people who get married think it is going to be for a long time. And I felt that way, but I still felt that . . . having it legalized would protect me." Her concerns seemed to be two-fold. As the nonbiological parent, she wished to establish a sense of obligation and commitment to her children. But her statement that second-parent adoption would "protect" her suggests a desire to establish a legal claim over the children so that her partner would also be committed to including her as a parent.

This notion of the law as making commitments was used not just to generate a greater sense of obligation on the part of parents to one another or to the children, but also to signal commitment to others. For example, Rhonda said that part of her motivation for second-parent adoption was to indicate that parenthood was an important commitment: "So I thought that [second-parent adoption] was a way to show that we were serious. You know, that the kids weren't puppies. We're not just getting some puppies because we're in a relationship, and how cute would that be? This was freakin' serious." She recalled that both the judge and the attorney also communicated the seriousness of the commitment that was generated by the legal process of adoption. For example, she remembered the judge saying: "'Regardless of your relationship you are committed to parenting these children. . . .' There are no documents that actually indicate that, but that was kind of his type of conversation with us and [we] were looking at each other like, 'OK, alright, this is real.'" The stories of these participants indicate that the making of commitment seemed to be an integral part of the adoption process for many—commitment between parent and child, and commitment to each other as a couple and as parents. This view of commitment as being generated by the law speaks to the perceived power of the law to establish ties that cannot be obtained through other mechanisms.

Participants also discussed the importance of legal marriage in creating commitment between partners, as well as to children. Traci and Vivian, a white, married lesbian couple residing in a legally neutral state, discussed the power of the law to bolster commitment and establish greater security:

> TRACI: [It is] the security. Yeah, that is true, because you can't back out of this now! I make fun of her all the time—you can't do it!
> VIVIAN: Whenever someone, like our friends, say something about it, . . . her comment is always that it really matters. Marriage matters. . . .
> TRACI: Yeah. Well, yeah. It really does matter. It really does make a difference. Because I think that if you know that you are married and you take that commitment seriously. . . . And, yes, people say they can do it [without marriage], but if you have that ceremony and you have that paper and you have that commitment, then maybe you are willing to stick out through a little more tougher times than you would otherwise. Otherwise you would be like—fuck, I'm sorry; I'm not married to them. I'm just going to pack up my shit and leave. You know people would do that. . . . There is no plan B.
> VIVIAN: Yeah, there isn't.
> TRACI: Because once you get married and you get the certificate and you have got that commitment, all of the insecurities—
> VIVIAN: They go away.

Legal marriage, as exemplified by having the certificate, is viewed by this couple as generating obstacles to separation, establishing or solidifying commitment, and removing emotional insecurities. This is a good deal of work that is done by a single legal undertaking. For those who view legal marriage as accomplishing so many tasks for a family, the lack of access to marriage could be powerfully felt.

Law Means My Family Is Valued

As prior research has argued, states that pass laws that curtail the rights or freedoms of a particular class of persons are sometimes perceived to be "othering" the group—dehumanizing or devaluing their lives or experiences (Cochran and Chamlin 2000). This "othering" process can be internalized by group members, affecting feelings of self-worth or a sense of legitimacy. It can also be internalized by individuals outside of the group who might view negative laws from an authority such as the government to sanction hate or violence against a group. Laws can be powerful, then, not just in terms of their direct effects on individuals' lives, but also in the manner in which they are perceived as being a reflection of whether authority figures value a group of persons. Approximately 10 percent of our participants referenced this idea of the law being an extension of the federal or state government, and serving as a benchmark for the status of their family in society. For those living in states with positive or protective laws regarding gay families, they at times described a feeling that the laws or legal procedures made them feel that the government cared about them and viewed their families as worthy of protection.

Janis and Laura described attending a wedding shortly after marriage was legalized in their state. They recalled being unexpectedly affected by the ceremony that was conducted by a justice of the peace. Laura explained:

> Some friends of ours got married right after and it was a justice of the peace who was this . . . sixty-five-year-old female judge in somebody's backyard, with a little ceremony and flowers around. And she administered their oath and then at the end she said, "By the power vested in me by the [state], I now pronounce you married." And it still chokes me up, to have the [state] actually back you. You feel like you don't care about state recognition until you get it, and then it seems like, ok, it's like [the state] is invested in this relationship. And that is moving to me, it really is. . . . At that time, especially when it first happened, the idea that the government would actually weigh in in favor of this relationship, like that seemed meaningful. So in that sense, the law worked.

For her, the marriage law did not just allocate rights; rather, the law seemed to communicate approval of the relationship and support of the family unit.

Alexandra and Dana communicated a similar sentiment. Alexandra attributed the feeling primarily to same-sex marriage being legalized in the state, saying:

I feel it has even impacted my view of the whole entire state legislature. . . . I feel like . . . the legislature is working to protect my family. . . . I don't think I would necessarily have said that before the marriage ruling came through. I even feel like [that] with the second-parent adoption. [I] remember reading on a message board or something like that [where] somebody was talking about . . . how they hated that they had to do a second-parent adoption and how angry it made them. And I feel sort of exactly the opposite. . . . I feel so grateful to have that opportunity and that the whole legal system would be interested that I can be a parent to my kids.

This idea that the legal system is interested in protecting her family echoes the feelings expressed by Laura. When new rights are afforded to a group that has been disadvantaged, and the rights appear to come about through the will of the state (rather than dictated by the courts or by the federal government), the law might be more readily perceived as working on the group's behalf with their betterment in mind. There are potentially important implications for how this legal sanctioning might affect the manner in which individuals operate within legal or administrative systems. As Alexandra went on to explain:

And I definitely [would] say . . . that it has a trickle-down impact to other things that I see as being benevolent forces in our lives. . . . So I was at the hospital with [my daughter] and . . . I told the guy at the desk that [her] other mother was coming and to let her know where we were. . . . I imagine if I was someplace else, this would feel really hard. . . . Am I sure I'm going to get this guy to let Dana into the hospital? . . . But I felt like, of course he wants to help me and my family! . . . I tend to assume that everybody is interested in supporting our family and I honestly think it's a direct result of the legal situation. The laws are in our favor; I assume everybody else is too and that people who are inside of systems that we interact with want to be supportive of us.

For Alexandra, the positive laws coming from the state generate a signal not just as to how the legislature might view her and her family, but also as to the type of treatment she anticipates receiving from a variety of the systems in which she operates. Essentially, the government has sanctioned equal treatment and there is a perceived trickle-down effect to other actors within the state.

This notion of the legal environment interacting with the sociopolitical environment was echoed by other participants, who described the manner in which the positive legal context provided their families with a different kind of everyday life than they might experience in other states without these protections. As Laura described, the law cleared many of the obstacles from their path as they sought to achieve their family goals: "We're so shielded here from the culture wars. That's the main thing I feel about living here. . . . We have health insurance coverage for our IVF, we had a gay lawyer who helped us navigate all the legal paperwork we needed before marriage became possible, then marriage became possible, and we joined in." These legal benefits translated into a type of barrier between them and the debates that were occurring in other states. Many participants living in legally positive states described this as a "bubble"; they were aware that their experience of gay parenthood was likely fundamentally different from that experienced by gay parents living elsewhere. As Tina, a partnered, white lesbian in her thirties who is a resident of a legally positive state, explained: "I feel very safe having a family here. I feel very safe bringing [my son] up here because I know that differences in family in [this state] are the norm versus the exception, and that is not true where he lived previously and where I grew up. . . . I want to be fair to my kids and I feel like living in [this state] provides them the same opportunities everyone else gets without a ton of discrimination. . . . It offers the most level playing field for our family." Similarly, Arnold, a partnered, white gay man in his sixties living in a legally neutral but friendly state, acknowledged how lucky he was to raise his daughter in a progressive sociopolitical environment: "[This] was an easy place, I think, to bring up a child in a gay relationship. . . . [My daughter] frequently told me it was cool to have gay dads here. There aren't many kids who could say that."

Because It's the Law!

Ewick and Silbey (1998) described the manner in which law can be viewed as constraining. By this, they mean that people often view rules and regulations as providing constraints on human action. We are powerless before the law, unable to modify it to a particular situation or to individuals' distinct needs. Legal actors, such as judges or administrators, are sometimes understood as being particularly constrained by the law; they might be thought of as having little discretion when interpreting legal doctrine (Ewick and Silbey 1998). This view of the law makes it predictable and reliable in many respects but, at the same time, also makes people more likely to "defer to the constraint of the law" (90). Our participants frequently articulated these constraints. In some cases (as discussed in chapter 6), they argued or acted against legal constraints even while they referenced their supposed intractability. For about 18 percent of our participants, however, constraints were met with either respect or acceptance, signaling a view of the law as external to human agency.

Birth certificates were a subject that frequently led to a discussion of the constraints posed by legal or administrative rules. Many of our participants wished to have both parents listed on the birth certificate in cases dealing with insemination or adoption, out of the belief that identifying an individual as a parent on a birth certificate conferred parenthood status (a belief that is not necessarily borne out by the law). When confronted with the document itself or a statement regarding rules or laws that regulate birth certificate completion, they often accepted the constraints as unchangeable or as something that could not be modified for their situation. Vivian, a married, white lesbian in her thirties who is a resident of a legally neutral state, described her desire to list herself as the second parent, saying: "So another parent was telling us to just to put my name as the father on the birth certificate. . . . I don't want the birth certificate to be invalid because we do that. We need to find out if that is legal. . . . Does the birth certificate actually say father? Or does it say parent?" Although she would have liked to modify the birth certificate to reflect her role in the parenting process, she seemed to feel constrained by the words on the form. If it says "father," she cannot put her name, but if it said "parent" this might be an indication that it would be legal to include her name. Rhonda articulated a similar view of the way in which the language on the birth certificate tied her hands in terms of adding her partner's name. She explained: "In [this state], it doesn't say 'parent' and 'parent,' it says 'mother' and 'father.' . . . [She] is not the father and there isn't one, so I don't want to identify her just to make ourselves feel better about having the two parents on there. To me it would cheapen the situation. You know, it clearly says we're trying to do something that we're not supposed to be doing. And I don't like that feel about it, so I didn't want to do it." Rhonda seemed to view the language on the form as constraining; it is "the law" and if you try to make modifications then you are doing something you are "not supposed to be doing." Accordingly, she later indicated that if the form had said "parent 1" and "parent 2," she would have put both names "because it would be permissible." The identification of her partner as a parent on the birth certificate was something she found appropriate, despite heteronormative notions regarding parenthood accruing through biological or legal ties; the form itself, however, curtailed her ability to take this step. As Beth, a resident in a legally neutral state, explained: "You know, I mean, it clearly says 'father' and that's it."

Legal constraints also frequently surfaced during discussions of relationship status. When asked their marital status, some of our participants discussed the manner in which their relationship status was determined by a set of rules that they seemed unable or unwilling to modify. Joann and Rhonda, who live in a legally neutral state, described their commitment ceremony, and then identified themselves as partnered. As Joann explained: "You know . . . there's rules, and . . . we haven't been able to be married by the law." Beth jokingly described her sexual orientation as "married," but when asked her marital status, responded: "Partnered. . . . Not legally married." Darrell, a partnered, white gay man in his forties in a legally neutral state, responded to the question about his marital status by saying, "Hmmmm, well I guess legally single," suggesting that it was important to describe his relationship status in terms of what was recognized by the law. And Kerry, a partnered, white gender queer person in her thirties who lives in a legally positive state, indicated her relationship status as single: "We're domestic partners, but under the federal law we're single."

For many individuals, context affected the appropriate response to this question. Those who were legally married in one state but moved to another state where marriage was not legal seemed uncertain as to which response to supply. For example, Ruth and Vicky had a ceremony in their legally neutral state, which does not provide legal marriage; they also were legally married in a legally positive state. When asked their marital status, Ruth responded: "Single." Vicky then qualified: "We are married in [this state]—we are not *legally* married here, but we got married here. . . . But we are married legally in [another state]." This uncertainty was common among those who had shifted legal contexts. As described by Ruth: "So, you know, I just went to a new dentist, and he says, 'Are you married?' I am like, now how do you answer that? In my mind I am married, in another state I'm married, but legally here in [my home state] I am not married. . . . Depending on the day, we probably say different things."

For a few individuals, there was confusion as to whether they were legally married due to the fluctuation in marriage laws. For example, Devin (who resides in a legally positive state other than California) expressed uncertainty about his marital status, saying: "I'm partnered. We got married in San Francisco but our marriage was nulled. I guess we're not married. So we're partnered." Although our question was open-ended regarding relationship status, participants often referred or alluded to legal constraints that limit the categories by which they could describe their relationship. Responses like these suggest that some participants define familial relationships by giving what they perceive to be the correct response because "it's the law."

LGBT parents did not just see *themselves* as subject to the constraints of the law. Other legal or administrative actors were viewed as similarly bound by external legal forces. Johanna described the manner in which the hospital personnel communicated that only the birth mother could be listed on the birth certificate, saying: "I'm not on [the birth certificate] and that is a state . . . thing. . . . The hospital, they did tell me, which I really respected, . . . that you can't be on the birth certificate and here's why, it's the law. It wasn't just that I was overlooked; they did explain it to me." She viewed the hospital personnel to perhaps be on her side, but limited by the law. This viewpoint of the law echoes Ewick and Silbey's (1998) description of the manner in which their participants viewed judges (for better or worse) to be constrained by laws as a disembodied doctrine. Marlon, who has a law-related career, also voiced this notion that legal actors were subject to the law rather than able to use the law as a tool. He discussed the way in which other states have a form that lists "parent a" and "parent b" which might permit identification of both members of a same-sex couple on a birth certificate. Although technically one could write the name of both parents on a birth certificate even if it said "mother" and "father," he indicated that persons who work within the field of law should not do that because they "need to follow the law, and the law doesn't permit that." As a legal actor, he also viewed the law as constraining rather than subject to modifications.

In many respects, some of our participants treat the law less as an abstract intellectual endeavor and more as a reified force that controls as well as constrains. Theresa, a single, white lesbian in her thirties who resides in a legally neutral state, indicated that she and her former partner had worked to write up an agreement governing custody arrangements for their child following their separation. They did not consult with an attorney or sign a formal agreement; rather, her former partner found a sample agreement and drafted guidelines for custody. She described a disagreement regarding the custody arrangement:

> Briefly, in an uncharitable mood, I said, "Well, what if I want [her] to take an after-school class? . . . Like, she can do that." Then [my ex] said, "no, she can't," and she went back and looked at this document she got and there is something called first right of refusal. It means that if I can't watch my child for a period of two hours or more, I have to first ask [my ex]—do you want her for that time? So [the after-school class] is like two hours long, so [my ex] is like, "No, that is first right of refusal."

The way in which she recounts this conflict and its resolution suggests that, once their arrangement was committed to paper, it became law. Although she emphasized this was an informal agreement and she did not view it as legal, her acquiescence to the terms of the agreement regarding the right of first refusal suggest that she felt powerless before the law. The document, in this way, had become something larger than the couple.

This sentiment of the law on paper being an entity of its own also surfaced during more positive interpretations of the role of the law in the family. Discussing her motivation for seeking marriage, Traci explained: "We went and got married in Canada. . . . I wanted to get married and I didn't care. That's what I wanted to do; I don't care if anybody else believes in it. And I said I want to even go somewhere where I can get a piece of paper. Even if no one else believes it. I have got that piece of paper; it is mounted on the wall." The piece of paper took on a life of its own, to some degree, in her eyes. Her motivation for marriage in Canada seemed less about making a commitment to another person or acquiring rights, and more about the acquisition of this piece of the law in paper form.

Conclusion

Approximately one quarter of our participants articulated interacting with the law as if it is a legitimate bestower of identities and obligations. Nonetheless, many of these participants simultaneously expressed resentment or frustration when the law did not serve their family goals. Because some participants viewed the law as immutable, rather than contingent, their ability to sway outcomes was constrained even in instances where they faced obstacles.

The belief that the law is unchangeable, objective, and legitimate was not expressed by those living in legally negative states, despite the fact that they perhaps confront more rigid legality. Rather, those who expressed this "before the law" mentality were almost equally located in legally positive states (45 percent) and legally neutral states (55 percent). Those participants in legally positive states often voiced seeing the benefit of the law for their families, whereas those in legally neutral states often encountered constraints that they believed could not be modified.

In addition, participants who expressed sentiments regarding the law as beneficial, powerful, and unchangeable were overwhelmingly white women. Approximately 90 percent of individuals articulating these ideas were non-Hispanic white, and approximately 85 percent female. These demographics closely mirror those of our overall sample, however, suggesting no strong relationship between demographic characteristics and an overall "before the law" stance. On the other hand, approximately 55 percent of those expressing "before the law" perspectives were married, 43 percent partnered, and only 2 percent single; this contrasts with our overall sample demographics, where 43 percent are married, 43 percent partnered, and 14 percent single. Viewing the law as legitimate or favorable, therefore, appears to be a sentiment that is tied to legal marriage for many of our participants.

Closer examination of the specific type of "before the law" perspectives that were shared by participants revealed that legal context, marital status, and gender appear to play a role in the cultural messages about the law that are received and embraced by participants. Those participants who conveyed the idea of the law as a maker of families and conveyer of identities were almost evenly split between legally positive and legally neutral states. Out of those expressing these ideas, almost all of those who lived in a state with legal marriage were, in fact, married. It is possible that individuals who view the law as important in forming family identities are likely to seek to do so via legal marriage; it is also possible that those who have been legally married are more likely to perceive the law as playing an important role in forming their family relationships and identities. None of those living in legally negative states voiced the same type of sentiments about the role of the law in defining their families and identities. This understanding of the law appears to be less common in situations where the law overtly excludes LGBT individuals from definitions of family. In terms of race and sex, this group of individuals closely mirrored our overall sample characteristics, with 84 percent white and 80 percent female. Understanding the law to play a powerful role in transmitting family identities, therefore, seems guided more so by legal context than by individual demographic characteristics.

Participants who articulated the notion that marriage serves to legitimate families were, unsurprisingly, overwhelmingly married. Almost 85 percent of those who communicated this conception of marriage were married, as opposed to only 43 percent of those in our overall sample. Understanding legal marriage as a legitimator is likely a reflection of both their own beliefs and rationales for getting marriage, as well as their experiences with the societal response to their own marriage. Given that legal marriage is more common for those in legally positive states, the individuals who communicated this idea of marriage were predominantly located in legally positive states, approximately 80 percent, with 20 percent residing in legally neutral states. In addition, this idea was only raised by women participants, and these women were slightly younger than the sample mean. This could suggest that nonheterosexual women are more likely to receive and, perhaps, to accept messages regarding the legitimizing force of marriage, as compared to nonheterosexual men—echoing the experiences of heterosexual women who experience greater societal disapproval than men for being unmarried (Thornton and Young-Demarco 2004).

Approximately 90 percent of the participants who indicated that the law plays an important role in establishing commitments between adults, or between adults and children, resided in legally neutral states. In addition, almost all of those in neutral states who voiced this sentiment were those who had married in another state, signaling the importance of seeking out that legal commitment even outside of their own state. Indeed, 75 percent of the individuals in this group were married, which is likely reflective of the fact that commitment was one of their rationales for securing marriage, even if it meant crossing state borders to do so. Those who were not married described the importance of utilizing second-parent adoption to establish legal commitments between parents and children. This group's racial, ethnic, and sex composition closely mirrored that of our sample as a whole.

Those who understood the law as signaling that the state cared about their families resided almost exclusively in legally positive states, at 72 percent, with the remainder in legally neutral, but generally gay-friendly, states. Their legal context had a direct relationship with their understanding of state actors as interested in the welfare of their families. All of the participants expressing this idea about legality are white.

Those participants that signaled adherence to the law because "it's the law" resided primarily in legally neutral states, with 80 percent in legally neutral and 20 percent in legally positive states. This suggests that those living in more ambiguous legal contexts are more likely to express the idea of adhering to the law, even when doing so might not be desirable for their family outcomes. Unlike participants in legally negative states, those in legally neutral states might articulate an adherence to the law out of respect for the law's authority given that they experience fewer direct conflicts between their family goals and legality. About 25 percent of those expressing this idea were male, making this one of the more popular "before the law" themes for men. These findings could reflect some of the gendered perceptions of legality found in other research. For example, some research has found that men are more likely than women to convey the idea of the law as rule-bound and inflexible, rather than considering what legal approach produces the most reasonable outcome for the parties involved (Baer 1999). This idea was also less strongly related to being married than some other "before the law" sentiments, with only 30 percent being married; this is likely due to the fact that this idea was expressed more by participants who reside in legally neutral states where marriage is less accessible.

Overall, legal context, gender, and marital status appear to play an important role in determining whether participants view the law as a legitimate conveyer of rights or meaning-maker. Further, these perceptions were colored by those of other legal actors, such as judges or legislators. The words or actions of these legal actors seemed to hold great significance for participants in conveying acceptance, social approval, or identities; this was particularly the case for participants who heard judges sanction their relationships with their partners or with their children. Similarly, participants described interactions with friends or family members that shaped their legal meanings, such as those participants who indicated that their relationships were afforded greater respect following legal marriage. Legal actors and social networks, therefore, acted alongside legal context and demographic characteristics, to shape a "before the law" approach to family law for our participants.

In chapter 5 we examine the manner in which viewing the law as contingent, rather than unchangeable, can dramatically shift interactions with the law for LGBT parents from acquiescence and toward modification.

5

Parenting with the Law

I think the law is useful. I think it provides a good framework and the vagueness of it is something we can work
within. I mean, second-parent adoption in [our state] exists
because of two words that are missing. It doesn't indicate
"mother" and "father" as parents specifically. . . . It was originally intended to protect a straight couple who had gotten
divorced and now one is remarried and that [new spouse] is
going to become a parent, so [it just says] "parent" and "parent." . . . And it is because of that loophole or nonlanguage
that you can kind of make second-parent adoption work in
[our state].
—Joann

In contrast to viewing the law as a reified object lacking in human
agency, many individuals understand the law as something that not
only *can* be manipulated but that *should* be manipulated. The law, in
this respect, can be viewed as contingent on individual circumstances
rather than as a fixed legality (Ewick and Silbey 1998). Conceiving of
the law as contingent and malleable raises the possibility of using the
law to achieve one's goals (Ewick and Silbey 1998). This picking and
choosing among legalities in order to achieve a particular end is seen as
the particular skill of attorneys, who might be understood as trained in
the art of legal gamesmanship. Viewing the law as changeable, however,
removes some of the mystery or power that comes with a "before the
law" perspective. Playing the game becomes something that anyone—
with the right resources—can do.

Approximately 58 percent of our participants described the contingency of the law, either as something that they recognized and used to
their benefit for their families or as a frustration in determining their
rights or identities. As indicated by Joann's story, vagueness or flexibility

can be understood as what makes the law useful or legitimate. Without this plasticity, the law is stable and individuals are subject to its whims for good or for bad. But the contextual and contingent nature of legal rights, particularly for LGBT families, can often make for guesswork and frustration when legal statuses or rights vary across geographic areas or time. This aspect of the social construction of legality is articulated as both a blessing and a curse for LGBT families.

When the law is viewed as a game, with outcomes that can be shifted based upon the particular facts of a case or resources employed, then individuals who are willing to play the game begin to consider various strategies for achieving their desired ends. Our participants sometimes expressed frustration with the need to play the games in order to form their families, and some felt that LGBT families were at a disadvantage in employing legal resources. But many made note of the fact that becoming parents involved throwing yourself into the legal ring, and attempting to come out the winner.

For some participants, strategizing and working with the legal system was described either with true enjoyment at "working the system" or in a positive light in terms of using one's resources to achieve a desired end. For example, Raymond, a partnered, white gay man in his forties who is a resident of a legally positive state, explained that he often strategized and manipulated the system when faced with legal or administrative obstacles to his parenthood goals. But this game playing was not, in his mind, indicative of ill intent or even disrespect of the legal system. He noted:

> You know, getting what you want in life is a lot about manipulation. And a lot of people think that manipulation is a negative word and I don't. We . . . manipulate our kids every day. . . . A three-year-old would stick his finger on a stove and get burned and if you say, "Don't do that, you're going to get burned," they may or may not listen. If you say, "Look, if you stick your finger there, it's going to get burned, you're going to get a blister and it's going to get really big and it's going to pop and ooze and really hurt and you may have to go to the hospital." . . . You're manipulating that kid to make sure that kid does not touch that stove. Is it really horrible? Well, that's a little extreme, but I think you get my point. We manipulate every day to get what we want. And hopefully if our motives are altruistic and proper, the manipulation is not a negative thing, it's a

positive thing. . . . So with the law it's the same thing. You work within the boundaries of the law and what you can get away with.

Manipulation of the system, within the boundaries of legality (i.e., "what you can get away with"), was seemingly normative for this participant. Rather than viewing the navigation of legal obstacles as particularly unique or burdensome, he appears to categorize legal manipulation as one of many other practical strategies that people engage in to achieve their desired ends.

Some other participants were quicker to point out the various costs associated with playing the game to form their families or acquire legal rights over their children. Marlon, a partnered, white gay man in his fifties residing in a legally neutral state, described the law as a "hurdle" that must be overcome:

[The law is]—the word that came to mind is a *hurdle* . . . . Sometimes it feels like putting a round peg in a square hole. The law is set up presuming you have a mommy and a daddy. And we don't. And our system . . . is not set up to handle that, in all respects. It's getting much better. People are understanding about gay families, but it's not there yet. And that's how I feel, that I'm trying to squeeze a round peg in a square hole. And usually it will fit, actually. A round peg will fit in a square hole. . . . It's not like a square peg in a round hole that just doesn't work. It works; it's just a little different. And sometimes you have to scratch things out and write in what fits. You have to find the right judge, you have to find the right person, and things like that. So, it's a little more work, it's a little more expensive, but you can do it if you really try.

While observing that he must take extra steps to work around a heteronormative legal system, he expresses both optimism in his ability to achieve his goals and, to some degree, optimism regarding the legal system moving toward more inclusiveness that would allow him to avoid these legal maneuvers. In this respect, while he acknowledged the labor involved in working the system, he did not express much resentment over the process.

Although participants like Raymond and Marlon seemed fairly at ease with playing the game, others expressed frustration at having to be players. Curt, a partnered, white gay man in his thirties who is a resident of a legally neutral state, discussed the manner in which he and his partner approached the foster-to-adopt process as having an uncertain outcome, in which they must strategize in order to win. This act of playing the game was, to him, an added burden placed upon them as a gay couple:

> I feel like we have to . . . we have to find ways to make [the law] work for us, rather than just being able to take it on face value. Gay people can adopt, you adopt as a single person and then there is a [second-] parent adoption. So one of us is on the birth certificate and there is a special [procedure] with the judge and they add the other as a coparent. It's like—yes, it can be done, but there are some judges that just won't do it. So we view it as it's almost more of a game and we have to play the game. And I mean, we can do it. We can play it, we can win it. But we *have* to play it. It's not like a straight couple that would go in and say, "I wanna adopt a child," and [they say], "OK, well, this is how it works." It's like, ohhh OK, there is *strategy*. And I think that is the best approach—you have to be strategic about it.

He not only was willing to work the system, but expressed confidence in his ability to do so successfully. Nonetheless, the fact that legal structures compelled him to take steps that he perceived could be avoided by his straight, married counterparts made the process distasteful to him.

Similarly, Traci and Vivian—a married, white lesbian couple residing in a legally neutral state—communicated resentment over their understanding that the law required additional work on their part as compared to a straight, married couple. Their exchange reveals the same tension voiced by Curt—the flexibility of the law often permitted them to achieve their family goals, but they expressed bitterness that they had to engage in these manipulations.

> VIVIAN: [The law] needs some tweaking but I can work with it. There are other things we can do. Like, . . . they are not going to consider me a parent of the child when the child is born. OK, that is just the law; that is the way it is. Now we have to work around the law, now we have to go through the [second-parent] adoption side. We can

work around it, even though here are one set of rules [and] you cannot change that rule, but there are other ways. . . .

TRACI: Yeah, we have to spend a lot of time and money getting around bullshit.

VIVIAN: So it is more difficult for us because we have to go around everything to get where we want to go. It is a lot easier for straight people.

TRACI: Because they are already granted it without thought.

These stories reveal that participants who express a "with the law" perspective about aspects of their parenting process are often optimistic about their ability to find a way to achieve their parenting ends, or to marshal available resources to advocate for their family. They recognize that the law is contingent and, being so, possesses flexibility that creates space for their family. At the same time, participants acknowledge that this space must be carved out of a heteronormative legal framework that is, at its core, often incompatible with or hostile to their families. Accordingly, their strategies for "playing the game" are simultaneously creative, effective, and result in bittersweet victories.

In this chapter we highlight several of the key strategies employed by our participants for working within the legal system. These include variations on forum shopping, employing workarounds, accessing heteronormative privilege, and marshaling one's resources. Some of our participants expressed multiple of these "with the law" strategies, resulting in the percentages across strategies summing to more than 58 percent of the overall sample. We conclude by assessing the manner in which legal context, legal actors, social networks, and demographic factors interact to produce a "with the law" approach to legality with respect to the family.

Forum Shopping and the Parenthood Process

By understanding the law as contingent, doors are opened for a greater variety of options for achieving family goals. One of the most common strategies our participants articulated for avoiding negative legal outcomes was engaging in some type of forum shopping. In the right court, before the right judge, in the right county, state, or country—parenthood goals can be achieved.

Forum Shopping for Judges

One of the most prevalent narratives among our participants involved selecting a particular court or judge that was favorable to LGBT families. Approximately 18 percent of participants described engaging in forum shopping as a strategy for working the system in order to achieve family goals. Forum shopping was extremely common for those seeking to engage in second-parent adoption in states that did not clearly permit such adoptions. Across states, there was surprising consistency in the stories that were told regarding finding the attorney with the inside knowledge, the jurisdiction or judge who was likely to grant the adoption, and trips made with a group of other LGBT parents to the friendly court for adoption day.

In states that might frequently seem unfriendly toward LGBT families, finding the judges who were perceived as focused on the welfare of children or LGBT rights was often argued as essential. Anthony, a single, white gay man in his thirties, was going through the foster-to-adopt process in a legally neutral state. He noted: "I have not at this point encountered any problems. I think my biggest stumbling block is going to be toward the end of the process, if I end up with a judge who's very conservative and against it, cause that's a real possibility in [our state]." Esther, a partnered, Hispanic woman in her forties who lives in a legally neutral state, similarly described the contingent nature of second-parent adoption within her city, stating: "I've heard that you get the right lawyer and the right court, . . . the right judge, it can go through. But I don't know if it's a matter of buying it or if it's a matter of . . . timing, the resources, and living in the right [place]." Dianna, a partnered, white lesbian in her forties, echoed this sentiment, observing that second-parent adoption in her legally neutral state "is kind of hit or miss, and certain judges would do it and certain judges won't and eventually no judges would." Sam, a married, white female-to-male transgender individual who lives in a legally negative state, attempted to explain why outcomes were perceived to differ so dramatically depending on in what part of the state you sought an adoption:

> It's a different demographic in [that part of the state]. It's primarily, first of all, much more Democrat-leaning. [My part of the state] is much more

the Republican-leaning center of the state. But I think also because of the metropolitan population [in that part of the state], they are much more leaning to anyone who is a financially viable adult person who is willing to take care of a child. You know, "Sign the paper, let's get it done," and it doesn't work that way as readily in [my part of the state]. You are more likely to run into conservative bias [here] where, in my opinion, they are less worried about the child than about politics. So I think there are many things going on in [that part of the state] that make it a little easier to find the judges who are not as, what's the word . . . rural, maybe. Do you know what I mean? I mean, they deal with such a diversity of situations constantly that you are less likely to run into, "This is my hometown and this ain't how we do it here."

While participants can be viewed as "playing the game" through this strategizing of selecting favorable jurisdictions, their perception of the rules of the game is decidedly negative, with many articulating a belief that the laws and many judges do not have their family's best interests at heart.

The understanding that family outcomes were dependent on finding the right judge led to strategizing on the part of many participants. They described the manner in which attorneys or adoption agencies directed them to the appropriate court where they would be most likely to obtain their adoption. Krystal, a married, white bisexual woman in her thirties was going through adoption in a legally positive state. She recalled that her court selection was entirely determined by her attorney's advice, indicating they did "what our lawyer said to do" in selecting a court. Other participants elaborated that their attorneys had the inside knowledge about which jurisdictions and which judges were likely to lead to the best outcomes for their LGBT clients. Katherine, a married, white lesbian in her forties, explained that second-parent adoptions were being done in her legally negative state, but that you had to have the right attorney with the right knowledge. As she explained: "The attorneys that are doing them know how to get in front of the right judge. I don't know how they do that. They know how to do that."

Similarly, Joann, a partnered, white lesbian in her thirties, recalled her attorney explaining the process in their legally neutral state as follows: "I asked, 'Well, how do you decide where it happens and why.' And she said, 'Quite frankly, we've got relationships with some judges that are going to be great, without question, when we take it to the court rooms. They are advocates for good family structure.'" Kendra, a married, white gay woman in her thirties, similarly described her attorney recommending a particular court in her legally positive state due to the perceived friendliness of the judges to LGBT parents: "All the lawyers, they all know the . . . sitting judges and some are more sympathetic than others and some are just more pain in the asses than others. And so the lawyer knew that the general feeling was that [this] court was letting a lot of cases go through without a lot of trouble." Along the same lines, Curt indicated that part of his strategizing in selecting an adoption agency involved considering the insider knowledge of the agency in selecting the right judges to process the adoption. He explained: "They tend to direct most of their gay adoptions to specific judges and they know those judges and they know how to make the system work in our favor. . . . That is kind of their reputation—that they know how to help us through the state."

In states that granted more latitude to forum selection, participants frequently recounted going to another city for their adoption. This forum shopping across cities was fairly commonplace, as described by Marlon who indicated that it was popular and widespread within his legally neutral state. He explained: "Do you understand [our state] law is silent regarding second-parent adoptions? It is something we do all the time, hundreds, thousands of them have been done in [our state]. We go to [another city] often to do them because the judges there are very permissive in doing that and it is very easy." Participants told of learning of these "friendly cities" from attorneys, organizations, and friends. For example, Beth, a partnered, white lesbian in her thirties, described how she was instructed by her attorneys to go to another city in her legally neutral state for second-parent adoption: "Like, our attorneys advised us, yeah, do this in [this other county]. . . . They never turn down a single-parent gay adoption. I mean, well, they don't turn you down because you're gay. . . . And so they said, 'Do it in [this other county].'" Similarly, Ben, a partnered, white homosexual man in his thirties, indicated that he learned about the friendly cities within his legally neutral state through his attorney. He recounted: "I knew there were some issues that could be gotten around by a certain judge in [another city] who's friendly to GLBT couples. Like, when I went to adopt, . . . we went straight to that judge. Our attorney is based in [our city], . . . so she knows exactly how to handle those snags. And they are not to be handled in [our city] apparently."

Although attorneys were a ready source of information about friendly jurisdictions, some individuals indicated that they learned of friendly cities from organizations. For example, Keith, a white gay man in his forties, was going through the foster-to-adopt process as a single parent in a legally neutral state. He was less concerned about his sexual orientation given that he did not have a partner which might more readily reveal him as gay. Nonetheless, at an orientation on fostering, he described how prevalent the forum shopping strategy was for gay parents: "[During the orientation], I heard a lot about—If you can, go to [another city]. [Laughs.] For the judges, don't go [here]. Don't do it, don't do it!" This strategy was readily communicated to potential adoptive parents by others who had the "inside knowledge" of how to work the system. Others learned about the friendly cities through friends sharing their own experiences with forum shopping. Kendra, for example, explained: "[At my work, there was a woman] who was a lesbian, and her and her partner had a child and she was telling me that . . . they had to go to [another city to adopt]. So I knew that. And then, also, I had this friend who has children . . . and one of them has a schoolmate that had lesbian parents, and she talked to them for me. And . . . they had to go to [the other city to adopt]."

Even participants residing in states that were more restrictive in terms of selecting jurisdictions sometimes were able to select different courts that were more beneficial to them. Sharon, for example, is a single, white lesbian in her forties who lives in a legally positive state. She described how she was able to select either the jurisdiction where she lived or the jurisdiction where the child they were adopting was born. She opted for a court where the child was born, explaining: "We didn't want an adoption in a county court where we lived because it was in a rural [part of the state]. . . . Our child was born in [a larger city], and they let us stay in [that city]. . . . We wanted to go to the [city] court as opposed to the rural court because we knew the [city] courts would be much more supportive."

After marshaling their resources to locate a potentially friendly forum, participants described the process of traveling to the jurisdiction and appearing before the judge. Many indicated that attorneys made trips with a group of LGBT parents to the chosen court, with all adopting on the same day. Johanna, a married, white homosexual woman in her forties who lives in a legally neutral state, described the process of completing adoptions in another city with a group of clients as a strategy engaged in by her attorney, saying, "If you haven't heard, there's this one attorney in town that's her M.O." Marlon described the adoption process as follows:

> Well, [my lawyer] took me there and [she] explained that [this city's] judges all determined that this is legal and proper and no big deal and there is an adoption attorney there who handles everything for the children, makes sure everything is proper for the kids. So, it's really all handled for you in advance. You go there and you have a five-minute little hearing. . . . In [my city], judges are more conservative, more concerned about their appearance with the religious right and those types of things. And since the law doesn't expressly authorize [second-parent adoption], my understanding and impression is that most of them wouldn't do it. The other problem is that . . . you can't pick your judge [in my city]. [In this other city], you go to any district judge you want, regardless of what court the case is filed in and you have that judge grant your adoption. . . . So you find the judge you want and a judge that has agreed ahead of time will approve it.

Once the judge was identified, the participants described appearing before the judge as part of a group of LGBT parents that were all clients of the same attorney. Joann, who was adopting in a legally neutral state, described the process, saying: "[The judge] . . . kind of looked like a deacon at a Southern Baptist church and he was great and we have a picture with him with the kids after the adoption. . . . He was a pretty good guy. The actual court interaction is pretty small. You are kind of herded in there with multiple families that are doing it and you get taken up one at a time." Similarly, Beth described a group of LGBT parents who went through adoption at the same court, explaining, "so we showed up and there were several couples, all women." Ben offered more details about how this group adoption was orchestrated by the attorney, saying:

BEN: Yeah, the adoption is a pretty joyous occasion. There's a couple dozen couples there all doing the same thing, some of them have three or four kids and have a baby in their arms and they brought their families and took photos with the judge. It was really nice.

INTERVIEWER: Were the other couples gay or lesbian?

BEN: All of them were.

INTERVIEWER: Were they all [the same attorney's] clients?

BEN: Yeah, they were. She does it once a month, one trip a month. She's got the second Tuesday—I don't know the day, but it is something like that, the same day every month. If no one is lined up for some month, she'll try to push people up or do it quicker so she doesn't waste any trips.

INTERVIEWER: Is it always the same judge?

BEN: Yeah.

Echoing this basic account, Margo, a married, white bisexual woman in her thirties, described her adoption process as a trip to another city in her legally neutral state with a different attorney and the attorney's clients. She recalled:

Well, we showed up with two other families. . . . She said she normally does them in groups like that, just to go bing, bing, bing. . . . We weren't supposed to see any particular judge, but [our attorney] was just planning to pop in and see who was around. But when we got there all the judges were at some conference doing a training. So we were thinking, like, "We came all the way to [another city] and now we're not going to be able to do it and what's going to happen?" But she found somebody who would do it on her lunch break.

These stories from participants emphasize that they understood the process of forum shopping to involve more than just picking a friendly forum. It was a multifaceted strategy on the part of the parents, attorneys, and judges.

A few participants indicated that forum shopping still proved beneficial within a legally positive state given the additional control they could gain over the process. For example, Heather, a married, white queer woman in her thirties, selected a particular court because it provided the option of selecting the social worker that would conduct the home study. She noted:

> [With this court], you get to choose who does your home study and we just felt more comfortable with that. I was prepared to get really offended with someone coming and doing the home study but the social worker was very nice. She was gay; [the lawyer] recommended somebody who was. . . . We did pay for the social worker, . . . and I think that if you don't want to use one you choose, they will appoint one and then I think that's free. But I felt . . . I wanted that control.

Selecting the social worker, more so than the potential judge, was an important factor for this participant in determining the court due to the additional control that it supplied over how your family is described in the home study.

For others in legally positive states, the perceived benefits of forum shopping were not always related to the outcome of the proceeding. Nellie, a partnered, white queer woman in her thirties from a legally positive state, described how she had explored options at two courts. When she went to get information at one court, she felt frustrated by the process, but at another the court clerk was very helpful. She explained: "We went to them and the guy was so nice and so much easier to comprehend. . . . And he was gay, so I liked that too. I felt comfortable so we decided to go with [that court] . . . because it was just—the clerk was easier." In ways such as this, participants reported varying benefits that could be gained by forum shopping as they went through the process of becoming a parent or acquiring legal rights over their child, including access to specific social workers or to friendly administrators.

Although participants often discussed forum shopping as a strategy, they also acknowledged potential obstacles in the process and (for some) the tenuous nature of this legal loophole. Curt, who selected his adoption agency in part due to its reputation for assisting in forum shopping, acknowledged that this was a tricky game to play. He explained:

> Apparently [selecting judges is] not as easy as it used to be. . . . These are kids who are wards of the state, so in theory you can go to any judge you want to but you have to be careful because there is a judge . . . who

has seen this child all the way through the foster system and all of a sudden you wanna pick up and use a different one for adoption. You are gonna piss the judge off. And [the adoption agency] has gotten their hand slapped for doing stuff like that. So that may not be much of an option anymore and they are going to have to start working with the judges that they have been assigned, and [our county] is tough. It's all pretty conservative Republican judges. We will see. It would be a shame to go through this entire thing, have all of this go our way, and get stopped at the end. You know, by some bigoted judge.

His story emphasizes that while forum shopping might on its face appear to be a means of treating the law as a game, there is a lot riding on this endeavor. Not only could an individual lose by angering the wrong judge, but the entire pipeline for adoptions could be negated if forum shopping is not navigated carefully. Some of our participants discussed this process less as strategizing and playing the game within the confines of the law, and more as a secret endeavor to subvert the legal system—one that could be exposed and shut down at any time. We discuss this view of forum shopping in more detail in chapter 6, given that it exemplifies many elements of the "against the law" schema.

Forum Shopping for Children

Although much of the forum shopping described by participants involved finding the right judge within the state in which they resided, approximately 9 percent of participants described strategies to cross state or national borders in order to select laws that were more favorable for the parenthood process. This was particularly important when state laws did not permit individuals to adopt children as an LGBT couple or to enter into surrogacy agreements. Some participants then chose to investigate whether and how they could use the laws or processes in other, friendlier states or countries in order to become parents.

For example, Ben, a white, partnered homosexual man in his thirties, explained that when he and his partner discussed options for having children, they decided that they were interested in surrogacy. They began to explore options for surrogacy within their own legally neutral state, and were disappointed in what they found: "We contacted some

GLBT family lawyers just to see if they could guide us in the right direction. Didn't have much luck in that area. The laws in [our state] at the time, or maybe the way they were being interpreted, was going to make it difficult. We actually didn't try too hard in [our state]. We actually found an agency and a surrogate in [another state]." After locating an agency and a surrogate out of state, the couple had the attorney who was part of the agency draw up the legal documents and oversee the process of locating a surrogate. Although the couple made some changes with subsequent pregnancies, they retained the original surrogate that they located outside of their state. By looking toward states with less restrictive laws on surrogacy, they were able to access legal rights that they perceived as not accessible within their own state.

Devin, a partnered, white gay man in his forties in a legally positive state, shared a similar story regarding surrogacy. When he and his partner decided to explore surrogacy, they began to investigate some of the agencies that assisted couples with the process. They were most drawn to options outside of their state. He described the manner in which he was impressed by the overall environment regarding both laws and activism surrounding reproduction within their chosen state:

> DEVIN: We had that legal security there and we liked that. There was this great idea for assisted reproduction work all over [the state]. Like, they were very gay-positive, all of the medical people. And then my family was there.
>
> INTERVIEWER: Ok, now, when you use the word *gay-positive*, do you mean something that's above and beyond, for example, a term such as *gay-friendly*? Or are they synonymous for you?
>
> DEVIN: You know, probably synonymous, but maybe a little bit more. Because, like, our IVF doctor was gay and he is, like, an advocate for gay surrogacy and gay men doing this, so he's like—whatever the opposite of effusive is. So he's not like, "Ah, that's great, you guys are doing this!" But I just felt like every step along the way, people were encouraging us and that felt great. . . . Subsequently, we talked to other couples to sort of give them advice about doing surrogacy, mostly here in [our home state], and it feels like even in the five or six years since we've gone through this process, the feeling around [our state] has changed, legally and all of this stuff. . . . So all this stuff

about, wow, [this other state] is so much better, might have been just
that moment we were in, you know?

As his recollection suggests, there are various factors that appeared
to encourage forum shopping across state lines for parenthood, including laws, the perception of a friendly and supportive environment, and
feasibility (in this case, having family located in the state helped). His
observation that the advantages offered by forum shopping might be
temporary emphasizes the contingent nature of the law—both geographically and temporally.

Yet another one of our gay male couples also opted to forum shop for
the friendliest surrogacy laws. Bobby (thirties) and Walter (forties) are
a partnered, white couple residing in a legally neutral state. When they
decided to pursue surrogacy, they found that California laws were the
most appealing due to their understanding that they could sever the surrogate's parental rights prior to the birth of the child. This was important
to them because their names would be placed on the birth certificate at
birth. The agency that they were working with originally matched them
with a surrogate in another state, but they indicated that they "wanted a
surrogate from a tier-one state," that is, a state with the friendliest laws.
In describing the process of forum shopping, Walter observed: "I kind of
wish the law were like . . . one-stop shopping and we didn't have to worry
about the details. . . . But I am grateful about the law in this country
because it allows us to choose the laws that favor us." Walter, like many
of our participants, felt simultaneously grateful that he had the freedom
to elect friendlier jurisdictions when forming his family, but frustrated
that legal inconsistencies required him to engage in forum shopping in
the first place.

In addition to surrogacy, some of our participants opted to adopt
in other states because of friendlier laws. For example, Katherine and
Nancy are married, white lesbians in their forties. They were married in
one state but currently reside in a legally negative state, and were considering adopting from the state where they were married. They had
identified a child that they were interested in adopting, and Katherine
explained: "Interestingly enough we have a choice; since [the child] lives
in [another] state, we have a choice whether to finalize in [our state] or
[the other state] and if we finalize in [the other state], automatic second

parent. . . . They'll recognize the marriage and it's pretty much set from there." Unlike in their home state, they would both be able to adopt the child as a married couple in the other state, and both of their names would be placed on the child's new birth certificate after the adoption. This was a huge incentive to adopting across state lines, given that they were uncertain of the degree to which second-parent adoptions could be readily obtained in their home state. Strategizing in this manner opened the door to an array of legal rights that they otherwise did not believe they could access.

Perhaps more expectedly, participants also described seeking more favorable legal environments for adoption in other countries. International adoption required researching shifting legalities regarding single parent or gay adoption in other countries, including greater obstacles to intercountry adoptions as a result of the bureaucratic restrictions and additional costs that resulted from the Hague Adoption Convention (Wardle and Robinson 2013). For example, Sharon considered international adoption while living in a legally positive state. She described the process of sifting through legal guidelines in several countries to settle on a place to pursue international adoption, saying: "There were obviously countries we couldn't go near and ones we wouldn't go near because they were not friendly so we picked countries that were supportive. But there are certain countries that wouldn't even let a single woman adopt so those were out to begin with anyway. . . . [We were looking for] someplace where we wouldn't have to completely lie and hide the relationship. Mentioning it is one thing, but having to completely lie—we were trying to find countries that were at least remotely friendly." While she was open to considering countries that might not permit both her and her partner to adopt the child, her search was focused on countries where she would not have to hide her relationship. Some participants who selected international adoption chose not to disclose a gay identity or the existence of a same-sex partner; some went a step further and described themselves essentially as heterosexual. This aspect of adoption is addressed more closely in chapter 6.

Other individuals saw the potential for both parents to adopt in other countries. Ruby, a partnered, multiracial lesbian in her thirties who is a resident of a legally positive state, was hopeful that joint adoption might be available in Mexico: "I know somebody who runs an orphanage in

Mexico, and Mexico City has same-sex adoption. And . . . this person believes that they're trying to . . . have national laws that will allow for [joint adoption]. So that may align with our situation when we will be married." In this respect, Ruby perceived greater options in another country for same-sex couples to pursue their desired legal outcomes of both parents adopting.

In addition to these more deliberative choices of pursuing adoption or surrogacy in more favorable legal environments, some participants ended up adopting across state lines due more to procedural mechanisms. For example, Carl, a married, white gay man in his thirties, resides in a small, legally positive state with limited children available for adoption. He explained that his pathway to adoption was circuitous, filled with some deliberate planning in terms of accessing greater legal rights but also some circumstantial outcomes that resulted in adopting from another state:

> You know, I think where it really began . . . [was] when we were both living . . . in Florida. It's where I had been working. And at that time Florida still had a ban on same-sex adoptions. . . . We were thinking, well, we want to move to a state that legally has some protection and that if . . . we were going through the adoption process, where that could happen. . . . And so that was one of the reasons—after doing a bit of research and looking at places I thought I might want to work—that was part of the reason we ended up coming to [this state].

Carl's path to adoption began by identifying a friendly state to move to where they would be able to adopt a child. After moving to the state, they made their profile as adoptive parents and sent it to a lawyer. As he described it, the lawyer had a relationship with a lawyer in another state that she often used for adoptions. He explained: "She has another lawyer that she does a lot of business with in [this other state], who is kind of the intake lawyer who does a lot of advertising and connects with potential birth moms. And our profile was sent out there." Ultimately, their profile was selected by a birth mother and they made a trip to the other state in order to pick up their son. By adopting across state lines, Carl indicated that they were obligated to fulfill some of the legal requirements in both states:

Part of the way this works, though, is that you have to satisfy all the regulations in each state, which is why when we went down for the birth and to pick up our son we had to stay there for several days because the legal stuff has to be cleared in both [states]. So, I mean, when the adoption is finalized and all that, it's all done in [our home state's] probate court. . . . You follow all the laws, to have a child that's going to be adopted in another state kind of exported successfully. . . . But also, . . . the fact that this is a private adoption kind of skirts some stuff too. . . . I mean, it obviously has to follow the adoption law but there's an element to it that it's kind of a private contract as well. . . . While we were there, oddly enough, [the other state] passed some sort of law restricting the right of unmarried couples to adopt. I think it's all very contingent, frankly. I think a lot of the reasons why we ended up making the decision we have and why we've followed the path that we have is because we came to the state that we did.

His account of his adoption experience reveals a rather complicated balance between finding an available child and navigating two legal systems—one less friendly than the other. Unlike in the previously described cases of forum shopping for adoption, Carl and his partner adopted a child who was located in a state with less friendly laws and a less friendly sociopolitical environment than the state in which they reside. But by engaging in cross-state adoption, the couple was able to put their adoption portfolio in front of a greater number of birth mothers and they perceived this approach as increasing the likelihood of adoption occurring. Carl, however, understood the status of these laws to constantly be in flux, meaning that routes to adoption were shifting—even, as in his case, during the course of the adoption process. These fluctuating legalities created a great deal of uncertainty for parents as to where to locate favorable jurisdictions.

Sheila, a partnered, white lesbian in her fifties, described another case of cross-state adoption. She and her partner were living in a legally positive state and were seeking to adopt a child. They began to research adoption agencies, looking both inside and outside of their state:

So we had done a lot of research online . . . on all different adoption agencies across the country, on where lesbians were adopting and how was that working. And we came down to five agencies that we liked. . . .

We made a grid, of how much does it cost, about how long does it take— kind of your really basic questions. . . . And we realized that at this other agency that our friends had gone to [in another state], we found a lot of information about the really basic stuff. So my partner called the agency, and the secretary realized . . . [that my partner] is African American from her voice. And she connected her to the executive director of the agency who talked to her some more. And it just seemed that on that day, an eight-and-a-half month pregnant African American woman had presented herself and wanted to have an African American family adopt her child. . . . She just presented that day, so I guess they didn't have any other families or any other appropriate families. So we're calling [to ask], like, how much does it cost, and then within twenty-four hours my part- ner had spoken to this birth mom and within twenty-eight days we had our child. So it was a story. I was not involved, I could not be involved because this was in [a negative-leaning state].

The couple was able to adopt, and adopt quite quickly, due to locating an available child where the birth mother's desire for an African American family moved her partner to the top of the list of possible adoptive par- ents. Being able to adopt quickly and successfully was a trade-off for adopting in a state where the legal and sociopolitical climate was much less accepting of LGBT parents. Not only was Sheila not able to adopt the child along with her partner due to their cross-state adoption, but she had to exclude herself from the entire adoption process so as not to endanger the outcome. For participants like Carl and Sheila, the process of cross-state adoption was a strategy in which couples perceived the benefits of a successful adoption to outweigh the costs of navigating a less friendly legal environment.

Forum Shopping for Friendly Home States

Most forum shopping strategies described by participants involved look- ing for ways to achieve parenting goals while remaining in their current residence. As Traci, a married, white lesbian in her thirties, explained regarding her decision to travel to Canada to get married: "Well, I went somewhere else to do what I wanted to do anyways, but I still live here. It's not like I'm moving to Canada to stay or anything." The majority of participants reported working with their legal limitations to find loopholes or employ their resources to achieve goals, rather than moving in order to access new rights. Approximately 15 percent of participants, however, reported that they selected residences due to legal rights, that they would have moved if they had not been able to become a parent within their state, or that if they were to move in the future then their residence choices would be determined by the available family laws.

Some participants considered their available legal parenting options when making moves to other cities or states. For example, Sheila noted that when she was selecting graduate schools she picked a school located in a state where she had heard they were permitting lesbians to adopt. Margarita, a married, Hispanic lesbian in her thirties who is a resident of a legally positive state, similarly explained that she selected her state because "it was important to move to a state where I could legally adopt being in a same-sex relationship." Some participants also investigated whether second-parent adoption was available in a state when choosing to move. For example, Kerry, a partnered, white gender queer person in her thirties, noted: "There's only a few states that will let you do second-parent adoption and I knew that [this state] was one of them. And that was actually one of the things that I had looked at when I was going to move here."

Other participants indicated that if they had been unable to find a way to have a child in their own state, they would have moved. For some, changes in the law opened options previously unavailable; without those changes, forum shopping through moving was a strategy they considered. For example, Anthony, a single, white gay man in his forties, was going the foster-to-adopt route within his legally neutral state, and observed that the situation had changed enough while he was living in the state that this became a viable option. But, had it not been possible, he said: "I was going to do it regardless. Even if it came down to me having to move to another state, I was going to do it." Similarly, Colin, a partnered, Hispanic gay man in his thirties, was living in a legally negative state and explained that he and his partner had delayed having kids because they felt stymied by the legal obstacles within their state. He observed: "It really was just a matter of the law. We had talked about, maybe two years into the relationship, you know—it doesn't look like the environment is going to change anytime soon; maybe we should get out of this state. And it was always just, 'Okay, next year, next year, next year' and there has always been one reason or another that has kept us here." Once laws changed, providing them with greater options for expanding their family, they moved forward with adoption. Had the law not changed, however, the idea of moving to have greater options was a strategy they considered. Notably, while moving was an option that some participants discussed, uprooting one's life to move to another state was not a simple task—resulting in most participants attempting to resolve their legal conflicts within their state.

Relatedly, some participants indicated that although they were able to have a child in a legally nonfriendly state, they would consider moving for second-parent adoption or if they had additional children. Discussing future moves for legal rights was fairly common for participants who had a child, but who were unable to obtain second-parent adoption in their current state. For example, Jody, a single, white lesbian in her forties, emphasized that access to second-parent adoption would be a priority for a move from her legally neutral state, saying: "I was not gonna move unless I moved to a state that I could get second-parent adoption. Why would I leave to get nothing? You know? I was already here with nothing."

Esther and Shelley, a partnered lesbian couple living in a legally neutral state, also indicated that they would consider a move for second-parent adoption. Each had a child with a former partner. Following their separations with their partners, they encountered a variety of legal and financial issues that posed challenges for their families. Shelley, a white lesbian in her thirties, in particular felt that if her former partner had adopted their child, then the partner might have felt more of an emotional and financial obligation toward the child upon separation. In discussing whether they would move to gain access to second-parent adoption if they decided to have additional children, both Esther and Shelley responded that this would be an important consideration. But, at the time they had their first children, this was less of a pressing concern. Esther, a Hispanic lesbian in her forties, explained this change of heart, saying: "I think at the time, at least for me, it was—this is my home, this is where I live and I've got to find a way to make this happen now, . . . where I live. And it was possible. But now after what we've been through, each of us, I realize ideally it would be great to live somewhere else." These stories reveal that many of our participants attempted to find a way to have a child within their state of residence, even if the available options were not ideal or left one of the partners without legal rights. Those who experienced the negative implications of lack of access to second-parent adoption articulated more often the desire to move to acquire these rights or the necessity of having them in place prior to having additional children.

For people living in positive states with access to the legal rights they want for their families, almost all indicated that they would not move to a state where they did not have recognition of their marriages or their parental rights. This fear of losing rights was described by Laura, a married, white lesbian in her forties:

> In states that have laws against gay adoption, we worried that [Janis's] adoption of the kids wouldn't be honored. You know, adoption is treaties between each state and we were worried that coparent adoption by [our home state] wouldn't be honored by a state like Florida or Arkansas that was outlawing gay adoption at that time. . . . We didn't know if we would actually be discriminated against in practice, but we worried about it. It did kind of give us a list of states we wouldn't move to.

Whether these fears were substantiated was unclear even to the participants themselves. But the notion of losing rights through a move was a strong deterrent for these individuals. Krystal, who lives in a legally positive state, initially seemed to describe the legal relationship between her partner and their child as being partially dependent on the agreement that she and her partner had regarding guardianship. She explained:

> It seems that we are fine . . . unless I for some reason try to challenge her legally, like—'I want to take away your rights.' . . . In which case, I may have some legal standing to do. . . . So it seems as though if we're united in the fact that she is the guardian, it's not going to be that much of a problem. It's really just that there may be some legal standing in [a more negative state] that she is like a legal stranger to our child.

This notion that the parental relationship could shift following a move emphasizes the perceived contextual nature of the law, where selecting a friendly state becomes a legal strategy for some participants in order to form and maintain family relationships.

Some participants seemed to realize how privileged they were to be living in a state that granted their families protection. For example, Dana, a married, white lesbian in her thirties, explained: "I think about those situations [where people are living in legally unfriendly states] and, like, how do people do that? Like why don't they move somewhere else if they can? And I recognize not everybody can move, but you know people who can. Like, why don't they move someplace else? I think [I look at it that way] because I'm here and because I have these rights and I feel like I can't, I *won't* do anything else."

The Workarounds

In addition to forum shopping, participants described strategies to imitate specific legal rights if they were barred from directly accessing them. Approximately 15 percent described strategies that involved drafting documents that provided an air of legality, or using legal mechanisms that were similar to the desired outcome. Badgett (2010) delineated approaches that LGBT individuals take in order to generate some of the protections of legal marriage, such as wills, power of attorneys, joint property ownership, joint bank accounts, and so on. Our participants identified many similar ways in which they worked to replicate the rights of marriage, as well as ways in which they attempted to mimic parental rights. In some respects, these workarounds reflect an understanding of legality as being a tool that can be creatively manipulated to achieve desired ends. These conversations particularly surfaced around the topic of second-parent adoption for participants living in locations where they were unable to access these rights.

For parents without a biological or legal tie to a child, second-parent adoption was viewed as worth pursuing—either through forum shopping, as we previously described, or through creative document drafting or manipulations of other legal provisions. Lynn and Malcolm are a partnered, white lesbian couple who resided in a legally neutral state at the time that they conceived their child. They assumed, given the overall negative sociopolitical climate in the state, that second-parent adoption was not an option. As a result, they considered possible ways to replicate the provisions of second-parent adoption for Malcolm, the nonbiological parent. As Lynn explained:

> We just discussed it among ourselves kind of what our agreement would be in terms of parenting and what our agreement would be in the case of a split and all those sorts of issues. . . . We didn't really look to the laws of the state as being expansive enough or limiting or giving us any sort of definitions of family. We just planned to operate outside of that. . . . But in this case, [once we discovered we could do second-parent adoption], we could see where the law would help us and we exploited it for that.

Recreating some of the rights and obligations that accompany parenthood was important to this couple, but they initially assumed they would have to creatively work outside of the legal system in order to produce a kind of informal parental agreement. Once they realized they could access "the real thing," they opted for second-parent adoption. Similarly, other participants described the belief that they could or would draw up documents that might establish parenthood rights in the absence of second-parent adoption. For example, Mark identifies as single, white, queer, and female-to-male transgender, and resides in a legally negative state where second-parent adoption was not an option. He indicated that if he were to have additional children, he would pursue second-parent adoption alternatives: "If I was someplace where second-parent adoption wasn't allowed, [I would] have some legal documents drawn up beforehand, before the child was even conceived or something, to be like, this is the plan if we should ever split." Thus, for some participants without access to second-parent adoption (or who believed they did not have access), the proposed workaround involved drawing up formal or informal documents that set forth a plan regarding the rights and obligations of each individual—particularly in the event of relationship dissolution.

Individuals residing in legal jurisdictions where second-parent adoption was not an option discussed other strategies that more directly sought to create legal rights and obligations. For example, Sharon, a single, white lesbian in her forties discussed a strategy employed in her former state of residence that she initially termed "second-parent guardianship." As she explained:

Guardianship is done when somebody besides the legal parent needs to have de facto parental rights to do schooling and medical care and stuff like that. . . . So that is how they manipulated the law in [my former state] to try to help gay and lesbian parents to do a second-parent adoption—second-parent guardianship. So the legal parent retains legal rights and grants guardianship to the other parent, which gives them some legal rights. . . . It can still be revoked at any time by the actual parent. . . . I think it is a regular guardianship thing, and when guardianships are used appropriately it makes sense. But because you are kind of contorting this other legal thing to do [second-parent adoption], it seems it doesn't really fit. But it was the only choice we had, the only legal vehicle we had at our disposal to do anything close to [second-parent adoption.]

Although second-parent adoption rights cannot be recreated through guardianship, the guardianship process was perceived by many of our participants to do some of the work typically provided through second-parent adoption. As Sharon observes, however, guardianships are not intended to establish full parental rights and are only "contorted" to do so by LGBT parents residing in states without second-parent adoption. They consequently are understood by participants to result in a pale imitation of parenthood, and one that can be revoked by the "real parent" at any time.

For a few participants, the need to draw up their own paperwork was described as permitting them greater control over the meaning and rights related to their relationship. For example, Ruth and Vicky, a married white lesbian couple living in a legally neutral state, indicated that if second-parent adoption had not proven an option, they would have drawn up paperwork that set forth legal rights over the children. The couple has two children together, with each of the women carrying one of the children. Vicky observed that it was important to have some type of document in place in case of a separation, saying: "We wouldn't want one of us to take one kid and one to take the other, or one having more rights than the other over a child as the biological parent. You know, the state makes you that way, and we didn't want to see it that way." Vicky understood the state to create a tension between biological and nonbiological parents, and she perceived that this tension could possibly be overcome through creative drafting of legal documents.

Another proposed strategy to deal with a lack of second-parent adoption was to travel to other states for the birth of the child in order to gain access to friendlier laws. A variant of forum shopping, this idea of giving birth in a friendlier state was contemplated by four of our participants—although none of them followed through on this plan. Julie, a partnered, white lesbian in her fifties who is a resident of a legally negative state, explained a possible plan that incorporated both traveling to other states or drawing up paperwork in order to access second-parent adoption or equivalent rights:

> [If I had not been able to access second-parent adoption,] I still would have wanted to have a child. I don't know if I would have tried to, like, give birth in Seattle or Massachusetts, or somewhere else. I probably would have tried to research a way that we could both legally be this child's parent. . . . Yeah, I would have looked for the loophole elsewhere or found a state where it was legit. Or go to a lawyer to draw up agreements that would be nonbinding. I mean, that was the frustrating thing with the lawyer. You know, you could go to these lawyers and draw up these agreements and sign them but they had no legs; they weren't binding.

Ultimately, this couple was able to access second-parent adoption so these options were not fully explored. But her discussion presents both the significance of acquiring parental rights for LGBT couples, and the lengths to which parents contemplated going to acquire such rights. Further, her story again reflects the notion that drafting documents that replicate second-parent adoption was often understood as a superficial fix. These documents generated the appearance of legality, and thus were often viewed as preferable over having no paperwork. But such documents failed to offer the protections promised by the law due to their perceived unenforceability.

Even for individuals who believed they had parental rights through same-sex marriage (a belief that was not necessarily valid for all jurisdictions), second-parent adoption or similar rights were viewed as desirable to acquire. This uncertainty regarding the relationship between marriage and parental rights resulted in five of our participants indicating that they would (or did) seek second-parent adoption despite their legal marriages. For example, Lula and Sherri are a white couple in their thirties who reside in a legally positive state and were able to get married. Nonetheless, they still intended to go through second-parent adoption procedures. Lula explained their rationale as follows: "I see it like getting insurance. Actually we went to a talk about it with a lawyer who described this situation: 'You're moving to a state that doesn't recognize your marriage or recognize your relationship to the child. You have parents who . . . would fight your custody.'" Although neither Lula nor Sherri was concerned about parents fighting for custody, the idea of moving or traveling to nonfriendly states raised concerns about how transferable parent-child relationships might be. Lula, the nonbiological parent, also had her name on the birth certificate and they carried the birth certificate with them when they traveled. This practice evidenced their concern that, outside of their jurisdiction, their marriage might not be enough to confer parental rights.

Henrietta and Patti, another married couple in their thirties living in a legally positive state, indicated that they were considering stepparent adoption as a means to strengthen the parental claims of the nonbiological parent. Their explanation mirrored that of couples attempting to mimic second-parent adoption rights, given that they expressed uncertainty as to whether stepparent adoption provided the sought-after protection. As Henrietta, a Middle Eastern queer woman who is the nonbiological parent of their child, explained:

> It's very weird, the whole stepparent adoption, because in [our state] I'm already on the birth certificate and I'm already his parent [given our marriage]. So the stepparent adoption is for in case we're out of state, but it's contingent on our marriage. And our attorney was saying that if somebody really cared, it actually doesn't do anything because it's contingent on a marriage that they might not recognize. But that nobody is going to pursue it that far, hopefully.

This couple, much like many residing in more legally negative environments, felt the desire to strengthen parental rights despite feeling reasonably secure within their own state due to their belief that marriage conferred parental rights. Their ability to replicate parental rights while living in a country where rights were so variable created challenges and insecurities for the couple, much like for many of our participants.

These stories of individuals seeking second-parent adoption even when they had same-sex marriage speaks in part to the function ultimately served by second-parent adoption. As discussed in chapter 4, second-parent adoption in many ways was understood as transforming individuals into parents—legitimizing, creating social recognition for, and protecting their parent-child relationships. Thus, in cases in which the parent-child relationship was threatened, the desire to pursue legal means to shore up the relationship seemed to surface for participants. Given the precarious and contextual nature of same-sex marriage and other family rights for LGBT parents, the use of creative approaches to replicate parenthood rights appears to be understood as a necessary strategy across all legal contexts.

Accessing Heteronormative Privilege

If family rights are typically dependent on heteronormative institutions, such as marriage, or assumptions regarding the straight, married household being the gold standard for raising children, then gaining access to heteronormative privilege might be viewed as a strategy in the legal game. Our participants frequently voiced their beliefs that straight couples faced fewer obstacles to family formation and to obtaining legal rights over their children. Some did so with resignation, whereas others responded by strategizing regarding the manner in which they might access similar rights.

Marriage was one of the most commonly voiced strategies for accessing heteronormative privilege, with approximately 9 percent of our participants specifically mentioning marriage as a tool to gain control over their legal relationship with their children. Julia and Alyssa are a married, white lesbian couple in their twenties who live in a legally negative state. They discussed the manner in which they included marriage as one of several steps that would potentially increase their odds of adoption. As Alyssa explained: "I think our first step was just the marriage. Because even though it's not legal in [our state], maybe the judge will take it into consideration. . . . We own a house together, we're married, power of attorney, all this stuff. We figured the more we had, the better we looked." Through generating various indicators of commitment and stability, they seemed to intend to create themselves in the image of the heteronormative married couple. They did this not for their own self-identities, but as a strategy to improve their standing during the adoption process. Their story exemplifies the manner in which marriage can be a strategy—not just for generating direct legal rights (e.g., permitting joint adoption), but also as a credential-building exercise that might bolster LGBT individuals' legal credibility as parents.

Some of our participants had not yet married, but voiced that they had considered marriage as a strategy. For example, Colin, a partnered, Hispanic gay man in his thirties, had contemplated marriage as an avenue to gain access to joint adoption within his legally negative state. He recounted: "We might [get legally married] because I understand that there's been a recent change in [state] law as far as adoptions are concerned. They're still not allowing us to adopt jointly but I have heard from one of the case workers that if you marry in another state they will recognize that for adoption purposes. . . . That's what my case worker told me, so we're very much considering going to New York or Washington to get married." Marriage, in this respect, was viewed as a strategy toward adoption rather than as the meaning-making (and family-making) institution that our participants described in chapter 4. When we followed up by asking whether he would be considering marriage if it were not for its potential effects on his adoption, he emphasized the strategic nature of his potential marriage by responding: "No, not until it is federally recognized."

Some participants recognized the potential benefits of marriage, but were unable to directly access its privileges. This led participants to consider other ways to mimic some of the benefits of marriage as part of their family strategies. For example, Shelley a partnered, white lesbian in her thirties, described the domestic partnership she had in her prior state as providing certain advantages in establishing familial relationships. She observed: "[The domestic partnership] still didn't give [my partner] any rights [to the child], but if I gave birth to her, [my partner] had the legal right to adopt and that was our plan. She was going to legally adopt her." Shelley understood domestic partnership in her state to not provide the same rights as would marriage, but it provided an avenue for legal adoption that conveyed additional protection; this rendered domestic partnership part of a strategy for family formation.

In areas without domestic partnerships or marriage, participants sometimes considered ways in which to generate the appearance of stability and commitment similar to marriage. For example, Beth and Hannah, a partnered, white lesbian couple in their forties who live in a legally neutral state, explained that they generated paperwork that they used both as protection for them as a couple and for their family at the birth of their child. Their exchange reveals the strategy involved in their decision:

> BETH: We went to some attorneys and got a bunch of legal paperwork signed up. So we got as much legal protection for us as a couple as you can. . . . Just I mean, like, you know, legal marriage.
> HANNAH: Then we made sure we had all the paperwork at the hospital in case there were any issues.

Their decision to generate paperwork that would establish similarities to "legal marriage" reveals the manner in which access to heteronormative legal privilege via the marital institution is understood to provide a blanket of rights that is difficult—but important—to recreate.

Although access to marriage was generally voiced as a useful strategy for acquiring family rights, in situations where same-sex marriage is legally tenuous this could prove not to be the case. Sandra, a married, white lesbian in her forties, described the manner in which she and her partner contemplated marriage when it became legal in their state. They were uncertain as to whether marriage would continue to be accessible, given that it was being challenged on various fronts. Since they were going through the adoption process, they ultimately decided to wait to marry, explaining:

> When we could have gone down to city hall and gotten married, . . . it was pretty clear that marriage was not going to be upheld and we wanted the protection of domestic partnership. So we didn't go down and take in the celebration and do this really fun thing because it felt risky. Because when you get married you are no longer domestic partners and . . . we were not sure and we didn't want to do anything legally questionable when we were going through this adoption process. We knew we were going to be going before a judge and didn't want to do anything legally questionable.

Thus, while participants viewed legal marriage as a plus in most instances, this participant voiced concerns that same-sex marriage might be viewed as legally subversive and could undermine her family plans. This story suggests the very contextual and shifting nature of family strategies, with differing legal frameworks and experiences with the law producing varied approaches—even with respect to the so-called marriage benefit.

The Transgender Case

Accessing heteronormative privilege was deliberate on the part of many of our participants who sought out marriage to improve their family outcomes. For our transgender participants, however, accessing heteronormative privilege was typically a less intentional act, and yet it was frequently noted as an advantage when forming families or accessing rights. Some of our transgender participants and their partners described this in terms of "luck," and typically expressed ambivalence or guilt regarding their access to legal privilege.

Clara is a separated, Hispanic queer woman in her thirties; her former partner identifies as female-to-male transgender. Clara described how she and her partner engaged in a fairly deliberate, strategic approach to gaining access to heteronormative privilege. Residing in a legally positive state, Clara explained: "Ultimately, what we ended up doing was he got his driver's license, the sex on his driver's license, changed in order so that he could sign the birth certificate as her father." Much like the couples who married in order to be able to place names on birth certificates or jointly adopt, Clara described a deliberate approach that permitted them to access particular legal rights—in this case, to engage with an administrative system as a different-sex couple.

Wyatt and Lauren are a married couple in their thirties, living in a legally negative state. Wyatt identifies as queer and female-to-male transgender. The couple detailed the manner in which the ability to change one's sex on official documents permitted access to legal marriage and, concomitantly, identification as a parent on a child's birth certificate. According to Lauren, Wyatt's decisions related to administrative documents generated access to these legal benefits. She recounted: "I feel like we lucked out, kind of, I guess. Because we live in [this legally negative state], but [he] was luckily born in the state of New York so he was able to change the gender marker on his birth certificate, which allowed us to be legally married [here]. . . . And then, luckily again, because he could sign the space of father on the birth certificate . . . I feel like it worked to our benefit." She recognized their access to heteronormative privilege and attributed it to "luck," but Wyatt was quick to point out that this advantage was relative:

> But . . . what if those laws weren't even there? Like, it's annoying that they're all there, so that's like a hindrance. . . . I've been really lucky. . . . I feel like we don't feel the repercussions of the laws very often, but I certainly feel like they're a hindrance. I mean, I don't feel like there are laws that are helping me, helping us, for having to do all this work, to work around them and with them. But I also feel like generally, the way I look at it, it just is how it is. . . . We don't really, like, fuck the system constantly. We just live our lives and do what we need to do to get by pretty much.

Although they both express the sentiment that they have been fortunate in accessing marriage and its accompanying rights, Wyatt observes that avoiding negative repercussions or flying under the radar is quite different from fully enjoying privilege.

Jacquelyn is a married, white queer woman in her thirties who lives in a legally positive state. She identified her partner as intersexed, with his birth certificate indicating a male sex. Much like Clara, Wyatt, and Lauren, Jacquelyn also noted the way in which the sex on administrative documents generated access to heteronormative privilege when creating their family:

> I guess he is—I'm pretty sure he is legally [our child's] father because we were legally essentially married at the time when I delivered and he signed the birth certificate saying he was the father. So it is pretty above board. And I think because, with his intersex status, it sort of changes the way— there's not as much technicalities around it. It is just more legally defensible because he's not really transgender. I mean, there is kind of a transgender narrative over whatever, but he's not—we kind of have it on this more legitimized transition. It is just not as legally problematic. . . . I feel like as far as the state is concerned, we're in a pretty legitimate heterosexual scenario in which my husband is unable, just doesn't have sperm, so we use the donor. It's more of just like a heterosexual donor insemination, legally.

Although she describes their legal relationship with the state as more "legitimate" than that of a transgender situation, her account reveals a similar tension between accessing privilege and being a full member of the privileged group. Her tenuous grip on heteronormativity is reflected by her use of phrases such as being "pretty sure" that her spouse is the child's legal father, being "legally essentially married," and their situation being "more legally defensible" than that of a transgender individual. She appeared to recognize the relative ease with which they could access legal privilege, but also noted that their inclusion in a heteronormative legal category was a state construct rather than something that reflected their lived experience.

Some of our participants specifically referenced the tenuous nature of their access to heteronormative privilege. For example, Clara indicated concerns regarding how concrete her partner's parental rights were given that they were based solely on the birth certificate. They had used a known donor, and she worried about the possibility that one day the biological father would make a claim for parental rights. She explained: "I'm her mother and that is indisputable, you know. If I were in the position of being her father and that were potentially disputable, I think I would probably want to do the second-parent adoption and do whatever I could possibly do to make that happen."

Similarly, Ellis, who is female-to-male transgender, and his wife Alice also recognized their advantage in gaining marriage and parental rights in their legally negative state as compared to a same-sex couple. Yet they seemed to view their access to these rights as subversive, and subject to change if the state became aware of their situation. Part of this concern originated from the fact that when the couple married in one state, Ellis was only required to show a driver's license in order to obtain a marriage license. He had changed his sex on the driver's license, but not on his birth certificate, and his understanding was that a change of the birth certificate was actually required by state law to be considered male and permitted to marry. We include a lengthy excerpt of the exchange between the couple below regarding the complexities and perceived tenuous nature of their access to heteronormative privilege:

ALICE: This is also another reason why we don't want to engage with institutions. The process is sort of unraveling things. And, in fact, we've even questioned whether we should be doing a second-parent adoption and if it would do more harm to our legal relationship to one another if we do that. Because it would call into question paternity in a way that otherwise it's not. . . . We also looked into [foster-to-adopt] here because now we could afford to adopt and we've considered it, but we can't as a couple. We're not allowed to, legally. So I could adopt. Ellis couldn't adopt. . . . It's not [an option] for same-sex relationships. . . .

INTERVIEWER: So you feel like even though you have a legal marriage, that you still need to operate within the system as if that legal marriage had not occurred?

ALICE: In a sense, yeah. At least, I don't take for granted our status as valid or honored anywhere. In a very real sense. I mean, we obviously pass. And so there's this way in which we're kind of riding it out, but it's just sort of opening the gates for me that I just sort of feel like could cause a lot of issues. And there's precedent of these things happening to trans people and their partners in terms of paternity issues.

ELLIS: But the fact is we operate 100 percent of the time in every legal situation that we enter into as though we are a heterosexual married couple, because we have a legal marriage because they didn't ask for the one form of ID that would have made it not possible for us to get married at the time. But they asked for the driver's licenses and that's what I gave them. So according to that requirement, our marriage is absolutely legal. I mean, we pay joint, married federal income tax; we have all the other trappings. The baby that she gave birth to is recognized as mine, legally, because we're legally married. So we just don't want to enter into any situation where there would be cause to question the validity of the marriage. . . . In every other capacity it's absolutely legal and functions the way every other straight person's marriage does, except that if you wanted to make an issue out of it, you probably could.

Their account reveals a different picture of the relationship between trans couples and the legal system. Ellis in particular pointed out the advantages that the couple has been able to gain by virtue of operating as a heterosexual married couple, including parental rights by default due to their marriage. At the same time, they view their hold on these rights as uncertain and subject to change. They voiced fears regarding attempting to operate as a straight couple in the adoption process in case an investigation were to disclose Ellis's birth certificate changes and thus "out" them as a nonheterosexual couple. They were also torn between further cementing Ellis's right to their child via a second-parent adoption, and perhaps weakening their current legal rights by revealing that he might not have a legitimate legal claim over the child in the first place. In some respects, their story suggests that they are more fearful of interacting with the legal system than a same-sex couple would be. The ability to access heteronormative privilege, therefore, did not carry with it the ability to fully enjoy that privilege. Rather, their account and that of Clara's indicates that these benefits were viewed in the more traditional notion of a privilege versus a right—something that you earn and that can be taken away if you fail to successfully perform heteronormativity.

Although their greater access to the legal system was sometimes viewed as shaky, few of our transgender participants indicated an unwillingness to use heteronormative privilege as a strategy. Mark, however, expressed hesitancy about following this route to privilege that might be available to him due to being female-to-male transgender. Identifying as single, white, and queer, Mark lives in a legally negative state. As he explained:

> There's a trans guy that's been about to legally change his gender so they can adopt in any state through any kind of adoption agency, whether it's religious-based or international adoption. There's just like, no questions. It's all changed; no one ever knows the difference. And that's kind of cool in a way, but I don't really like that either because I feel like, well, there's plenty of other queer families out there who are having problems so I don't think that the—I don't know. It's one of the things that kind of bothers me about trans in general. Like, well, I'm just going to completely transition and fit completely into the hetero world and it sort of leaves everyone else behind in a way.

The accounts of other trans participants belie this notion of fitting completely into the heteronormative legal world. Nonetheless, this participant's observation raises the critique expressed by some gay and lesbian individuals regarding the trans population's ability to access heteronormative privilege (Halberstam and Hale 1998). Although heteronormativity can be a strategy of playing the legal game, it is one that perhaps most readily reveals the disparities across legal players in accessing rights.

Marshaling Your Resources

Strategies in game playing involve talents and skills, as well as collecting and utilizing valued resources. Navigating legality is no exception, and our participants often described the manner in which they employed good attorneys, social networks, money, education, or other tools to achieve a victory. This is as a central feature of the "with the law" perspective, given that actors perceive that they have the capacity to influence the outcome of the legal process (Ewick and Silbey 1998). Our participants acknowledged their own agency in the process by seeking out and utilizing resources in order to form their families or secure parenting rights.

A Good Attorney

For approximately 15 percent of our participants, finding the right attorney was specifically mentioned as a good starting point for accomplishing family goals. Although approximately half of our participants consulted with attorneys at some point during the parenting process (see chapter 3), this particular group of participants specifically indicated that knowing the right attorney was part of their strategy for success. Attorneys, unlike most of our participants, are "professional players" (Ewick and Silbey 1998) in the legal game. They not only speak the right language, but they often have the right connections in order to operate inside the system to accomplish goals.

For some participants, there seemed to be almost a comfort in recognizing that a good attorney could potentially produce the desired outcome. For example, Esther who lives in a legally neutral state, explained: "I don't have a problem with the law so much, but I also know it's kind of a game and it depends on who's ruling and who's listening and all that stuff. . . . It's just like having the right attorney and representation." Similarly, Marlene, a partnered, white lesbian in her forties who also lives in a legally neutral state, indicated: "That is the whole country I think. If you know the right person, the right lawyer, the right judge, to grant things."

Many participants assumed attorneys would be able to create rights or mirror legal rights through creative document drafting. For example, Curt and Willie, a partnered, interracial gay couple in their thirties, discussed the obstacles they potentially faced to securing second-parent adoption in their legally neutral state. They indicated that, even if second-parent adoption itself was impossible to secure, there would likely be other legal alternatives that a creative attorney could generate that would give equivalent rights:

> CURT: I would think there would be ways that you could get around it and you could effectively have [second-parent adoption], where it may not be in name but you have kind of created it.
>
> WILLIE: I would think that if one of us adopted, the other one would be the legal guardian.
>
> CURT: Somehow a good attorney should be able to get around it. . . . I am optimistic, yes, that a good attorney would find a way, would be able to create or draft documents.

This belief that attorneys are able to draft documents to generate or mimic rights was echoed by other participants. Colin, for example, described his desire to mimic second-parent adoption rights prior to recognizing that second-parent adoption might be an option in his legally negative state. He explained: "We were told that there were some documents that you could draw up that wouldn't really be as effective as second-parent adoption but still would provide you with some better circumstances than not having any rights at all. So we were willing to have whatever legal documents drawn up that we could to best protect [the child's] interests and to best protect [my partner's] interests." Even if the law did not permit second-parent adoption, then, there was the possibility to create rights through creative document drafting.

Similarly, Joyce and Jenny, a married, white couple in their thirties who were living in a legally negative state, expressed concern about whether Joyce's children would be returned to the biological father if Joyce passed away. They were attempting to take preemptive steps through their attorney to preserve access to the children for Jenny. Joyce explained: "I have a good attorney and I talked to him about what we can do as far as drawing up in my will and my power of attorney and how much involvement Jenny can have in the kids' lives. . . . [I learned about the attorney] through a friend. They told me they knew about a really liberal nice attorney that would be helpful and that is how I found him." For this couple, like many other participants, having a "good attorney" was viewed as a means to craft legal rights or take preemptive measures to avoid negative implications of the law.

Other participants described specific feats that their attorneys were able to accomplish in a manner that suggested their attorneys' specialized skills and information about the legal system enabled them to "do the impossible." For example, Ben described the manner in which his attorney was able to have his name added to the birth certificate in the space for "mother." He recalled: "The putting both names on the birth certificate, that is possible . . . and it was a surprise. [My attorney] actually arranged that, I didn't expect my name to be on it and I was kind of tickled to get one saying I was the mother."

The "right attorney" was also deemed as essential for learning about the proper forums for acquiring legal rights. Much like forum shopping for friendly jurisdictions for adoption and second-parent adoption, there was often one attorney (or a handful of attorneys) who seemed to know the ins and outs of achieving second-parent adoption. This theme emerged in virtually every state, but particularly in states that were legally neutral or negative. In these cases, knowing the right attorney could mean the difference between knowing that adoption is even an option within the state and believing it is impossible. For example, Dian, a partnered, white queer woman in her forties who lives in a legally positive state, explained: "[In my state], since 1994 there has been one lawyer that pretty much every lesbian or gay family goes to. I think there may be some others, but really she's the one you want. She was the one who was arguing a custody case when the judge actually changed the precedent, changed the legal treatments in terms of second-parent adoption. . . . So she was representing us in this case." Undoubtedly, in her mind, she had the "right attorney" to assist her in her case, given that the attorney was well-known and well-versed within the area of LGBT family law matters. This ability to locate the attorney who is "in the know" was repeatedly raised by our participants, emphasizing the manner in which the ability to acquire a skilled legal player was viewed to weigh the odds in one's favor.

Socioeconomic Resources

Although finding the "right attorney" was viewed as beneficial for gaining access to insider's knowledge of the legal game, many of our participants discussed using their own personal skills or resources to be successful in their family goals. In particular, approximately 10 percent referenced the pervasive cultural discourse that the law can be bought, or at least the outcome strongly influenced, by money, education, or other socioeconomic resources. Viewing law as a commodity, to be bought and sold, is possible only if law is understood as contingent (Ewick and Silbey 1998). Our participants acknowledged the manner in which legal outcomes were contingent on the ways in which they used (or understood that they could use) their socioeconomic status to increase their odds of achieving their family goals. For example, Margarita, a married, Hispanic lesbian in her thirties, described the law as "something that can be worked around. Given the right resources. I mean I don't know that I could necessarily work around it. Because I might not have all the resources I need." Because she resided in a legally positive state, she did not feel that her lack of resources had proven to be too much of a burden. Nonetheless, she acknowledged that legal obstacles were navigated more successfully if a person was well-equipped to find the loopholes or manipulate the system.

Some participants were accepting of the fact that the law was contingent on individual resources, whereas others expressed resentment. For example, Allison, a married, white lesbian in her thirties who lives in a legally positive state, expressed frustration about the process that permitted her partner to adopt their child. She stated: "I see it as a work-around, like the idea that we had to do documents [for adoption]. . . . And the way that works . . . is that I, the biological mom, had to adopt my own child so that [my partner] could be the legal parent—it is just stupid. I will do that because I can pay money for that, but people get pregnant all the time who aren't married legally and they don't have to do things like that." Although she had the financial resources to go through the adoption process and obtain legal rights for her partner, she expressed bitterness that she *had* to do so. Her understanding was that different-sex couples are not required to take this additional step in order to establish legal relationships to their children, particularly if they are married. Her ability to access the legal system, therefore, was not viewed with pleasure given that it served as a reminder that her family was viewed as nonnormative by the legal system.

Similarly, Michelle and Sabrina expressed these competing views of frustration with "working" the legal system, and feeling fortunate that they had the resources to do so. Michelle identifies as a nonlegally married, white lesbian in her thirties, and Sabrina as a nonlegally married, Persian lesbian who is also in her thirties. Residing in a legally neutral state, they explained:

MICHELLE: It really bothers me that we can't just get married and have a baby like anybody else can. . . . It drives me crazy that we can't have both our names on the birth certificate. But otherwise, it's just something we have to deal with. I always like to [take the available legal steps like second-parent adoption]. I mean, luckily we can take advantage of the tax credits [for second-parent adoption]; it's like a zero sum.

SABRINA: And luckily we have the means to be educated about what we're up against and take the steps necessary to protect our family. And some people don't have that opportunity. So we're lucky; we're in a good position financially and with the education that we have.

There was almost a sense of guilt expressed by participants, like this couple, for complaining about heteronormative biases within the legal system if they had the capacity to work around those obstacles. Although Michelle indicated that she felt the burden of the additional requirements placed upon her both to have children and establish legal rights over the children, both of the women were quick to qualify their criticisms with how "lucky" they were that they had the opportunity to use their resources to achieve their goals. The game aspect of the legal process was also reinforced by Michelle's observation that the ability to write off adoption expenditures on their taxes resulted in a "zero sum" effect. Her comment serves as a claim that, while they wished they could avoid the game, they were fortunate to be able to play and to know how to operate within the rules in order to avoid some of the costs.

In addition to frustration and resentment over using financial resources to work around the law, many participants indicated that they felt their money bought them a second-class product. For example, Antonia, a partnered, white queer woman in her thirties who lives in a legally positive state, expressed her opinion about the law and her family life, saying: "I guess I see it as something that sucks. Probably not the most sophisticated answer. But I feel like it definitely has a negative impact on our sense of our family. It feels like something you have to pay a lot of money to kind of get around. And even in the ways you get around it, it's largely imperfect." This idea that your money and extra work buys your family protection that is legally tenuous surfaced throughout our interviews, including when participants described paying attorneys to draft "workarounds" that attempted to mimic other legal rights. The ability to use financial resources to acquire legal protections, therefore, did not always mean that participants felt that legal protection was actually achieved.

Using Knowledge to Navigate Legal Forms and Procedures

Some participants cited the ability to use their own education or intellect as a tool to complete legal documents, obtain legal information, or identify a legal strategy that helped improve their outcomes. Approximately 11 percent of participants specifically referenced using their backgrounds or their initiatives in order to complete documents on their own. For example, Traci described how she was able to bypass attorneys and complete her divorce paperwork. She recounted: "Back then I wasn't making any money or doing anything. So then finally I figured out I could fill out my own divorce papers. It cost sixty-eight dollars here. So eventually I did it and I went and met [my ex-husband] and said, 'sign these.'" The manner in which she recalled this event suggested a sense of victory over the seemingly inaccessible nature of the legal system. Initially, it seemed that she had to wait until she was financially able to access the legal system via an attorney, but ultimately she was able to utilize her own initiative to gain an understanding of the legal and administrative processes and accomplish her goals on her own.

Similarly, several of our participants described using books or the Internet as resources to locate forms and information about legal procedures in order to avoid attorneys. For example, Kristina, a married, Hispanic queer woman in her fifties who lives in a legally positive state, was going through second-parent adoption and opted to handle the process on her own. Expressing her comfort with doing so, she stated: "No attorney; we are doing it all ourselves. . . . I went to [a website]. . . . It's pretty well documented." Although she evidenced confidence in her ability to navigate the process successfully, other participants were more uncertain about completing legal paperwork on their own. For example, Andrea, a single, white lesbian in her forties living in a legally positive state, recalled setting up wills and guardianship paperwork during her pregnancy, saying: "I did that through, like, a Nolo Press. . . . Nolo Press, it gives you legal documents. . . . They recommend like a Quicken will document and I did that online, which I probably shouldn't. And I have thought often times since then that I should probably go to an actual attorney, but I haven't." She was able to complete her documents on her own by educating herself through books and forms designed for self-representation in legal matters.

While Andrea elected to go the self-help route, she expressed a sentiment shared by many who used online forms—that they are doing something wrong or that their documents are less legitimate or more subject to being contested. As reflected in chapter 3, many of our participants used resources other than attorneys to gain information about the law or complete documents, but often seemed apologetic about this approach. This is perhaps explained by the fact that, for most, their election of self-representation is a result of financial constraints. Thus, they appear to feel a certain amount of shame or uneasiness at using a more affordable approach given that they perceive some value added from an "expert's" involvement. For one of our participants, Henrietta, this uncertainty led to her consulting with an attorney regarding the documents that she produced. She explained: "What I ultimately did was . . . I e-mailed the attorney and I explained what we needed and she said that I could [do it myself] because I wanted to do this as cheaply as possible. And I had said, 'If I put something together will you look at it?' and she was like, 'Yeah, I'll totally do that.' So that is what we ended up doing. . . . I drafted it off the Internet." In this respect, she was able to use her own resources to access and draft the document, but then also call upon external legal knowledge from an attorney to rubber-stamp her work and increase her confidence in its legitimacy. As her wife, Patti, proudly related: "And [her draft] turned out to be almost perfect. She did our second-parent adoption too!" This statement reflects pleasure in accessing the legal system on their own, as well as the belief that attorneys are perhaps uniquely suited to determining whether legal processes are completed correctly. These stories regarding legal self-help reveal the tension that often exists between a belief that the legal game can be accessed by lay participants, and the sentiment that the law is a murky, complicated field that requires an expert.

In addition to completing legal documents on their own, some participants indicated that their knowledge of the legal system served as a resource for acquiring the desired outcome. This knowledge came from several sources, including prior experience, occupation within the legal field, and self-education. We discuss sources for legal knowledge in greater depth in chapter 3, but highlight here an example of each of these sources as an illustration of how legal knowledge was marshaled as a resource. Four of our participants specifically mentioned prior experience with the legal system as something that produced an advantage for them during their parenthood process. For example, Dana and Alexandra, a married, white lesbian couple living in a legally positive state, explained that they had originally opted not to use a known donor due to fears regarding the possible legal claims that individual might have over their child. At this point, however, they both indicated they might be more comfortable with a known donor. For Alexandra, this was directly related to their prior experience with the law and how she felt this gave them an advantage in establishing control over a known donor situation. She relayed: "We've navigated a lot of the legal situations—so we've done a second-parent adoption, and obviously with a known donor the legal situation would be a little different, but I feel like we've navigated the legal situation and it feels a little less intimidating." She viewed this prior experience as an asset that could be mustered as a tool to assist in managing future legal hurdles. In this respect, their experience with the law in their parenting situation opened doors for additional possibilities given that they felt the law could be more easily accessed than they once anticipated.

Eight of our participants identified as working directly in the legal field, either currently or in the recent past. They cited this experience and knowledge about the law as a resource that they were able to utilize to achieve legal ends. For example, Lula, a married, white lesbian in her thirties who lives in a legally positive state, explained that she had decided not to have formal wills drawn up due to her knowledge about wills and estates law that she received as part of her legal training. She commented: "I think there's an automatic assumption where your assets will go and it starts with the spouse. . . . Then it goes to children after the spouse and, because she is my spouse, I was sure that the family would be protected. . . . I don't feel the need to take care of it at this point because I don't think what we'd do would be outside of what the law would normally do." Even though her work was removed from this area of the law, her general legal knowledge was used as a tool to assess whether and how she would use the law on behalf of her family. Similarly, Marlon, a partnered, white gay man in his fifties who lives in a legally neutral state, is employed in the legal field and was able to strategize about how to use the legal system on his own behalf. He adopted a child internationally and wished to have an in-state birth certificate. He was familiar enough with the law to know that if they readopted the child in the United States, then he could obtain a birth certificate from his own state—which would make it easier to obtain social security, passports, and so on. His legal background allowed him to make strategic decisions in order to make his parenting life easier.

Some individuals cited self-education as an asset when playing the legal game. Specifically, some participants expressed the notion that seeking out legal knowledge in order to know their rights allowed them to apply pressure when needed in order to accomplish their family goals. A story from Jody illustrates this concept of using self-taught legal knowledge as a tool. Jody, a white lesbian in her thirties, described her desire, as the nonbiological parent, to be listed on the birth certificate when her child was born. She is married and lives in a legally positive state where she believed it was possible for her to be listed, but she was nonetheless concerned she might face resistance from individuals at the hospital. As she explained: "I knew my rights. I knew that legally I should and could be on the birth certificate, so I would have won. And they say that this is the nexus for lesbian moms so I was like, nobody's going to give me any shit, and if they do I'm going to pitch a fit." Her feeling that she was familiar with the law and her rights was, in many ways, a weapon that she could employ if she faced opposition in achieving the desired outcome. She believed that she "knew [her] rights," and this knowledge prepared her to challenge authority figures if need be.

In these ways, participants articulated that education about the legal system (whether a byproduct of one's occupation, prior legal experience, or something that was sought out) and the ability to understand and complete legal documents were resources that could be employed on behalf of their family. These tools allowed participants to circumvent the role of attorneys in their family formation. Accordingly, participants were able to maintain some distance between themselves and legality with regard to their family. Although still operating within the legal system, the ability to act on their own behalf provided a sense of agency that might be more desirable when dealing with familial legal matters.

It's Who You Know: Using Social Networks as a Resource

Participants voiced that achieving legal ends is not just about buying outcomes, but about using connections—in other words, who you know can be a large predictor of whether you will be able to achieve your legal goals. In chapter 3 we discussed the role of social networks in serving as a source of legal information for our participants. In addition to using networks to gain information, participants also used their contacts in order to achieve special treatment or expedite procedures.

The type of networks that were most frequently cited were ones established in the workplace. Approximately 8 percent of our participants specifically mentioned that they used workplace networks in order to expedite procedures, request particular judges, or gain access to other benefits. For example, Michelle, a nonlegally married, white lesbian in her thirties who lives in a legally neutral state, worked on a political campaign where she made contact with a particular judge. She recalled: "So, since [I met this judge], I was like, 'When I have a baby I want to come to your court,' you know because it's civil, family court. So I had asked our attorney, 'What do you know about [this] judge?' And she was like, 'Oh, yeah, we've wanted to get in with her courtroom because I want to establish [relationships in this county] a little bit more.' And so we just got her to do it with [the judge's] schedule." Rather than relying on the insider knowledge of an attorney, she used her professional networks to identify a judge that she perceived to be friendly and worked with her attorney to set up the second-parent adoption proceeding with the judge. If she had relied only on her attorney's knowledge and connections, the adoption would have happened in another city—as the attorney typically went to another court where she knew the judges. Her network enabled her to both select a friendly judge and to select a convenient venue for the adoption proceeding.

Similarly, Kerry, a white, partnered, gender queer person in her thirties who lives in a legally positive state, described the manner in which her partner was able to use her professional network within the legal field at various stages of their second-parent adoption proceedings:

> Before we had kids, we started proceedings for second-parent adoption. And because [of my partner's job], she has major connections, so we were able to speed that process up. . . . I think the adoption [occurred about four months after they were born]. So that was pretty quick. . . . [It was so quick] only because we had a [judge] in family court who [my partner] knew. . . . [My partner] asked if it could be put on a specific judge's calendar because she was friendly with the judge and it's just an adoption. So she said, "Hey, do you think this judge would hear the case rather than some random person who does all the adoptions?" And the judge said, "Sure, my calendar's open during this week." . . . The judge was, like, so tickled pink and honored that [my partner] wanted her children to be adopted in front of her. She opened her calendar and said, "Let's do it now." So we got in a lot quicker than we would have.

Given that this couple resided in a legally positive state, the ultimate adoption outcome was not necessarily predicated on finding a friendly judge. But the speed at which the adoption could be accomplished appeared to be directly connected to her relationship with the judge. Although expediting the second-parent adoption process might seem like a small accomplishment, many of our nonbiological parents highly valued completing the second-parent adoption as soon as possible following the birth of the child. In some respects, their parenthood identity (as well as their rights over the child) was in limbo until the adoption was finalized. This resulted in strategies regarding finding ways to expedite the adoption proceeding, such as using concerns regarding health insurance or visits from family members to acquire earlier adoption dates (as related by participants such as Marlon, Michelle, and Johanna). Thus, what might appear on its face to be a minor victory, in terms of accomplishing the adoption more quickly, was actually a very desirable outcome for many participants.

One perhaps surprising use of a professional network to acquire legal rights involved Julia and Alyssa, a married, white lesbian couple in their twenties who live in a legally negative state, who were able to use legal resources from the military base at which they were stationed. Given that their baby was born prior to the repeal of Don't Ask, Don't Tell, they were in some ways cautious about revealing their relationship in the work place. Nonetheless, they used the resources available to them in order to complete power of attorney documents, wills, and related documents. As Alyssa explained: "You walk in with the paper, you leave it, doot, doot, they stamp it and that's it. Getting it done." Even though the utilization of these resources could have placed them in a precarious position with regard to work, they felt that the strategic benefits of acquiring these legal documents outweighed the dangers.

Another couple discussed the manner in which they were able to call on several networks both within the workplace and outside in order to raise awareness of trans-related issues—including things that affected their family. Residing in a legally negative state, Wyatt is female-to-male transgender and works in an educational setting. He discussed the manner in which networks had often allowed them to avoid the negative implications of state law for their family:

> I've been really lucky in that, because of where I work, I'm at the front-end of information a lot of the time. . . . And if something comes up, I can e-mail the head of HR at [my employer] and they're going to take it a lot differently . . . you know, because I'm a voice of a community . . . so I think they get more serious. Like, oh, well if there's press about this. . . . We've definitely been known to shoot some things off to our friends at the newspaper if there's an issue. So I think I've just been really privileged in my work. And for a lot of different reasons, I mean, to have an education, to be able to read even a little bit of the documents we see.

His story emphasizes that having access to powerful networks is only part of this particular legal tool. The ability to use networks effectively is a skill, and one which some individuals are able to deploy more effectively than others.

Overall, for those able to employ networks as a resource in the legal process, the notion that law is about who you know was viewed fairly positively. These individuals were successful in organizing their resources to achieve their family goals. But for those without networks, there was more critique of this particular contingency in legal outcomes. As Brenda, a married, white lesbian in her forties who resides in a legally negative state, explained:

> I mean some people just have more access. I mean, we don't have a network. . . . We don't go to a church where people might volunteer and know of children in need that need to have a home, you know, that kind of thing. I think there's a lot of network involved when you are adopting kids. Or kind of, I hate to say this, but finding kids, you know, there is a certain amount of networking that you have to do. Not just through the state, but just through people you know.

She perceived adoption as particularly problematic given their lack of social networks that would gain them access to children or assist in the adoption process. She later described a friend who was an adoption attorney and was able to use her resources in order to adopt, even when it was difficult for LGBT persons to do so in their state. She recalled: "It's really difficult [to adopt]. It's almost, not political, but it's like almost based on the luck lottery, you know. Like we have a friend who has adopted three children, mostly because she is in the system, she works with an agency. . . . She's deeply involved [with the system], and so has access to the birth mother and is involved with her and the birth mother is involved with the children." Although she used language regarding luck to describe how some people are winners in the adoption game, her explanation illustrates that it is less about luck per se, and more about networks that enable some individuals to gain access to the legal system. In states with negative laws regarding LGBT parents, lack of access to strategic networks can generate barriers to achieving family goals and, accordingly, produce resentment regarding this aspect of the legal sport.

Persistence, Persistence: Using Personality as a Resource

Some participants described their good fortune in the legal process as a byproduct of certain personality traits. In particular, the notion of persistence or refusing to accept "no" was perceived as part of the reason for their success. Approximately 6 percent of our participants made particular references to the use of personality traits as a resource.

Colin, a partnered, Hispanic gay man in his thirties who lives in a legally negative state, described many of the obstacles that he and his partner faced when adopting their son, an older boy who was close to aging out of the system. The child's age made the couple particularly anxious to complete the adoption process quickly, given that he had lived so much of his life within the system. Prior to the adoption being finalized, administrative procedures called for the boy to have several visits with his would-be adoptive parents, after which he would have to return to the orphanage. Concerned that workers at the orphanage were unfairly treating the child, Colin became determined to expedite the adoption process. Through repeated inquiry and pushing the issue, he found a way to move up the date by which their son could come to live with them. He explained:

> What we ended up doing was we picked him up on the fourteenth and we kept him. And we did that by his agency getting our agency here locally to allow us to go to [another place] to get finger printed because they can obtain the backgrounds in about forty-eight hours versus our agency that was six plus weeks. . . . So we went [there] to be fingerprinted and, while we were there, we also took advantage of the fact that we had a court date set to ask the judge for extended visitations.

The telling of his story revealed that several accommodations were made to the process for them, including changing procedures regarding background checks and visitation lengths. But the resource employed to gain these accommodations was primarily persistence, where he described himself as pushing the agencies to move forward and not letting their case fall through the cracks.

In much the same way, Carlton, a partnered, white homosexual man in his forties living in a legally neutral state, described how he utilized persistence and pressure in order to solidify his adoption of his son.

Carlton's son was being fostered by an older different-sex couple who did not want to adopt a newborn. According to Carlton:

> They were fine with [my son] being adopted until they found out he was going to go to a same-sex couple. And then, so like a week before we were supposed to get him, they started calling and trying to block us, saying that they hadn't been given the opportunity to adopt the baby. . . . And then I started off a big stink, because I got on the phone and I started calling *everybody*. I mean, state senators, the state attorney, the Human Rights Campaign. . . . You know, I just started raising all this holy hell, and finally the department called me and said, "Hey, stop calling, he's yours! Stop it!"

Carlton viewed his being proactive and aggressive in solidifying his adoption as an important component to achieving his family goals.

Marlon, a partnered, white gay man in his fifties who lives in a legally neutral state, similarly described how persistence in interactions with the Social Security office could pay off. As he explained:

> Social Security is the only place that historically gives same-sex couples problems. Now we have a birth certificate with both our names on it. We gave them a birth certificate, which should make it easier, but they said, "What is this? We can't do this. What are you talking about? This isn't legal." And I said, "Look, get me a supervisor, blah, blah, blah." And so this is the common problem that people do have when they go to Social Security is the [workers there] are not used to [same-sex relationships], they don't know what it is, they don't think its legal. . . . Get a supervisor or go to a different Social Security office. Eventually it will be done; don't be offended by it, they're not insulting you, they're just not used to it, they don't know what it's like.

His overall message of not giving up, being persistent, and achieving your desired outcome reflects his perception that legality is something that can be accessed with enough "know how" and willingness to push the system.

Some individuals used this persistence as a tool not just to acquire their own desired outcome but also to push for legal or political changes.

Merle, a single, white homosexual man in his fifties who lives in a legally negative state, observed that he has domestic partner benefits with his employer because, "I pushed that through myself at my office and everyone embraced it wholeheartedly." Similarly, Tiffany, a married, Asian lesbian in her thirties who resides in a legally negative state, described her activism as a tool to pressure for change in order to avoid the negative implications of the law: "There are [legal] issues and there are obstacles. I guess they haven't affected us as much. But there are obstacles and I'm sure there are bigger obstacles for some people, but I think that is why we try to be a little more proactive in the research studies, in the rallies, in you know, whatever we can, to throw our hat in the arena. And, you know, this might not directly be affecting me and my family right now today, but in the bigger picture it is an issue, it is an obstacle." In this respect, being proactive and being involved in politics and research was viewed to be a mechanism by which legal ends might be, ultimately, achieved.

These strategic uses of persistence and activism are a complicated mix of marshaling resources and resistance—resistance through going up the chain of authority to achieve one's desired ends or engaging in social movements for legal change. In the next chapter, we examine acts of resistance more closely, finding that many of our participants turn to operating against the law's intent when they are frustrated in their attempts to play the legal game.

Conclusion

The majority of our participants reported recognizing the contingency of the law, and drawing upon strategies to manipulate the law to their family's benefit. This perception of the law as malleable was voiced by participants across all legal contexts. Nonetheless, those residing in legally neutral and legally positive states were somewhat disproportionately more likely to describe their legal interactions in these "with the law" terms. Approximately 36 percent of participants within this group were from legally neutral states (34 percent of the overall sample). Participants from legally positive states were 34 percent of this group (33 percent of the overall sample). Approximately 30 percent of individuals in this group were from legally negative states (34 percent of the overall sample), rendering participants from these states somewhat underrepresented in expressing a "with the law" approach to navigating legality. Nonetheless, this is a far greater representation of individuals from legally negative states than was reflected in the "before the law" theme, which contained no participants from negative states.

It is perhaps unsurprising that this idea of playing the legal game would be most commonly expressed by those in legally neutral or positive states, given that legal manipulations might prove more successful in these environments. In legally negative states, where there are overt laws against LGBT families, the notion of being able to work within a perceived hostile system to get around legal obstacles is less prevalent. In legally neutral states, however, there is more ambiguity in the outcome due to the lack of decisive laws on the books. It is in these situations where creative approaches to working with the legal system seem to become a notable part of the legal discourse, shaping the legal landscape for LGBT parents.

In addition to legal context, gender and marital status appear to influence whether participants viewed the law as contingent on individual circumstances. Men were overrepresented in this group of participants, at 25 percent, as compared to their representation in the overall sample, at 17 percent. Accordingly, women were underrepresented at 69 percent (78 percent of the overall sample), and transgender participants were represented about on par at 6 percent (5 percent of the overall sample). Men's overrepresentation could reflect a greater confidence in manipulating the system for favorable outcomes, due to both popular gender messages regarding competitiveness and aggression, as well as higher socioeconomic status. In addition, we find that married participants are somewhat overrepresented in this group as compared to the sample composition, with 50 percent married, 38 percent partnered, and 12 percent single. It is possible that participants within the "with the law" group are particularly likely to take advantage of all legal protections to which they can gain access, including legal marriage. For some of our participants, marriage was even utilized as a strategy for family formation.

Taking a closer look at the four specific strategies used by our participants to work with the law, we found that legal context, marital status, and gender shaped the particular strategies employed. The type of forum shopping used by participants varied across legal context and demographic factors. Approximately 62 percent of those who used this type of forum shopping for friendly judges or jurisdictions resided in legally neutral states, 28 percent in legally positive states, and only 10 percent in legally negative states. As previously noted, forum shopping for friendly judges is most likely to produce favorable outcomes in states with ambiguous laws, where finding the right forum can make the difference in whether rights are accessed or denied. Notably, additional participants in legally negative states did forum shop for friendly judges; the manner in which they discussed this process, however, was quite different than those in legally neutral or positive states. Accordingly, we discuss in chapter 6 the way in which these participants engaged with "secretive" forum shopping.

Participants who reported forum shopping for friendly home states were, similarly, grouped disproportionately in legally neutral states (55 percent), as compared to positive (33 percent) or negative (12 percent) states. In addition, participants falling into this group were disproportionately partnered (60 percent), rather than married (20 percent) or single (20 percent). This appeared to be connected with the desire to move to a friendlier state in order to gain access to second-parent adoption. Participants who reported being unmarried were, overall, more concerned about accessing second-parent adoption than those who were legally married.

Those who forum shopped across state or international lines for children were primarily located in legally positive states (55 percent, as compared to 33 percent in neutral and 12 percent in negative states). Individuals in legally positive states who were forum shopping for children were often looking for even more favorable laws (in the case of surrogacy), or their forum shopping was almost accidental in terms of being unexpectedly connected with a child in another state. Given the predominance of those seeking friendly surrogacy laws within this category, males were also overrepresented at 55 percent as compared to their 17 percent composition in the overall sample.

In terms of those using workarounds to mimic legal rights, participants were fairly evenly distributed across legal contexts: 36 percent in legally neutral, 36 percent in legally positive, and 28 percent in legally negative states. The fact that this distribution closely reflects that of the overall sample suggests that legal context might play less of a role in shaping whether an individual will employ one of these workarounds. Approximately 90 percent of participants in this group identified as female, and 10 percent as female-to-male transgender; none of the gay male participants discussed these types of workarounds. Although this could be a peculiarity of our particular sample, it raises questions regarding the role that gender might play in influencing the use of legal workarounds.

Legal context appeared to play an important role in shaping whether participants would utilize heteronormative privilege as a strategy for achieving their family goals. Excluding our discussion of heteronormative privilege related to our trans participants, 42 percent of the participants who reported using heteronormative privilege resided in legally negative states, 29 percent resided in legally positive states, and 29 percent in legally neutral states. Similarly, over two-thirds of those in the trans group who used heteronormative privilege resided in legally negative states. This suggests that in states without access to legal rights and in which there exist outright prohibitions related to LGBT parenting, participants may rely on heteronormativity—particularly related to marriage—in order to "play the legal game." In these legal contexts, it is possible that there exist few other legal tools at LGBT parents' disposal. In chapter 6 we discuss the more subversive ways in which participants reported using heteronormativity to resist legality.

Finally, participants discussed several ways in which they marshaled resources in order to maneuver within the legal system. Having a "good attorney" as a resource was overwhelmingly voiced as important for those living in legally neutral states (72 percent, as compared to 14 percent each in legally positive and negative states). Related to forum shopping, it is within these uncertain legal environments that having the right attorney who can place you in a friendly courtroom becomes important. In addition, males were disproportionately more likely to voice the importance of having a good attorney, with 55 percent of individuals in this group being male and 45 percent being female. Further, approximately 45 percent of participants in this group were nonwhite, raising questions regarding whether access to a good attorney was understood to be an important mechanism for achieving power and privilege for these participants.

For those participants who discussed using socioeconomic status as a resource, 60 percent resided in legally positive states. The idea of being able to "buy a victory" is typically attributed to individuals in privileged positions; for LGBT parents, it is possible that this sense of privilege is more common for those living in legally friendly environments. Bolstered by a positive legal environment, the idea of utilizing income or education to play the system might be understood as more of an option. Similarly, for those who reported using legal knowledge or self-taught knowledge as a resource, almost 80 percent resided in legally positive and 20 percent in legally neutral states. These participants were also predominantly female (88 percent), suggesting that women might be more likely to rely on legal knowledge or self-taught completion of legal documents in order to accomplish parenting goals.

Participants who reported using social networks as a tool were overwhelmingly located in legally negative states (66 percent, as compared to 17 percent each in legally positive and neutral states). In legal environments with few legal options, social networks might prove more important in order to gain access to legal rights. In addition, 95 percent of those who mentioned using social networks as a tool were non-Hispanic white; this does not necessarily mean that nonwhite participants were unlikely to use networks, but networks were not discussed as a tool in the same way as for non-Hispanic white participants. Additional participants reported using social networks as part of their process of becoming parents, but these individuals did so more for informational purposes (see chapter 4) than as a legal tool.

Finally, participants who used persistence as a legal tool were disproportionately located in legally negative states (60 percent) and legally neutral states (40 percent). For these participants, the feeling that their legal victory was uncertain or unlikely due to their legal environment resulted in the use of pressure and persistence to ensure certain things went their way. Gender also played a role in whether persistence was employed, with 80 percent of participants in this group being gay men. Given that the use of persistence, as described, conveyed constructs often associated with masculinity (e.g., aggressiveness), then male participants might be more likely to use—or to admit to using—these tactics to achieve parenting goals.

Overall, legal context and gender appeared to play an important role in shaping whether and how the law was manipulated by participants. In addition, interactions with legal actors and social networks affected the manner in which participants "played the legal game." In particular, for individuals engaged in forum shopping, attorneys were an important resource in identifying friendly jurisdictions and overseeing the process. Social networks were also important, given that connections to attorneys and friends aided participants in identifying ways to work within the legal system. Connections with coworkers or judges sometimes also provided assistance in achieving favorable legal outcomes. These interactions with legal actors and social networks, alongside legal context and demographic characteristics, served to form a "with the law" framework for interacting with the legal system.

In chapter 6 we examine situations when our participants described being unable to truly work with the legal system to achieve their parenting goals. Unlike the participants discussed in this chapter who utilize the flexibility of the legal system to maneuver toward their parenting goals, the participants discussed in chapter 6 describe ways in which they engaged in more subversive acts of resistance during the process of becoming parents or parenting.

6

Parenting against the Law

Any time it comes to my gender status and the things that flow from it, I think of [the law] as incredibly antagonistic. I'm suspicious, I'm avoidant, I am *resentful*. That's the one. And I kind of think of it as the way you kind of shut your body down in preparing for a long flight. That's my visceral feeling when I prepare to do something administrative. Like, you can't stand up for yourself. You can't make waves, you can't demand respectful treatment. . . . You have to passively allow yourself to pass time with other people. And then hopefully if you do all the things right, you get out in the end. . . . [S]elf-advocacy leads to punishment because you then name yourself as a problematic category. . . . And in the case that I do that, I risk losing the very thing I went there to resolve.

—Ellis

For many of our participants, legality saturates their daily lives. Much as Sarat (1990, 343) described in his study of legal consciousness and the welfare poor, "the law is all over" for LGBT parents—its presence is felt in routine tasks such as completing forms, traveling, and children's school assignments, as well is in direct interactions with administrative or judicial bodies. Approximately 50 percent of our participants responded to the law's invasion into their family life with resignation, resentment, and—at times—resistance. For some, such as Ellis quoted above, the notion of openly resisting an unfair practice was impractical, as it was easier to feign submission in order to accomplish a desired outcome. Nonetheless, some types of resistance were accomplished more subversively so as to maintain the appearance of cooperation, all the while rejecting the authority of the law in determining their family lives.

These forms of resistance were often subtle, involving the everyday resistance tactics described by Ewick and Silbey (1998) that are frequently overlooked or unlabeled as resistance. Although most of these practices were unlikely to lead to social change, their very use signaled a recognition of the oppressive nature of the legal system, a rejection of the basis for legal authority, and a defiance of the current social order. Our participants recounted several types of resistance: using the law against itself through literal adherence to the law as written; performing roles of single heterosexual individuals in order to achieve family goals; making modifications to legal or administrative documents; challenging perceived unfair practices through political or formal legal channels; and deliberate violations of legality. Some of our participants expressed multiple of these strategies, resulting in the summation of the percentages across these strategies exceeding the 50 percent of participants falling into the "against the law" category. Legal context played an important role in determining whether resistance would be enacted by LGBT parents and, if so, in what format.

Just Following the Rules

One type of resistance expressed by our participants involved a technical adherence to the rules, but in a manner that knowingly stretched or defied the purpose of the law. Ewick and Silbey (1998) described this practice of resistance as "rule literalness," wherein individuals essentially turn the rules against the system and, by doing so, subvert its claim to power. For our participants, resistance by following the rules or using the legal system against itself was a more common approach than directly challenging or rejecting the law. Participants sometimes described these approaches with a certain amount of glee at subverting the system. But some participants expressed a degree of fear or uncertainty regarding their using the rules (or lack thereof) to achieve their family goals, articulating concern that their resistance could be discovered and punished.

"Secret" Adoptions

One of the recurring themes in our interviews was the manner in which individuals residing in legally negative or legally neutral states took part in what they believed to be secretive adoptions or second-parent adoptions. As we discuss in chapter 5, many of our participants engaged in strategic forum shopping to look for favorable outcomes for their adoption procedures. However, these individuals felt that forum shopping was part of "playing the game"—recognizing that legal outcomes were contingent on the particular legal actors and avenues, and that the law could be manipulated in your favor if you selected the right court. Approximately 9 percent of participants, however, discussed that they had found particular judges or jurisdictions that might grant an adoption and, while this was not outright prohibited by the law, they were fearful that their loophole could be discovered.

Along these lines, several participants indicated that they were informed second-parent adoption was an option if it was done quietly. For example, Colin, a partnered, Hispanic gay man in his thirties, described his discovery that second-parent adoption was available within his legally negative state: "I [was told] to contact this lawyer [in a different jurisdiction]; she's been doing second-parent adoptions. And so I contacted her and she said, 'Yes, under the radar we are doing it.'" Katherine, a married, white lesbian in her thirties, also described the secretive way that second-parent adoptions were being processed in her legally negative state. She explained: "Yeah, [those] counties are the places to go. Now, once the adoption has been processed, . . . it's nationwide, it's solid, you're done. Nobody can take it back; you just aren't going to find a judge or attorney [in this county] that's going to touch it with a ten-foot pole. . . . Second-parent adoptions are being done, even now. They're just being done quietly." Her account reveals her understanding that securing the second-parent adoption unobtrusively could gain her firm legal rights that were unlikely to be challenged even by the more conservative judges in her jurisdiction. Thus, keeping the process quiet so as to permit continued adoptions was important in that she believed she could secure a strong legal standing if she could make it through the system before the option was dismantled.

Many of our participants echoed this idea, describing the manner in which the attorneys themselves communicated the importance of not publicizing second-parent adoptions. Theresa, a single, white lesbian in her thirties, currently resides in a legally neutral state, but was located in a legally positive state when second-parent adoptions were viewed as a more secretive process. She described a meeting where an attorney instructed a group of lesbian couples about legal issues related to parenting. She recalled:

> The possibility of successful second-parent, same-sex partner adoptions—like, people don't hear about it and that's by design. The attorney also said that those of us in this community do this in places where we can get it through and are managing. You know, we don't publicize it because we feel like that would be dangerous because the people after you want to do it too. We want to protect this as long as we can, and right now that means keeping it under the radar. Like the average Republican probably has no idea that my child has two legal parents and [they're] women.

Katherine told a similar story regarding an attorney cautioning her to maintain secrecy regarding the second-parent adoption process:

> [An attorney] was on the panel and the question that I asked . . . was, "What is the status of second-parent adoption in the state?" And I explained what my situation was and such and she said, "Let me talk to you after the meeting." And she said, "The reason I want to talk to you privately is that, you know, I'm just begging you, please don't do any interviews . . . with the media, don't raise any ruckus about it. Just please, very quietly, go do your second-parent adoption because we are working on trying to find *the* perfect case." . . . [The attorney] indicated when I talked to her [later] that they are just trying to get as many second-parent adoptions done as they can because the larger pool you have to deal with, the stronger your case is. So in the event that there is a couple that really can't afford the legal fees, there are attorneys that are doing them pro bono just to get them done.

Similarly, Tiffany, a married, Asian lesbian in her thirties, described the manner in which there was a multigroup effort to quietly complete adoptions within her legally negative state. She explained: "If it comes down to adopting, from what we've heard through the network of attorneys and special interest groups and stuff that are helping with the whole situation, it is kind of low key. . . . It's kind of like, you've got to kind of keep it down, keep it on the down low. Like you can't make a big deal out of it and make it into a big publicity thing or whatever because then they are afraid they will start enforcing [prohibitions]." The descriptions of these participants, and others with similar stories, emphasize the manner in which second-parent adoptions are both secretly orchestrated by attorneys and LGBT parents, and are viewed as tenuous. The law does not directly prohibit the granting of second-parent adoption in these cases, thus the law is being followed as written. But there is an awareness that if this particular use of the law were to come to light, there would likely be a backlash given that second-parent adoptions for LGBT couples subverted the intention of the adoption laws. Accordingly, participants understood that protective measures were implemented in order to both keep second-parent adoptions accessible through secrecy, as well as to begin to build support in the event of a challenge.

This fear regarding a possible backlash or closing of the option for second-parent adoption was not unfounded, according to several of our participants. Participants in two states indicated that this very thing had occurred when awareness of second-parent adoptions surfaced. Several of our participants residing in a legally neutral state indicated that second-parent adoptions were being done quietly, but that recently this had changed when many of the other judges became aware of what was happening. As Jody, a single, white lesbian in her forties, described: "Although [second-parent adoptions] had been performed in [our city], the . . . judges had gotten together at some point and agreed none of them were going to do this. This was what the lawyer told us—that it had been done a few times, but all the judges had gotten together and they said, 'Look, we're gonna be firm and not do this anymore.' And so that option was no longer available." She essentially described a pact that was made among judges to not engage in a practice that was technically legal, but ran contrary to the perceived intent of adoption laws in the state. Although the law was legally neutral on this subject, the overall sociopolitical climate in the state was fairly negative on LGBT issues. According to Jody's understanding (and that of four other participants from the same state), this generated a sense among the judges, lawyers, and LGBT parents that the granting of second-parent adoptions was a subversive practice.

Participants also reported second-parent adoptions being halted in a legally negative state once officials were made aware of what was occurring. June, who identifies as a partnered, white "not straight" woman in her thirties, indicated: "The judge who granted [second-parent adoptions] just recently had to stop. . . . He was able to grant them, kind of on the down-low, and they came in and said, 'No, you can't do it at all anymore.'" Julie, a partnered, white lesbian in her fifties who resides in the same state as June, also discussed the manner in which the cessation of second-parent adoptions had occurred, saying: "It was never really clearly legal or illegal. It was a loophole. So I don't think there was any legislation passed that said adoption could only occur between a man and a woman or between a married couple. . . . I think it was where someone brought to light that this was going on and the governor said, well, that needs to stop." Although participants across the board in this state told a similar story regarding second-parent adoptions halting, two participants also indicated that there might be a second "secret" approach of being successful in second-parent adoption. After explaining that second-parent adoptions were no longer permissible, Carol (a partnered, white lesbian in her thirties) followed up by indicating that she was uncertain as to whether the door was completely shut:

> There's actually a law that says [second-parent adoption is] not something [our] judges can do. . . . I know the whole point of it was to prevent gays and lesbians from adopting a child with their same-gender partners. But I don't remember if that language is in there or not. I do know . . . I don't know if I should tell anybody this. . . . There's an attorney . . . who's found a loophole and is helping people do it. So that may be possible because the language of the law [is vague]. We actually have a meeting with her in a couple of weeks.

Although Carol seemed uncertain as to the exact language of the law, she was convinced that the intent was to prevent same-sex couples from engaging in second-parent adoption. Much like other participants described in this chapter, this sense that legal actors were working against her family engendered a desire to attain her family goals through seemingly underground, secretive means.

These stories of quiet opposition, coupled with fear of being "found out" and actual backlash when their resistance was discovered, signal tactical resistance practices. Ewick and Silbey (1998, 184) indicate that due to the power inequalities present, "resistant practices are often hidden, intentionally designed and executed to remain unrecognized and undetected by those against whom they are directed." One of the implications of not openly confronting the system through more direct opposition is that the semblance of the power status quo is preserved. Quiet, undercover opposition serves as no direct challenge to the legitimacy of the legal system's authority. When these practices are brought to light, however, a disruption in the system is revealed, albeit momentarily. A new reassertion of power is provoked; in this case, by orchestrating a cease and desist on the granting of second-parent adoptions in these two states.

Although these participants overwhelmingly expressed a degree of fear or concern regarding the disclosure of their resistant acts, there was also an element of pleasure at the thought of hoodwinking the legal system—an institution in which, so frequently, things did not play out in their favor. This aspect of bending the rules of the game in their favor was captured by Julie, who said that these secretive second-parent adoptions were "all like a tricky way we could get around the fact that we were not allowed to adopt as lesbians." While the laws might be against their family interests in many respects, the ability to quietly twist the rules allowed a small amount of reclamation of control over the course of their family lives and relationships.

Unexpected Health Benefits

Forum shopping was not the only situation in which participants reported quietly utilizing the letter of the law against itself. In several health scenarios involving parenthood, approximately 5 percent of participants described situations in which policies or laws could be manipulated to benefit their family. Although following the strict letter of the law or policy, participants nonetheless believed they were using these legalities in a manner that ran contrary to the intended purpose. In this respect, their practices signaled a degree of resistance to a legal structure that they felt was designed without their interests at heart.

Several of our participants discussed the manner in which loopholes within insurance provisions or other health benefits permitted them to access fertility treatments. These were primarily raised by women who were undergoing insemination. For example, Brenda, a married, white lesbian in her forties who is a resident of a legally negative state, discussed the manner in which both she and her partner were able to access fertility treatments through her insurance following their marriage. She recalled: "The company I work for . . . has fertility treatments covered as part of the insurance. So we have fifteen thousand dollars—this is kind of funny. So we have fifteen thousand dollars covered for fertility treatments. And I know they didn't intend it this way, but part of the reason that [we] got married was because when she got on my insurance, she was eligible for fertility treatments too. So we basically got thirty thousand dollars in treatments." As a married couple, her spouse was entitled to be added to her insurance. And, as the insured, both were entitled to fertility treatments. She perceived their use of the benefits to be permitted by the employer and insurance policies. Nonetheless, they expressed skepticism that this particular use of the fertility treatment benefits was intended, given that it effectively doubled their available resources for pregnancy as a couple. In this respect, they had more resources available through the policy for a single pregnancy than would a heterosexual couple. Her language regarding this outcome being "funny" and unintended indicates the manner in which they viewed their use of the benefits to be a somewhat subversive strategy that benefited their family.

Similarly, Kerry, a partnered, white gender queer person in her thirties who resides in a legally positive state, described the manner in which she and her partner were able to take advantage of a state grant to assist in their fertility treatments. Although they qualified for the particular funding, they felt that the money was clearly not intended to assist lesbians with achieving pregnancy:

> Because her insurance doesn't cover anything and my insurance doesn't cover domestic partners, . . . we were like, what are we going to do? And then we happened to run into a friend who had gotten pregnant and told us about this grant from the state . . . that's like an infertility thing. It's like this Republican agenda to get straight couples pregnant and it's an IVF grant, and you apply. . . . It's this awesome, awesome thing. It's this Republican agenda, I think money given, but the state . . . does it, and it runs through . . . these big reproductive hospitals. . . . We applied and we got accepted, and you have to furnish your tax returns and then they

figure out based on income—there's an income cap, you have to make under two hundred thousand dollars a year. And then they prorate what you will pay based on your income. . . . Everybody I know who's used the grant is a poor lesbian—everyone I know who has gotten this grant, because lesbians in this city make the least amount of money.

Once again, the participant described the manner in which she clearly qualified for the infertility treatments under the particular policy. Yet her understanding was that these funds were very much targeted toward families unlike her own. She repeatedly expressed satisfaction at gaining access to funds that she understood to be part of a Republican agenda to assist heterosexual couples with infertility treatments. Her pleasure at using the system against itself in this manner was evident, and emphasizes the way in which this "playing by the rules" was in fact a moment of resistance for her and her partner.

Picking a Friendly Social Worker

Approximately 9 percent of participants also reported "following the rules" when they selected social workers as part of their parenting process. In most jurisdictions, participants who were going through an adoption procedure had to have a social worker evaluate the parents and the home environment as part of a home study. And in some locations, social worker or psychologist evaluations were required prior to insemination. In many of these jurisdictions, the policies permit parents a degree of flexibility in selecting the particular social worker. Many of our participants used this flexibility to select a social worker who they knew might produce a particularly positive account of their home environment. In some respects, this process is similar to forum shopping because participants strategically identify and select actors who they believe will provide them with a favorable outcome. This process, however, is qualitatively different in terms of how participants discuss their selection of social workers. In many respects, they describe their selection of a gay or gay-friendly social worker as a subversive act. The system might require them to be evaluated as "good parents," but they reject the legitimacy of this authority for determining their fitness for parenthood by selecting an individual who is predisposed to describe them favorably. By doing so, they are not just going to a legal venue that permits second-parent adoptions, for example, but are superficially following "the rules" regarding a home study while simultaneously undermining the intent of the home study.

Theresa, a single, white lesbian in her thirties living in a legally neutral state, described the way that she and her partner were required to be evaluated by a social worker prior to going through the insemination process with a clinic. They not only selected their social worker, but rejected the one initially offered to them. She recalled:

> They had their own person and that is who they wanted us to use and we were like, "No, your people might be, like, homophobes. Can we use our own?" And they were like, "Fine." They have probably never been asked that before; it was great! And so we had to do that, but then we got in there and just flat out rejected all the other stuff and said we don't want drugs, we don't want this, we don't want that. And they agreed to it, and they made no money off us I'm sure.

For Theresa, the selection of their own social worker was clearly viewed as an act of defiance of the policies that they perceived as requiring additional scrutiny of their parenting process. Although they accepted that they had to be evaluated by a social worker prior to insemination, they resented this intrusion into their personal lives as part of the process of becoming pregnant. Rejecting the clinic's social workers, as well as their fertility medications and other medical options, seemed to serve as a means to reclaim some power over the process.

Other participants described locating social workers or psychologists through friends or gay-friendly organizations, or selecting social workers who were gay themselves. For example, Dianna, a partnered, white lesbian in her forties, discussed the work put into locating an appropriate social worker for her adoption in her legally neutral state:

> I can't go through Catholic charities, that is for sure. . . . [I used someone who] had done home studies for other gay couples that I knew. I asked some other gay couples and they used her and she was great, but then she ended up [being unable to complete the process]. . . . So, I had to get a new social worker. . . . So that is when I was like—Jewish people are gay-

friendly. I am going to call Jewish family services. . . . I was worried about calling anyone else because you just never know if you are going to get someone that is homophobic. . . . I was paranoid.

Although grounded in a stereotype, Dianna's perception that Jewish people would be less homophobic led to a strategic choice to select a social worker that she believed would generate a more positive portrayal of her family. While some participants, such as this one, looked for social workers who might be gay-friendly or who were not homophobic, others seemed to search for people they thought would be particularly gay-positive (as opposed to just neutral). For example, Kerry indicated: "We picked a lesbian. And we wrote the home study ourselves." Their selection of a lesbian, echoed by eight other participants, indicated the perception that they had weighed the cards in their favor by selecting a social worker who might work the system on their behalf. Indeed, in this instance, Kerry gained an advantage in terms of being able to craft much of the home study. As we explore in greater depth shortly, this practice of writing or influencing the home study more directly than through the selection of a friendly social worker, indicated a more delib-erate manipulation as opposed to a bending of the existing rules. The coupling, however, of the selection of a lesbian with the statement that they wrote part of the study suggests the way in which the social worker selection was viewed as part of a process of subverting the home study procedures.

Indeed, the manner in which the social worker selection could work in one's favor was explained by Colin, a Hispanic, gay man in his thirties living in a legally negative state. He recalled a story that illustrated his perception regarding the importance of a friendly social worker: "When my lesbian friend was looking at adoption, . . . they were going to work with a particular caseworker who was a lesbian and would have been supportive of them adopting and kept her mouth shut as long as they were willing to lie on the application [about being single and straight]. Because nobody else comes out here, just the caseworker. So they are the ones that choose to see or not see." The decision "not to see" a couple's sexuality, and thus not reflect it in the home study, permitted partici-pants to manipulate legal outcomes by using the policies (i.e., the home study requirement) to their advantage to tell the story as they wished it to be told. This act of resistance allowed them to technically play by the rules, but at the same time to reject the authority of the home study to determine what constitutes a good family.

Masquerading as Single

Although our participants were primarily having children while in a same-sex relationship, legal restrictions in many jurisdictions did not permit both individuals in a couple to adopt children. In most jurisdictions, however, gay men or lesbians could adopt as single persons. Taking on the role of a single person, described by approximately 15 percent of our participants, often involved creative presentations of family in home studies or, at times, outright misrepresentation of relationships or sexual orientation. In many respects, this process of resistance involved "masquerade," as described by Ewick and Silbey (1998), whereby individuals engage in a strategic co-opting of a role in order to achieve their desired outcome. In the eyes of the law, these individuals are in fact single given their lack of legal marriage. Their claims of being single, therefore, are technically accurate, meaning that they "do not lie about a role as much as they selectively invoke or present themselves in a role to which they might, in fact, lay legitimate claim" (Ewick and Silbey 1998, 206).

When couples pursued adoption via the single-parent route, they considered the manner in which their family would be represented in the home study paperwork. The manner in which they chose to represent their families was dependent, in part, on the legal context in which they resided. In some states, unmarried persons were not permitted to coadopt, but gay adoption was not explicitly prohibited; thus, some participants did not obscure their relationship. Even where gay individuals were not prohibited from adopting, however, many felt that presenting yourself as a gay person was unwise.

Hannah and Beth, a partnered, white lesbian couple living in a legally neutral state, exemplified a common response given by participants when describing how their relationships were categorized in a home study. They indicated that their social worker described their relationship in nonromantic terms, with Beth explaining: "[The social worker made it clear] that she would purely be a roommate. And so . . . anything beyond like a friendly, you know, relationship was not mentioned." Esther, a partnered, Hispanic lesbian in her forties who adopted in a legally neutral state, described the manner in which her partner was identified in the home study as a "nonmarried coresident or something." She and her partner did not select the terminology, but the social worker described their household arrangement in vague terms. As Esther explained: "They worded it the way they were supposed to word it. . . . Like, not this is her gay homosexual lesbian partner, you know, but they were like this is her nonmarried coresident roommate. . . . I mean she's a social worker, she does home studies, she gets paid to do them. So, I think, you know, she's aware that you can't say this is your big lesbo roommate person." Although technically gay individuals were not prohibited from adopting a child in their state, she later explained that the true nature of the relationship was masked in order to avoid any complications in the adoption process, stating: "You don't want to throw it into a tailspin where they question—you know, if you have some conservative judge questioning whether that's the right environment for a child. . . . So I think you just don't go there, you just don't say that. And see, that's the thing. Like, having a baby. I mean, shoot, anyone can have a baby—look at Britney Spears, anyone can have a baby and no one questions is this a good home. . . . You're in control, you know. You're not being judged."

Participants typically did not view omission of the nature of the relationship as a lie or a direct attempt to subvert the law. These reframings of the relationship, however, were understood as necessary nonetheless by many participants. Taking on the role of a single person was, in some respects, a form of resistance, but was often undertaken with resignation or resentment. As Esther indicated—for straight couples having a baby via intercourse, the suitability of their home remains unquestioned as part of the process. But for same-sex couples, the presentation of the adoptive parent as single and morally respectable (i.e., heterosexual) was often understood by participants to be required.

Similarly, Jody, a single, white lesbian in her forties living in a legally neutral state, described the way that home study presentations must be made through convincingly playing the single role. She stated:

> Well, you know you have to do a home study, and one of the big things . . .
> is you find a social worker who is okay with you being lesbians, but won't
> write that you're lesbians. You cannot write that you are a lesbian couple.

So the way it's written up, I mean you're totally honest with the home study social worker, but the way that she writes it up is that I'm another female living in the home, like a roommate. And as a roommate, I still have to go through all of the same legal checks. You know, you have to get the sheriff's reports for state and local infractions. There might actually be—I don't remember if there was a federal investigation, I don't think so. But you definitely had to get like your fingerprints done from immigration. All of this came with cost.

Her story echoes that of Esther's, in that she describes it as an imperative to present the adoptive parent as single in order to be successful. But, much as Esther noted, this masquerade comes with both financial and emotional costs in that it is an extra step that is required as compared to a heterosexual couple, and one in which she believes the law requires them to misrepresent the true nature of their family. Although the assumption of the single role was distasteful for many, it was nonetheless viewed as an essential method of using the system in order to achieve the desired end. As Dianna explained, being presented as roommates in the home study was necessary for a successful adoption: "Even I had huge problems about that. It felt a little dishonest, but it was also my only option."

This assumption of the role of a single person was not isolated to the process of adoption, although it was most commonly cited by our participants in the adoption context. Some participants mentioned approaching insemination as a single individual in order to facilitate the process. For example, Rhonda, a partnered, Hispanic lesbian in her thirties living in a legally neutral state, discussed the manner in which the single persona was utilized during her completion of the sperm bank paperwork. She explained: "I knew that it was legal for a single person to buy a tank of sperm. I couldn't have, on the paperwork, said I'm partnered with a woman. Like, you know, that was an automatic, they probably wouldn't do it. . . . We know enough to know that we can't approach it with two people." Whether accurate or not, her perception was that this was a necessary facade to accomplish parenthood.

These stories reveal that in legally positive or legally neutral jurisdictions, participants frequently reported playing the part of a single parent, who was seemingly divorced from sexuality, perhaps residing with a roommate. By contrast, participants residing in legally negative jurisdictions reported more explicitly taking on the role of a heterosexual. Colin, for example, described the manner in which adoptions were occurring in his legally negative state despite laws against gay adoption:

> Well, gay adoptions were happening under the radar for a long time. Couples too; they just lied about their relationship and went into a spare bedroom and said, "Oh, this is my friend now." I talked to caseworkers who were like, you know, "We're not stupid people, we realize what is going on. But we know a good home when we see a good home." And so, the caseworkers kept their mouths shut, the applicants lied on their applications, because there was an application question that said, "Are you a homosexual?" You checked "no" and you hoped that you had a caseworker that was supportive. Not always did you get one that was supportive.

In contrast to legally positive or legally neutral states, his story suggests that social workers and adoptive parents were not working together openly in order to process adoptions. Rather, he believed that lies or omissions were required both on the part of the social workers and on the part of the would-be parents. Further, Colin and other participants in legally negative states indicated that the adoptive parent must go beyond recasting the relationship with his or her partner, and must also complete a form that explicitly rejected that she or he was gay.

The manner in which more deliberate lying became a part of playing the single, heterosexual role when residing in negative jurisdictions was echoed by other participants. Sam, who identifies as married, white, female-to-male transgender and is in his forties, lives in a legally negative state. Sam described friends who wrote letters proclaiming their heterosexuality in order to be able to adopt, saying: "You have to write the heterosexual letter attesting to being straight and submit that to the state. . . . So you would have to not just omit things, you would have to out and out lie on paper." Sam understood the assumption of the heterosexual role to be temporary, however, explaining: "As I understand it, if you had lied previously and adopted as a single person, once you had the adoption enforced for at least a year, it is very unlikely that the state would overturn it for any reason. So if you were already established as a legal parent for over a year and then—oops, no, it turns out that you're gay and you end up in a relationship with someone, that's plausible. It could happen, and I know some people who have sort of gone that route."

Although most of the descriptions of performing heterosexuality occurred primarily on paper (e.g., presentation as roommates in the documents, checking a box or writing a letter indicating heterosexuality), some participants reported engaging in more prolonged, in-person demonstrations of heterosexuality in order to adopt. For example, Sheila, a partnered, white lesbian in her fifties, lives in a legally positive state, but her partner was able to adopt a child from a legally neutral state with a conservative sociopolitical climate. The agency from which she adopted was religious and conservative, and this required the adoptive parent to present both as single and as heterosexual. Sheila recounted the experience:

> SHEILA: So my partner never has worn a dress or anything like that. We kind of took a picture of her, she looked in drag. She was wearing a pair of my earrings, some lipstick, and some bad jacket that I had and we took the picture of her . . . and sent that in. . . . [When we went there,] we were in the hotel room in [a city] that was an hour away and I figured that's where you want to sleep. We just didn't want anybody to run into us. . . . A couple of days into it, [the agency] wanted to visit her [at the hotel]. . . . So I hurried up and got another room and I cleared anything that had to do with me out of there and went to another room. . . . The agency [asked her], "Who's this [other woman in the home study]?" . . . It felt like they wanted my partner to come up with her whole dating history and talk about who I was and how I was going to be involved with the child and kind of a nightmare.
> INTERVIEWER: Her heterosexual dating history?
> SHEILA: Oh absolutely. Oh, that was a given. . . .
> INTERVIEWER: So did you go with her to pick up the baby?
> SHEILA: Noooo. I discovered the Container Store. So every time she went [there], I was dropped at the Container Store and I shopped and I shopped.

Her story is one of a fairly complicated performance of heterosexuality that served to circumvent the legal and administrative guidelines that prevented same-sex couples from adopting. The maintenance work required in creating this image of heterosexuality was burdensome in many respects, but was nonetheless an act of concerted resistance. By her partner playing the part of a single, gender-conforming, straight woman, the couple was able to achieve family goals that might have been otherwise impossible within this state.

International adoptions often presented situations similar to those of participants residing in legally negative states, in that gay men and lesbians were explicitly prohibited from adopting in many jurisdictions. Some participants were nonetheless able to adopt internationally by presenting themselves as single with roommates, much like those in domestic adoptions. For example, Marlon, a partnered, white gay man in his fifties, lives in a legally neutral state and adopted internationally from a South American country. He explained:

> First of all, it was a single-parent adoption and I did not disclose my homosexuality. . . . [Our adoption agency] knows the reality of the world and what they will do is they will come and prepare a home study that is appropriate for the reviewing body. So the [country's] government and court needs a home study that is acceptable to them. And they don't lie about anything material in the home, but instead of [presenting us as] married, he's my "roommate" and it can be portrayed in a very nonsexual manner, as it was.

Some individuals seemed comfortable with portraying themselves as single for international adoptions and casting their partner in the roommate role, and others either rejected the option of doing so or rationalized that their approach did not constitute lying per se. For example, Jody, a single, white lesbian in her forties, lives in a legally neutral state. She indicated that she and her partner opted to adopt from a country in Africa over a country in Eurasia because the African country did not require a statement of heterosexuality for adoption purposes. She explained:

> [In the African country,] they would not adopt to lesbians, but . . . [the Eurasian country] required you to write a letter, a certified letter, to say that you are not lesbian and that you are actively seeking a husband. . . .

But I didn't feel good about lying. I mean, I didn't mind not telling, but I didn't wanna have a certified letter. . . . And the big reason was that I didn't want anybody to come back later and say, "Look, this is a certified letter, and you lied, and now we're takin' 'em." And this way, we were able to say, "You know what, we didn't admit, but we didn't certify, you know, this is the case." And, you know, as far as we are concerned, and the US laws are concerned, all we are is roommates, you know. We have no legal status, so all we can be is roommates.

Adopting the role of roommates or single was viewed as technically accurate, and thus less legally problematic than an overt statement denying one's sexual orientation. Although Jody and her partner were subverting what they recognized as the true intention of the law, they were doing so by what they perceived to be truthful representations. These acts coincided with their understanding of the legal system as something that can be manipulated, but that should not be explicitly violated.

Pamela, a married, white lesbian in her forties, faced the same predicament regarding making a statement of heterosexuality in order to complete an international adoption. She and her partner, Louise, live in a legally positive state and were adopting from a Eurasian country that prohibited lesbians from adopting. She recalled:

So we were open with the social worker, who said that that [our sexual orientation] was fine, but she was going to write the home study as if I was a single person and had a deadbeat roommate. Because that's what Louise always calls herself, the deadbeat roommate. So we did the home study as if it were my home. And then we had originally planned on traveling to [the country] together and when the trip was actually getting organized, they were like, "Um, you can't do that."

Their adoption process involved a more overt effort to take on the single role, given that Pamela had to do more than identify herself as a single adoptive parent or present Louise as her roommate. She was additionally required to hide Louise as part of the adoption process by not traveling to the country together so as to preserve her image as single. After traveling alone to adopt her child, Pamela then met with a judge where she was asked questions related to marriage and heterosexuality. She responded creatively, so as to maintain her masquerade as single and yet to avoid technically lying in court:

> And then when I was in [the other country], they did ask me about getting married and I had to lie to the judge. Actually, I didn't really lie. What I said was the absolute truth. It was kind of scary; . . . I thought I was going to jail. Because adoptions in [this country] are presided over by the court and the prosecutor, so it seems not sort of a happy occurrence when they have a prosecuting attorney there. So they said, "What happens if you decide to get married?" And I said, "If I ever met a man that I wanted to marry, then he would become part of my child's life." Which is true. It's never going to happen, but I gave an honest answer. And the interesting thing is, my cousin adopted also from [the same country] and was on a trip with a single woman who also had a roommate, and my cousin was like, "Come on, you can tell me." And this single woman was not telling anybody, which they tell you not to say a word while you're in the country. So to the woman, she goes, "You know, this is what my cousin said about her roommate, in case it helps you." And that woman also used the same line.

This ability to take on certain aspects of the single role, and yet technically remain true to one's sexual identity, signals an almost playful resistance to the law. Although she recounts a degree of fear both in her own representations in court, and in her cousin's experience with the other "single" woman, her response to the judge also signals satisfaction at side-stepping the dangerous implications of the judge's question through her technically truthful response.

In many of these accounts, participants describe the manner in which their social workers or agencies played a role in crafting their presentations of self. Participants often indicated that their social workers or agencies had a vested interest in presenting them in a positive light, so as to facilitate forming families or placing children in homes. For example, Pamela indicated that she believed her social workers were assisting in presenting her as single in order to expedite the placement of children in need. She observed that when they went to adopt their second child, their US agency no longer provided dual-home studies for gay parents in which the parent was portrayed as single for purposes of the foreign country but as partnered in the United States for purposes of second-parent adoption. Accordingly, they were told that representing oneself as single for the international adoption was no longer an option. She believed that this change was due to a fear of losing accreditation, explaining: "I think they had a group of very open-minded social workers who were willing to sort of bend the home study rules. . . . And I think the social workers were just trying to do what social workers do, which is be supportive of different families and open-minded, and I don't think they had been thinking about [the risk of losing accreditation]." Carl, a married, white gay man in his thirties who was living in a legally positive state and adopting from a legally negative state, explained his perception of the social workers and agencies' roles in crafting these single, heterosexual personas:

> But you know, this whole notion that states can even ban same-sex couples from adopting, it's ridiculous. . . . Basically, you know, if you want to adopt a child and are an upstanding person, I think in 99 percent plus of states, the social service workers will work to make that happen, regardless of what you are. And if you're gay or whatever and it's a state where it's illegal it's just like, don't talk about that. Don't say that. We're going to make this happen for you. . . . It really just dawned on me that the worst-seeming laws, at least in this area, . . . they seem just like a polite fiction. It makes people feel like there are certain things that are being protected, but really most of the people who are working in that system, they're going to do what they can for the kids. And, you know, if there's a gay couple who want to adopt a kid, they're going to help [make] that happen.

Although many participants were willing to take on the role of single, and even the role of heterosexual, others indicated that they were deterred from pursuing adoption from a particular jurisdiction due to this necessity. For example, Nellie and Susie, a partnered, white couple residing in a legally positive state, indicated that they opted not to pursue international adoption because they did not want to lie about their identity as a couple. As Nellie described:

> And then when we went to the international adoption . . . they'd told us that we'd have to lie; only one of us would be able to adopt. There's not a single

country that would allow you to openly adopt as a couple. We said to them like, "How do you guys do this if you have queer couples that are adopting internationally? How does that happen?" Cause they have to come to your house, do extensive interviews with social workers and they just pretend to not see your roommate. . . . And so I would go by myself to [the other country] or something and [Susie] would come as my friend to help. . . . It's crazy.

Ultimately, the idea that they would have to lie about their relationship discouraged them from international adoption, and they later were successful with insemination. Maxine and Allison, a married, white couple in their thirties living in a legally positive state, similarly described how they were deterred from international adoption due to the idea of having to lie about their relationship. Allison explained:

When you used to be able to adopt from China, they wouldn't let lesbians adopt but they would let single women adopt. So lesbian couples used to just lie and say that they were single and only one person's name was on the adoption paperwork when you go to China and everything. And this was . . . a possibility [for us]. But that's how you did it—you lied and said that you were single. And [Maxine] really, really didn't like that part. For her, that was like the worst she ever felt about being gay. And we couldn't be legally married in order to adopt internationally because the adoption social worker will lie, but they can't lie if it is legally true.

For this couple, presenting oneself as single felt fraudulent and not worth the costs incurred regarding the implied inferiority of their same-sex relationship. Further, the incongruences with legal marriage in the United States and required singlehood for the international adoption presented additional obstacles to assuming the single role. Ruby, a partnered, multiracial lesbian in her thirties who was residing in a legally positive state, echoed this concern when she explained that she also contemplated the strategic implications of legal marriage for her parenthood goals. She noted: "We did at one point talk about should we not get married legally so we can pursue international adoption. But I think we were just like, you know, we can't."

Residing in a legally positive state and having relatively easy access to legal marriage perhaps affected some participants' willingness to masquerade as single and heterosexual. In situations where alternative means of family formation were more widely available, taking on the single role in order to achieve family goals was only one of many options. Further, the option of legal marriage resulted in situations where couples were not readily able to adopt the single persona if they wished to also take advantage of legal marriage. Living in a more positive sociopolitical and legal environment, where their relationship was more legitimated on a daily basis, could have also presented a greater conflict for some of these couples in adopting a single, heterosexual identity. By contrast, for those living in states where they often felt the need to mask their sexual orientation or their relationships, taking on the single role perhaps felt like an opportunity to use this daily practice to their advantage.

In prior research, the masquerade process is one in which persons typically assume a role that carries less status or more vulnerability in order to make claims of greater need (Ewick and Silbey 1998). For our participants, this is not the case. Although they are assuming the role of a single person, which usually implies lesser power or privilege than that of a married individual, the action is undertaken to increase rather than decrease social standing. Even in cases where they are not explicitly required to denounce homosexuality or identify as heterosexual, the assumption of the single role is a performance of heterosexuality and thus a claim to greater privilege. It is perhaps this aspect of role-playing that leads to some of the ambivalence expressed both by those who choose to assume the single, heterosexual role, and those who do not. There is a taking of privilege involved and, through it, a reminder of one's status as an inferior would-be parent. Thus, while our participants discussed "tricking" those in power through taking on the expected role of a heterosexual parent, they nonetheless expressed resentment and hostility along with their resistance.

Disrupting Recorded Documents

Power is both reified and rearticulated through writings (Foucault 1978), inscribed within the laws themselves, as well as within writings that are related to legal or administrative processes. Approximately 20 percent of our participants enacted resistance through manipulations of legal documents, either by making changes to documents or by completing documents themselves rather than using the proper procedures. Through these forms of resistance, they effectively reject the legitimate authority of the power embodied in the documents (Ewick and Silbey 1998; Marshall 2005).

As same-sex couples, our participants frequently encountered documents that did not accurately reflect their family relationships or experiences. In these situations, some of our participants attempted to imagine what the legal or administrative body wanted them to communicate and completed the documents accordingly (Baumle and Compton 2014). Others, however, used the moment in which they experienced a conflict with their own lives and those of the document as a point in time to challenge the power structure reflected in the documentation.

The most common paperwork-related experience reported by our participants involved being confronted by a survey or form that asked them to identify family relationships that are not entirely compatible with their family structure. Many of the forms coming home from children's schools require modification by parents due to their use of gendered parenting labels. Ruth, a married, white lesbian in her thirties living in a legally neutral state, described the common practice of modifying these documents: "I have to fill out every year the same forms, and they always say 'mother' and 'father.' And we write 'parent one,' 'parent two.' . . . I would write 'mother'/'mother' on everything, and be so annoyed. Even still, when we go to the dentist, I have to do it."

Similarly, participants described modifying administrative paperwork in order to make it work for their family. For example, Louise and Pamela, who live in a legally positive state, described completing passport paperwork for their children that contained lines for the names of the mother and father. Pamela detailed their exchange with the postal worker:

> I've got all of my documentation with me and I said to this postal worker, and he's about, I don't know, maybe about sixty, big guy, he looks like he drinks beer quite a bit. . . . I get down to the parent stuff and it says mother and father and so I said, "She has two mothers." And he goes, "What?" And I said, "Yeah, she has two mothers." He goes, "Is that even legal?" and I go, "Yeah" and he goes, "Get out of here!" And he was just

looking at it, like, "Well, I don't know what to tell you to put." So we just
crossed out father and put a second mother, which we do all the time.

This process of changing forms was commonplace for our participants
and, while seemingly minor, signaled an open rejection of the expectation of the heteronormative, nuclear family. Crossing out or modifying
forms in this way served as an act of resistance both in the actual completion of the form and in the manner in which the form served as a
communication about family data. The type of knowledge that is sought
via the fields of "mother" and "father" is more than a simple data point,
but is also a means by which to regulate whom and what constitutes
a family. By changing the forms, participants are taking control over
the data collected about their family and, in doing so, taking control of
themselves as a subject of administrative power. Further, their changes
to documents do not exist in a vacuum, but are an interactive form of
resistance. Through the dialogue with the postal worker, for example,
Pamela's change to the form becomes a type of resistance via the act of
telling the story of their family (and the "legality" of their family structure) to an administrative worker. In this respect, the change to the form
is a more complicated act of resistance than it first appears.

In addition to changing the "mother" and "father" categories on administrative or school paperwork, participants also recounted the manner in which they chose to identify as spouses on forms despite their
lack of a legal marriage. For example, Willa and Wanda, a partnered,
white lesbian couple, were completing paperwork as part of the process
of Wanda undergoing insemination with a clinic in a legally neutral state.
Willa recalled: "You have to sign a consent for treatment, a consent sayin'
that this and this and this could go wrong. . . . It would say spouse, and
I just signed it. . . . I just signed it, whether they wanted me to or not. I
just did it." Through both her act of signing the document, as well as her
retelling of the story, she indicated resistance to the seeming exclusion
of her—as a nonlegal spouse—from the process of creating their child.
Even though she understood her signature might lack formal legal implications, by signing the paperwork as the spouse she rejected the way
in which the paperwork sought to regulate the legitimacy of her family.

Similarly, many of our participants described the manner in which
they classified their relationships with their partners or with their chil-

dren on the US census in a manner that was contrary to the formal legal relationship (Baumle and Compton 2014). For example, Malcolm and Lynn, a partnered, white couple living in a legally positive state, were attempting to identify their child's relationship to Malcolm on the census. They indicated that they selected the biological relationship category. In explaining their logic, they said that even though Malcolm had completed a second-parent adoption of Lynn's biological child, they did not view the child as adopted. Ultimately, they utilized heteronormative constructions of the family to validate their identification choice. Lynn explained: "That's what ended up being our justification for filling out bio-kids. How would have we filled it out if we were straight individuals?" Given that the child was conceived during their relationship and as a joint undertaking, they believed that a heterosexual couple would have considered this to be their biological child (despite the use of donor sperm). Although they understood that the legal relationship of the child to Malcolm was that of adopted, they rejected this conception of their family and, in selecting the biological category, they further rejected heteronormative definitions of parenthood. Selecting "unexpected" relationship categories on the census forms was more prevalent for individuals residing in legally negative or neutral states, given that individuals in these states were more likely to have ambiguous legal or biological relationships with their children. For example, in states without marriage or second-parent adoption, nonbiological or nonadoptive parents had no clear way to legally identify their relationship to their partner's child (Baumle and Compton 2014). Thus, they were more likely to resist the census categories and to choose parent-child relationship identities that reflected their lived experience (e.g., biological child).

Acts such as these signal resistance to the implied authority of the legal system to legitimize some family relationships over others. At the same time, the survey completion is often a one-sided form of resistance given that the recipients of the surveys do not necessarily know that the response category selected was one of defiance. Some couples reported more overtly communicating their resistance through participation in the National Gay and Lesbian Taskforce's "Queer the Census" project. As part of this project, the NGLTF asked same-sex couples to place a "Count Me In! Queer the Census" sticker on their census forms. Many of our participants had heard of this campaign and participated by placing the sticker on their form. For example, Carol and Maria, a partnered, white lesbian couple living in a legally negative state, indicated: "We put a sticker on ours! This is a gay family!" Participants who engaged in this project seemed to convey a belief that their process of modification of the official forms might momentarily disrupt the power dynamic in a manner akin to spray painting graffiti on the wall of an administrative building.

All of the previously described modifications to documents were undertaken in order to correct or to protest their inadequacy in reflecting same-sex family structures. In some cases, however, participants described manipulating or modifying documents to more deliberately subvert the legal process. For example, five of our couples reported significantly writing or revising their own home studies in order to portray their family structure in the most positive light. The home study document is intended to be undertaken by an objective third party in order to evaluate the suitability of the home environment for a child. As previously noted in our discussion of selecting social workers for the home study, many participants rejected the authority of the administrative or legal systems to evaluate their suitability for raising children. This resulted in their selection of social workers that were predisposed to describe their households favorably, rather than the "objective" actors that the process intended.

As further evidence of their resistance to this process, however, five couples indicated that they engaged in the manipulation or writing of their own documentation to facilitate their adoption. For example, Katie, a married, white lesbian in her fifties, had a prior relationship with a licensed social worker who she was able to use for her home study in her legally negative state. She explained: "I basically wrote the home study and I gave it to her, had her do whatever she needed to do to edit, and then she submitted the home study. That way, you know, um, I wasn't really focused on my partner in the home study. . . . I wasn't hiding that she was there. I didn't say, 'Oh, take your stuff and leave while we do this.' No. But I wasn't necessarily eager to describe the nature of the relationship either, you know." This manipulation of the documentation was echoed by four of our other participants, all of whom reported either writing or substantially revising their own home study reports. For example, Dianna, a partnered, white lesbian in her forties living in a legally neutral state, stated, "I wrote it for [the social worker] and she just copied it and added a few things." The ability to take control over the manner in which their households were portrayed was not only resistance to the requirement of being evaluated, but was a way in which participants were directly able to intervene in the process and have a potential effect on the outcome. In this respect, they were able to gain access to legal texts and modify them, thus undermining the manner in which the texts would potentially otherwise be used to objectify their families.

Rejecting Legal Heteronormativity

In order to express resistance to legality, most participants have on some level rejected that the law's power is derived from a superior claim on morality. As Ewick and Silbey (1998, 189) observe, resistance involves a realization that "legal authority does not come from moral principles that legitimate the power, but power produces normative grounds upon which power is exercised." As described in prior legal consciousness studies, when the law's authority is not viewed as deriving from morality, then the power that flows from the law might often be understood as arbitrary (Fritsvold 2009; Marshall 2005; Hull 2003; Ewick and Silbey 1998). Many of our participants understood that although the laws that affect their family were justified through moral claims, these moral claims were a reflection of the power dynamics that permit heteronormativity to dictate the terms of morality. As explained by Felicia, a single, white lesbian in her forties who is a resident of a legally neutral state: "[The law is] definitely part of a hegemonic system that doesn't have my interest in mind. The law was written by [straight] white guys for [straight] white guys and so folks that don't fall into that demographic are disadvantaged and manipulated." Rebecca, a single, Hispanic queer woman in her thirties who is a resident of a legally neutral state, echoed this idea:

I think [the law is] fundamentally flawed and a pillar of, like, the colonial legacy of this country. And I don't mean colonial in a kind of charming, architecture kind of way. I mean, like, colonization and conquest. . . . And so that's the way that I feel about my sexual orientation and the law. Like,

I feel like I have an interest in seeing people being able to live with dignity and being self-determined and being able to create families and homes and communities in a way that's keeping with their integrity as human beings. And it's not about accessing privilege or accessing middle-class values or the American dream. And I really resent and get frustrated with the fact that the LGBT rights movement is dictated by something that is rotten at its core, which is American values, you know? I feel like the lack of critique of oppression and the way it relates to what people imagine as accessing civil rights is just very disheartening and alienating. So, um, yeah. That's how I feel about it.

Rebecca more directly identifies the problem with legality as being her perception that there is a lack of true morality within the so-called American values that are argued to undergird the law. Accessing the law, she argues, is more about accessing a privilege that is used to oppress her family and others like her. For approximately 18 percent of our participants, this realization that the law is neither justified nor legitimized by morality led to avoidance of the law through various mechanisms whereby they were able to operate outside of the heteronormative legal framework.

In terms of forming families, several of our participants opted for approaches where they were able to exclude much of the law from the process. Approaches involving insemination, which were primarily available to women, were one of the simpler mechanisms whereby participants could sidestep some of the ways in which legality directly affects family formation. For example, Jody, a single, white lesbian in her forties living in a legally neutral state, discussed how she and her partner pursued insemination as a first choice for forming their family. She explained: "The only laws that I investigated [were] . . . I went and found this cryobank and went and talked to them. And I said, 'Do we have to go through a physician for this?' And she said no. . . . You know, so we were trying to keep a doctor out of it. We were trying to keep as much of the law out of it as possible."

This idea that the law should be relatively absent from the private process of having children was raised by many of our participants. Katie, a married, white lesbian in her fifties who lives in a legally negative state, expressed her belief that laws have no place in determining whether or how she is inseminated within her home. She argued: "Law or no law, if I'm not hurting somebody or killing somebody or whatever, then I think I should have the right to make certain decisions. And the law to me, at that point, becomes a suggestion, not what will dictate what I do." Her rejection of legality in this process evidences a belief that the laws on the books carry little moral authority. If she is not engaged in an act with moral ramifications, such as hurting another individual, then she contends that laws have little legitimacy in regulating her behaviors. Similarly, Lynn, a partnered, white lesbian in her thirties living in a legally positive state, indicated that she and her partner did not consider laws regarding at-home insemination as a barrier in having children. She stated, "I think somebody did tell me that it wasn't legal in all places, but we just totally didn't care and disregarded the law." Although this was not the approach they ultimately pursued to having children, her response indicated that legal prohibitions against what they deemed a private matter would not have proven an obstacle.

Others described going a step further and creating a family without involving doctors, sperm banks, or other legalities. These approaches typically involved insemination using donor sperm from friends or family. For example, Marlene, a partnered, white lesbian in her forties, described a group of her friends in her legally neutral state that had a baby together: "We had a mutual friend that wanted to have a child too, and they all agreed to parent. He provided the sperm and her and her partner would just call him and he would come over and they would do the insemination. She got pregnant using a turkey baster, which is pretty miraculous. . . . Now they all four parent. There are two dads and two moms." This approach not only removed much of the administrative and legal oversight that is a part of family formation for same-sex couples; it also more subtly challenges the moral underpinnings of such laws and regulations by rejecting the very definition of what constitutes maternity and paternity. The raising of a child by two same-sex couples, rather than by one mom and one dad, evokes an act of everyday resistance.

Similarly, some of our participants considered or pursued using donor sperm from family members in order to have a child. For example, Lynette, a single, black lesbian in her twenties living in a legally neutral state, indicated that she and her ex-partner had discussed this route, saying: "The way we planned on it was she had a brother and we were gonna use his sperm to impregnate me. So that way, you know, the child could have both of us." Similarly, Jacquelyn, a married, white queer woman in her thirties living in a legally positive state, indicated that they used her partner's brother as their donor. Although paperwork was signed at a fertility clinic in order to store sperm samples, they did not have a legal agreement with their donor regarding paternity rights. She explained: "To me, and this is a real benefit to me in having a donor that is part of our family, . . . there are a lot of people in our family that would just completely try to shut it down if our donor ever tried to assert any sort of place. Yeah, it's not really a concern because it feels so far out of the realm of possibility. I would say that it's not really a legal concern." By using a family donor, she felt that they were able to bypass much of the legality involved in using a known donor in terms of fears of challenging parental rights. In this respect, she indicated that they had replaced the role of the formal legal system with familial rules that regulated the behavior of the involved parties.

Other participants similarly had children in ways that were not entirely divorced from legality, but that challenged the traditional approaches. For example, Marlene explained that she and her partner did not learn about the child that they adopted from a public or private adoption agency, but from a chance meeting in a feed store:

> I was in . . . a feed store for animals. Someone walked up to me, an acquaintance of mine, and said: "My niece is pregnant. Do you know anyone or anything about the services available, because we have absolutely no services in town. Do you know anyone that wants to adopt a kid?" I said, "I do." She said, "All right. Write my niece a letter and I will give it to her." . . . So it was private adoption. Three months and it was over, done. Piece of cake, fell in my lap. Whatever you believe in.

Although formal law was required to process the private adoption, the typical administrative and legal processes were sidestepped in identifying a child and selecting and approving a prospective parent. This participant, therefore, was able to employ connections that permitted her to avoid some of the potential obstacles that a LGBT parent might face in being selected as the adoptive parent of a newborn.

Another example of avoiding some of the legal formalities of family formation involved male couples who pursued surrogacy. Ben, a partnered, white homosexual man in his thirties who lives in a legally neutral state, described how he and his partner initially worked with an attorney in locating their surrogate and in the birth of their first child. They decided to continue to use the same surrogate when they had more children, but opted to exclude the attorney from the process. The children who were born from this second surrogacy experience did not yet have birth certificates. He explained: "It's a little more complicated this time [to get the birth certificates] because if the attorney finds out that we did it without him then we have to pay him. We have to file in the court or district where the babies were born which is where he works, so it is kind of a risk on that one. . . . So, we are having to figure out the way to do it where we don't get in trouble."

Similarly, Bobby and Walter, a partnered, white gay couple in a legally neutral state, described their desire to exclude their agency from the process when pursuing a second child with their surrogate. Bobby explained that they were worried the agency would say "that we may not have a relationship with her and try to claim the rights of this upcoming pregnancy." Ben and Bobby's stories reveal the desire, in many cases, to avoid the role of attorneys, administrators, or formal elements of the law in family formation processes. Some of these desires are financial considerations, but nonetheless reveal the manner in which LGBT parents might wish to reject the legal trappings that are placed on them, but not on the majority of their heterosexual counterparts who do not use alternative reproduction.

By rejecting the law in some aspects of their family lives, LGBT parents also lose access to some of the protections that the law might provide. For example, in cases in which known donors or in which surrogates are used, formal law often provides the ability to safeguard the parental rights of LGBT parents against other parental claims. But for some participants, the law is viewed as either an unnecessary obstacle or as an oppressive force in their family lives. Thus, finding ways to operate outside of the formal legal system when forming families offers attractions that might offset the loss of claims to legal rights.

Challenging Unfair Practices

Many of the types of resistance described thus far have taken the form of acts that tend to be smaller, informal, and not readily recognized as opposition to the law. This type of resistance was the most common that was described by our participants. Nonetheless, approximately 10 percent of our participants also engaged in more obvious forms of resistance, including challenging administrative or bureaucratic procedures, employment policies, or legal outcomes via more formal processes.

Some of our participants described smaller challenges that precipitated the exploration of more formal legal challenges to unfair practices. Several of these involved the assertion of rights based upon their marriages or partnerships. For example, Rhonda, a partnered, Hispanic lesbian in her thirties who resides in a legally neutral state, discussed the manner in which she opted to enroll her partner for health benefits. The HR company that was administering her employer's benefits offered a domestic partner benefits policy. Her act was intended as a direct challenge to her employer's practices, and was undertaken with the expectation that it could result in her employment being terminated. As she recounted:

> So, for fun, I signed Joann up and I thought, well, we'll just see what happens. . . . And that went haywire. I actually ended up consulting with [an attorney] because the company ended up coming to me; they sent their pseudo-HR person to ask me to take Joann off the benefits. And I listened to them and then I thought, you know what, they can't do that. So they can't fire me because I'm gay. I mean, they can, but I'd walk away with a severance. But they can't deny me a benefit that exists. That's their problem for (A) not knowing and (B) providing it. So, I could take them to court on this contractually. . . . [But] I thought, I'm not going down this road.

Ultimately, she opted not to sue her employer for refusing to allow her to add her partner to the health insurance plan. But signing up Joann was an overt act of resistance to what she perceived as an unfair employment practice, and her consultation with an attorney indicated the seriousness at which she contemplated pursuing formal action against her employer.

Similarly, Katherine and Nancy, a married, white lesbian couple who reside in a legally negative state, described how they invoked their legal marriage as a means to push their way into a class for adopting parents. Katherine recalled that they were unable to find a local class and, instead, traveled to a nearby county to take a class in an area that she described as "rednecksville squared":

> So we show up at this training class that's being held at a Catholic church and walk up. I had been the one to get all the information about when the class was and all this kind of stuff and I did not say anything about the fact that it was me and my wife, because that wasn't relevant at that moment. So we got there and the lady greets us at the door. . . . And I said, "And this is my wife." And she says, "Oh, um, are y'all married?" And I said, "Yes, we are," and she says, "Oh, okay." And there was this not-stated thing in the air. And I found out later . . . they had had one other lesbian couple that had come in and tried to take the class [who were not legally married]. . . . And so she had told them they couldn't legally adopt because they weren't legally married. And so they didn't come back.

In this situation, Katherine was able to marshal her marriage as a strategic weapon in order to assert her right to be in the class. Her marriage did not entitle the couple to both adopt, and neither did the lack of marriage prevent the other lesbian couple from adopting as single individuals. Nonetheless, this invocation of the privilege associated with legal marriage was employed to challenge what appeared to be an unfair exclusion of the couple from the course.

Other participants described challenging heteronormative practices within their children's schools, including forms, homework assignments, or holiday activities. For example, Devin, a partnered, white gay man in his forties living in a legally positive state, described the manner in which his child's school effectively excluded families without mothers from a school holiday. He recalled:

> You know, we started [our child at his school] when he was three years old, and we quickly found out they celebrated Mother's Day as part of the school curriculum. They didn't celebrate Father's Day because it comes after the school year. And I kind of went in to talk to the principals about it,

to say I didn't like it, could they get rid of it. And ultimately they changed it. They turned Mother's Day to Family Day, and I think actually it's been really successful around the school. But there was a part of me where I resented that I had to do that work. You know, that I had to put in energy to advocate on behalf of our family. You know, the principal's like, "Wow, you're the first parent who's ever come in and raised this issue for us." . . . I feel that way about, like, our taxes and who owns what in our family and we have to do two and three times as much work to kind of clarify all that stuff. And if the law—the law could take care of that much more easily.

Rather than working within the heteronormative framework, or making modifications to forms, participants like Devin made a direct appeal to those in power to change what they perceived to be unfair or biased practices. Although successful, Devin observed that this was just one more instance in which he was compelled to take extra steps or challenge unfair practices because the law failed to provide for his family in the absence of his intervention.

Only six of our participants indicated that they directly challenged unfair practices through more formal legal channels, such as contacting attorneys, sending demand letters, or filing lawsuits. This differs from using the law to facilitate family formation or the acquisition of legal rights or benefits through adoption. Instead, these are instances in which participants challenged the status quo in an attempt to alter an unfair practice. These types of legal challenges are what people most often categorize as legal resistance, as opposed to the everyday acts that our participants more commonly employed. Almost all of the cases in which legal challenges were pursued, such as contacting attorneys or filing lawsuits, involved participants who resided in legally positive states. For example, Janis and Laura, a married, white lesbian couple, live in a legally positive state and were interested in using known donor sperm in a fertility clinic setting. They were told that they would need to pay additional money to quarantine the sperm prior to use because they were not sexual partners with the donor. They objected that this provided a burden in the form of time and expense that they believed would not be felt by a heterosexual couple that was not using donor sperm. As Laura explained: "If we had been a straight couple who had just met each other and wanted to have kids, they would have helped us. Which is what we were angry about.

We actually protested that and had a whole process of writing petitions to their practice and sent it to their lawyers and their lawyers said no, it has to be quarantined." This perception of unfair treatment in relation to a heterosexual couple, who perhaps had less commitment to each other, provoked the pursuit of a legal remedy for this couple. Although unsuccessful in obtaining their desired outcome, they nonetheless took action to alter a policy that created barriers to their family goals.

Even in cases where participants believed that they might be able to challenge an unfair law or practice, they sometimes felt that a legal battle conflicted with their ultimate family goals and thus was not worth pursuing. For example, Maxine and Allison, a married, white lesbian couple, were going through the process of Maxine completing a second-parent adoption of their child in a legally positive state. During the process, they faced an unexpected obstacle when the judge required them to marry prior to completing the adoption. As Allison recalled, this caused her to contemplate pursuing a legal challenge:

> Like, I have no idea if it was the judge and just his personal view that people should be married when they have children, or if there was a legal basis to what he was saying, like, "I can't approve this adoption unless you guys are married." . . . I'm really curious about what would have happened if we had had a more experienced lawyer and if we would have tried to fight it. But again, Maxine was very uncomfortable with not having done the adoption so we just did whatever we needed to do to make it go faster. But if I had the time and the money to make political statements, I'm pretty curious about what would have happened. I'm just curious if the judge was holding to a moral code or if it is actually law.

Allison was suspicious of the legitimacy of the judge's requirement that they marry, and the couple had not intended to marry otherwise. Rather than find another lawyer and pursue a legal challenge, however, Maxine's need to have the adoption completed in order to solidify her relationship with their child took precedence. A cost-benefit analysis such as this might serve to explain, in part, the relative absence of more traditional legal challenges to perceived unfair laws. For LGBT parents who perceive some avenue to achieve their family goals, the potential costs of resistance might appear to be too high.

Overall, one might view the lack of appeal to formal legal channels as a reflection of a lack of faith in the law. In particular, the lack of reliance on formal legal challenges could signal a rejection of the moral authority of a legal system that many perceive to be simply a product of a heteronormative society in which LGBT families are viewed as unequal. If individuals feel that pursuing a remedy through the legal system is unlikely to result in the desired outcome, then there is little motivation to go through the time and expense of challenging an unfair practice. The fact that the majority of appeals to formal law occur in states that have a more positive legal environment for LGBT families lends further support to this interpretation, given that individuals in friendlier legal environments might be more apt to view the legal system as a potentially effective route for change.

Rejecting the Law

Some participants skirted the line of legality without outright rejecting its authority. For instance, individuals who assumed the single, heterosexual role for adoption were hesitant to lie outright, yet nonetheless chose to present their relationships in an ambiguous manner or to avoid the issue of heterosexuality. For example, Keith, a white, gay man in his forties, was adopting as a single dad in a legally neutral state. He indicated that his sexual orientation was never raised during the process, perhaps because he was single, but if it had been an issue he would have presented himself as single and straight. Laughing, he said: "Yeah, I would have done that! Put my butch cap on, and gone in there. . . . Yes, I would have duped the system. Definitely. I pay my taxes, so . . ." Although he said he would have "duped the system" and expressed almost an entitlement to do so in his comment regarding taxes, he ultimately gave a response similar to many of our other participants who presented themselves as single and straight—they would perform heterosexuality, but would not necessarily lie outright in order to achieve adoption. Approximately 8 percent of our participants, however, reported conscious and blatant violations of legal requirements in connection with their families. When they did occur, they were typically minor in nature—consisting of ignoring administrative procedures or misrepresenting qualifications in order to gain access to rights or benefits.

For example, Theresa, a single, white lesbian in her thirties living in a legally neutral state, recounted a story about good friends who misrepresented their residence in order to gain access to second-parent adoption:

> We had good friends going through [second-parent adoption] at the same time who were living in an apartment complex in [a state without second-parent adoption], but they really wanted to stay there because they had limited financial needs. . . . They set up an address in [a neighboring state that permitted second-parent adoption], and I know for a fact that they didn't reside there permanently full time. They may have spent some nights there and they got mail there. They got legal correspondence there and their adoption went through and they moved out of the state.

Misrepresenting a legal residence in order to gain access to legal rights signals a willingness to take on a certain degree of risk in order to attain familial benefits. While arguably similar to parents misrepresenting a legal residence in order to gain access to a preferred school for their child, this particular misrepresentation is perhaps riskier because it is more tangibly tied to parental rights over the child. Second-parent adoption is undertaken by most participants in order to secure rights for the nonbiological or nonadoptive parent. However, in cases where the rights were obtained through subterfuge, the adoption perhaps becomes more tenuous. This fact likely accounts for the rarity of our participants in reporting the use of misrepresentations or subterfuge to obtain parental rights or custody. As cited by some of our participants in our discussion of presenting themselves as single or heterosexual, there is a fear not just of being caught but of risking claims to the child as a result. In instances of second-parent adoption, however, where the alternative is no legal claim over the child, the risk might be viewed as worthwhile.

Similarly, four of our participants who engaged in international adoption reported following norms regarding bribery or other black market activities that were part of adoption within the particular country. For example, Pamela and Louise, a married, white lesbian couple, adopted from a Eurasian country and described the manner in which they were expected to bring bribes to the orphanage. Pamela recalled: "Remember the bribes? So each time you went, you had to bring stuff to the orphanage. I had to bring clothes. I had to buy cigarettes, which nearly killed me to have to buy cigarettes. Diapers. You know, so you had to bring stuff. . . . You don't tip in money, you tip in stuff."

Other participants reported avoiding legality in order to have children in ways that rejected legal authority and were, perhaps, violations of the law. For example, Ben and his partner had children through surrogacy and did not have a legal surrogacy contract. They were attempting to avoid the legal system in terms of filing birth certificate records with the local court. At the time their twin children were born, they were unable to take them from the hospital because they did not have a birth certificate naming them as parents and hospital regulations would not release the children in the absence of a birth certificate. In order to be able to take the children home, Ben explained that "[the surrogate] took the babies out the front door and put them in our car." This telling of the bypassing of hospital regulations suggested a deliberate decision to reject legality by circumventing policies.

Rhonda, a partnered, Hispanic lesbian in her thirties who resides in a legally neutral state, detailed the manner in which many lesbians sold or distributed fertility drugs illegally in order to assist others in achieving pregnancy. She described the way in which medications were distributed through an online forum connected with a cryobank, stating: "People have leftover [fertility medication], and it's totally illegal to sell prescription drugs not through people who do it. That's the one thing I found, in this whole underworld, I found that people want a baby so much they will help each other out. You get pregnant with the medication and people would sell out or people would give stuff away." This was not the only instance of participants describing violations of the law undertaken to facilitate the family goals of other individuals. For example, Yanni, is a single, white queer woman in her thirties living in a legally positive state and a self-described anarchist. She disclosed: "I'm a doula, so I've done home birth and water birth for seventeen years. And so I've been delivering babies in homes, knowing that it's totally illegal." Although this was a career, rather than a purely altruistic endeavor, she describes the law as "cumbersome" as it relates to her "advocacy work for woman and children. Lactation, home birth, all of it." Her story, much like Rhonda's, indicates the willingness to violate the law on matters related to other people's family goals—even if not when it comes to one's own family.

Conclusion

Approximately 50 percent of our participants engaged in acts of everyday resistance to perceived injustices, such as following the letter of the law but not the intent, masquerading as single and/or heterosexual to achieve goals, and modifying legal or administrative documents. These everyday acts of resistance primarily function to assist individuals in achieving family goals, but are arguably less effective in transforming legality via resistance.

Much as Hull (2003) found in her study of LGBT couples contemplating commitment ceremonies, we find that LGBT parents rarely reject legality entirely—even when they express resentment or dissatisfaction about the way in which the law provides for their families. A few of our participants, however, did engage in more overt legal challenges or disregard of the law. These forms of resistance were undertaken more so when individuals perceived little risk to their family goals. For example, parents might challenge law or procedures when residing in a legally positive state in which a favorable outcome was more likely. Further, they might do so when pushing for second-parent adoption, given that they began from a place of no rights over their child; this meant that they had much to gain, and little to lose, in challenging or disregarding the law.

In addition, participants might be more willing to disregard the law or to engage in perceived illegal activities in order to assist other individuals with forming their families. This willingness to do so for other individuals suggests that willful violations of the law might be viewed by some participants as part of a collective action that challenges the legitimacy of legal obstacles to their family goals. These challenges occurred, however, after the participants had secured their own family outcomes—either after they had their children or after they had finalized marriage or adoption. In these cases, they were perhaps more willing to take risks to challenge perceived unfair laws because they were able to shift from a focus on individual claims and toward a collective mentality.

These findings suggest that, for most, the desire to formally challenge legality was offset by the potential for delays or barriers to their family plans that could result from challenges. The hesitancy to challenge the law in this manner, thus, does not necessarily signal that participants respected the authority or legitimacy of the law. Rather, participants, un-surprisingly, prioritized family protection over advocacy work or legal challenges, in manners ranging from small everyday acts to larger legal challenges. For example, Tabitha, a single, white lesbian in her fifties residing in a legally negative state, observed: "I will tell you, now that I have a child, I don't put any rainbow paraphernalia on my car because I have a child. His safety is more important than me waving my little rainbow flag." Similarly, Jacquelyn explained the manner in which she weighed risks to her family before deciding to challenge the law, stating: "I feel like I've certainly broken the law plenty and I'm not worried about it. Especially at this point in my life, I'm concerned with the security of myself and my family and I'm not going to do anything . . . with dis-regard for the law with knowledge that there would probably be really damaging consequences. To the extent that I feel like there's not going to be a legal consequence, I'm not concerned at all." Jacquelyn, much like Tabitha, indicated that she has become less likely to challenge the law since she has become a parent. These concerns regarding potential harm to one's family are powerful deterrents to challenging legality for LGBT parents, contributing toward few of our participants knowingly violating the law when forming their own families.

Participants engaged in resistance practices closely mirrored the overall sample characteristics with respect to gender and race/ethnicity. Compared to the sample, however, this group was disproportionately less married (30 percent vs. 43 percent) and more partnered (52 percent vs. 43 percent) and single (17 percent vs. 14 percent). This pattern could signal that those who have pursued legal marriage are less likely to reject law in other aspects of their lives, and are more likely to view the law as legitimate. In addition, individuals with legal marriage might be less likely to encounter obstacles in which they must enact resistance than those who are partnered or single (see Hull 2003, 2006 for a similar discussion regarding the reciprocal relationship between marriage and legal consciousness for LGBT individuals).

With regard to legal context, we found that participants who ex-pressed resistance or rejection of legality were somewhat disproportion-ately overrepresented in legally neutral states (38 percent as compared to 34 percent of the overall sample) and legally positive states (34 percent compared to 33 percent), and underrepresented in legally negative states

(28 percent as compared to 34 percent). A friendlier legal and sociopolitical environment is less likely to produce the need to engage in some of the resistance practices we identified, yet we still see that individuals in legally positive states discussed engaging in many of these practices. In some respects, however, it is more surprising that participants in legally negative states are underrepresented in this group, given that the lack of legal protections could generate more instances in which resistance practices would be contemplated. Residing in a state that is more overtly hostile to LGBT parents, however, could produce greater caution in engaging in acts of resistance that might endanger the family.

In legally neutral states, however, LGBT parents might feel more empowered to engage in resistance due to greater ambiguity in the legal environment. This ambiguity could provoke more "testing" of legal limits through resistance practices than the more clearly defined legality of a negative state. Nonetheless, as we describe in the following paragraphs, there is variation in this pattern across types of resistance practices, with some being more common in legally negative or legally positive states.

Participants who described "secret adoptions" were overwhelmingly located in legally negative states (75 percent); in addition, approximately 25 percent were located in legally neutral states and none in legally positive states. In legally positive or legally neutral states, forum shopping sometimes occurred as part of second-parent adoptions (see chapter 5), but this was viewed as a legitimate strategy of manipulating the law to achieve favorable outcomes. By contrast, those involved in more secretive second-parent adoptions were engaged in a practice that they understood to be in violation of, at the very least, the intent of state adoption laws. Their discussion about forum shopping, therefore, involved secrecy and fear which was not present in the forum shopping stories we discuss in chapter 5. Given that these participants were overwhelmingly located in legally negative states, where LGBT parenting laws were not in their favor, their understanding that they were subverting the law makes sense. Their embeddedness within an oppositional sociopolitical environment engendered a skepticism regarding any route by which the law might assist them in achieving rights over their children. These participants were mostly women and mostly white, but in keeping with the overall sample characteristics. Married participants were underrepresented, at 25 percent, whereas partnered (50 percent) and single (25 percent) were overrepresented in this group. This is probably tied to legal context, where married participants are more likely to reside in legally positive states and second-parent adoptions are often also overtly legal. The need for secrecy in forum shopping, therefore, is relatively absent in legally positive states.

Participants who relied on rule literalness to attain unexpected health benefits were small in number, making it difficult to observe patterns in their demographic characteristics or legal context. Significantly, however, this group was almost entirely women; this can be explained by the fact that participants were typically accessing fertility treatments or services.

Approximately 50 percent of the group of participants who selected favorable social workers were located in legally neutral states, with 25 percent each in legally positive and legally negative states. Within legally positive states, participants expressed fewer concerns about the manner in which social workers described their families. In legally neutral states, by contrast, participants seemed to feel there was more ambiguity in their outcome and that having a social worker put the right spin on their home study was important. In terms of individual demographics, gender and race/ethnicity closely mirrored that of the sample. Marital status, however, was important within this group, which was comprised of 75 percent partnered individuals. Individuals who are legally married face difficulty in obscuring the nature of their relationship in a home study; individuals who are single are less likely to need to do so, given that they are not residing with a partner. Thus, partnered individuals are overwhelmingly those who find selecting the right social worker to be an important component of their family plans.

Approximately 45 percent of participants masquerading as single were located in legally neutral states, 40 percent in legally positive states, and 15 percent in legally negative states. Those in legally neutral states might be overrepresented in the group masquerading as single due to the perception that their adoption outcome is uncertain and masking their relationship to their partner can improve chances of success. Those located in legally positive states were almost exclusively engaged in international adoption, where identifying as single was typically mandatory; outside of the international adoption context, most participants in legally positive states expressed less concern about masking their sexuality or relationships with their partners. The low proportion of individuals located in legally negative states who masquerade as single is perhaps surprising, given that adoption as single individuals would seem to be a promising approach for family formation within these states. The relative absence of individuals discussing this approach could be an artifact of our particular sample, or could indicate that individuals are less likely to frame their single adoptions in resistance terms within legally negative states. Participants who more overtly rejected their sexuality, however, *were* located in legally negative states, which reflects the requirement in some of these states to make a statement of heterosexuality in order to adopt.

Much like with those selecting social workers, the group of individuals masquerading as single is disproportionately partnered. When individuals are married, it is more difficult to present as single, as expressed by some of our married participants contemplating international adoption. The gender composition of this group mirrored that of the overall sample, but the group was less white than the overall sample. Approximately 28 percent of individuals in this group were nonwhite, with Hispanics standing out as particularly likely to masquerade as single. Nonwhite participants might feel more compelled to masquerade as single as a strategy to navigate multiple stigmatized identities during the adoption process.

Participants modifying documents were fairly evenly distributed across legal contexts, with 30 percent in legally negative states, 30 percent in legally positive states, and 40 percent in legally neutral states. Participants were overrepresented from legally neutral states and slightly underrepresented from legally positive and legally negative states, but overall this pattern suggests that document modification is not strongly linked to a particular legal context. LGBT parents residing in all types of states encounter documents that do not fit their family structure, provoking modifications. In addition, the group of participants that discussed modifying documents was 90 percent women and 90 percent white.

Almost two-thirds of participants who rejected the heteronormativity of the law as part of their family formation were located in legally neutral states, with 24 percent in legally positive and 10 percent in legally negative states. Those residing in legally neutral states were overwhelmingly more likely to describe creative strategies to form their families, or to compare their situation to that of a straight couple in evaluating their legal choices. Approximately 90 percent of the participants in this group were women, which reflects in part that women are able to implement more creative family formation options via insemination. In addition, this group was disproportionately single (45 percent), 20 percent were married, and 35 percent were partnered. Married participants seem to be less likely to reject the heteronormativity of the law, which could be tied to the manner in which many married participants choose legal marriage out of recognition of the power tied with heteronormative marriage. Single individuals, by contrast, might be more likely to reject legal heteronormativity due to their lived experiences of being single and being excluded from some of the benefits of legal marriage.

Our last two groups of participants involved individuals who engaged in more traditional challenges of the law. The first group challenged unfair practices; these individuals were overwhelmingly located in legally positive states at 70 percent, with 15 percent each in legally neutral and legally negative states. It is perhaps ironic that those who are most likely to challenge unfair practices are those with the greatest current protection. These participants in legally positive states, however, appeared to have expectations of better treatment and felt that their legal environment would support them if they made a direct challenge. The gender and race/ethnicity of this group mirrored that of the overall sample. However, with 72 percent married and only 28 percent partnered, the group had disproportionately more married couples than the overall sample. This combination of legal marriage and residing in a legally positive state could generate greater empowerment to make demands of the legal system.

Participants who rejected legality were overwhelmingly in legally neutral states, at 75 percent, with 25 percent in legally positive and none in legally negative states. One might expect that those in legally negative states would be most apt to reject legality in their family lives, given that they might have the least to lose in terms of other legal protections. Nonetheless, participants in legally negative states seemed cautious about engaging in actions that might subject their families to punishment. Their nesting within a seemingly hostile environment rendered them hesitant to engage in direct opposition to legality. Of those who did reject legality, approximately 50 percent were men and 50 percent women; men were, then, disproportionately overrepresented in this group. Men might be more likely to engage in direct opposition to the law, or might be more likely to talk about their interactions with legality in a fashion reflecting direct opposition. In addition, married individuals were underrepresented in this group, with 15 percent being married, 70 percent partnered, and 15 percent single. The choice of legal marriage often signals at least some willingness to work within the legal system; thus, married participants might be unlikely to outwardly reject legality. Further, the relationship between legal marriage and an overall positive legal environment likely produces less conflict with legality, which serves to discourage a rejection of the law.

Overall, the willingness to engage in acts of resistance or rejection of the law appears to be shaped primarily by legal context and marital status (and the relationship that exists between the two). In addition, the ability to call upon social networks to gain access to information about secret adoptions, favorable social workers, or ways in which to present oneself as single proved particularly pertinent for this group of participants. Further, interactions with administrative workers served to shape whether and how participants would engage in resistance.

Next, we conclude by taking a closer look at how interactions across legal context, demographic characteristics, and mediators like social networks and legal actors work together to shape the legal consciousness of LGBT parents.

Conclusion

LGBT Parents Constructing Legality

Everybody we knew did [second-parent adoption] in [the legally positive state we used to live in]. But when we moved here, we realized there were a lot of lesbians and plenty with kids, but [second-parent adoption] wasn't something that people talked about as crucial. That makes sense in this cognitive dissonance way. Why would you say that this is really necessary if it's outside the realm of possibility for you?
—Theresa

For LGBT parents, legal consciousness is constructed through complex interactions that occur between circulating discourses about the law, legal context, mediating factors like social networks, and individual desires and resources. Our participants' stories reveal the manner in which these factors intertwine to produce outcomes for an individual, with legal context emerging as an important determinant of how LGBT individuals form understandings about the role that the law can or should play in their families. As exemplified by Theresa, quoted at the introduction to this chapter, participants' ideas about what they want or need from the law with regard to their families is largely formed by the sociolegal environment in which they are embedded. When second-parent adoption is unavailable, for example, individuals are less likely to view it as a necessary component for forming families or parenting. They are unlikely to move in order to attain this right, or to defer childrearing until they can access second-parent adoption in another jurisdiction. Rather, they proceed with family formation and parenting by utilizing the resources and legal mechanisms that are available to them.

This does not mean that LGBT parents living in less friendly legal environments are unaffected by their lack of access to many legal rights.

As shown in chapters 5 and 6, participants residing in legally neutral or legally negative states are often powerfully aware of the manner in which their families are disadvantaged as a result of their sociolegal context. But the available social, political, or legal rights serve to shape expectations about what family formation and parenting entails for LGBT individuals. Accordingly, in jurisdictions that lack many of these rights, the notion of what is *necessary* is often modified to align with what is *possible*.

In this conclusion, we examine these ideas more closely by presenting an overview of our key substantive findings regarding how LGBT individuals navigate and construct legality related to their families. We then describe the theory that has emerged from our research that explains the manner in which legal consciousness is constructed for LGBT parents. We finish by exploring the contributions of our findings to sociolegal research and for policy surrounding LGBT families and the law.

Overview of Key Substantive Findings

Despite their unique position as persons often centered outside of the heteronormative legal structure, we find that larger cultural discourses about the law are not significantly modified by LGBT parents. Rather, discourses regarding the law as a just arbiter, a meaning-making system, and a creator of rights and privileges are supported and reaffirmed by many living in legally positive or neutral states. For example, participants evoked a "before the law" consciousness in the way in which they viewed the law as making families or relationships, such as generating a parent or spouse identity. Further, they described the law as creating commitments that were otherwise lacking, or signaling that their families were valued or deemed legitimate by those in power. These ideas emphasize the manner in which the law is understood as having the unique ability to confer identities and legitimacy, rather than simply to grant legal rights or privileges. The law is powerful, in this respect, and a force that is located external to the individual.

Our participants also described a "with the law" legal consciousness through which they viewed or used the law as if it was contingent, malleable, and "a game." Employed by individuals located across all legal contexts, playing the game was used as a means by which to navigate obstacles by working within the legal system rather than through challenges to the system. Participants described forum shopping for friendly jurisdictions or judges for adoption, as well as forum shopping for children (e.g., adopting from other jurisdictions). They also employed strategies such as finding workarounds that mimicked the legal rights they wished to achieve or accessing heteronormative legal privilege. Further, many marshaled their resources—including attorneys, the ability to read or decipher the law, social networks, or a persistent personality—in order to achieve family goals. Although playing the system was described in all legal contexts, those living in legally neutral states were more likely to rely on a variety of such practices; this appeared to result from not having access to clear-cut laws that either guaranteed or prohibited their desired outcomes. Finding the right jurisdiction or judge, or having the ability to access resources such as a good attorney or a social network, was imperative in these states where legal outcomes were uncertain.

Although many participants in legally neutral or legally negative states expressed resentment of the law, they engaged in little collective action that eschewed legal authority or sought to disable or dismantle an oppressive system. In this respect, there appears to be a mismatch between individuals' awareness of oppression and their behavior in response to that oppression (Wilson 2011; Collins 1986). Oppressed persons' behavior might be outwardly conforming, but more covertly resistant. This was the case for many of our participants, who engaged in everyday acts of resistance more so than formal legal challenges. These acts of resistance primarily involved technically adhering to the law while using it in an unintended manner; masquerading as single or heterosexual or both; or modifying documents. These acts were more common for those residing in legally neutral states. The sociolegal environment in such states produced a simultaneous resentment of the legal condition, along with a perceived need to remain at least superficially cooperative in order to achieve family objectives.

Challenges of oppression or perceived unfair practices were rare and, when they occurred, they focused more on achieving individual family goals rather than group victories. Relatedly, those who chose not to pursue formal legal challenges often referenced a fear of compromising their ultimate family goals for a momentary legal victory. The limited reporting of outright challenges is, thus, influenced in part by concern for one's family. As Kimberly, a married, white lesbian in her thirties living in a legally positive state, explained: "It's vulnerable to be a gay family and it's especially so with a child. You want to protect your kid as much as you can." When law can be safely invoked in order to reduce perceived vulnerabilities, such as through second-parent adoptions, participants do so—particularly those located in legally friendly jurisdictions. However, participants consciously chose to avoid many formal legal interactions or challenges due to this same desire to protect their children and their family goals. For this reason, those who reside in legally negative or legally neutral (but negative-leaning) states are hesitant to pursue legal challenges or place themselves within a legally vulnerable position because they remain much less certain about the likely outcome. These findings are similar to those of other legal consciousness studies that found that oppressed groups might favor more covert resistance tactics in order to avoid being perceived as a threat to the legal or political system (see, e.g., Chua 2012; Fritsvold 2009).

Our participants' experiences indicate that LGBT parents face obstacles because they defy the manner in which the law has constructed family and parent-child relationships. Simultaneously, however, many perceived that they acquire rights and legitimacy primarily through seeking legal recognition of their family by referencing and appealing to heteronormative legal standards. Family rights, including same-sex marriage and parenting rights, are thus pursued within a system of oppression and (largely) through the language and definitions of oppression. Through this approach, LGBT parents are ultimately subject to the legal system to define who they are in relation to their child and what rights they might have, rather than engaging in collective resistance that expresses a rejection of legality in their family lives.

Hull (2003) questioned whether "the concept of resistant legal consciousness [should] be refined to allow for the fact that actors may be 'against the law' in important ways but at the same time embrace rather than reject legality as part of their resistance." By contrast, Fritsvold (2009) coined the term "under the law" to refer to individuals who went beyond resistance and engaged in a true rejection of legality in their lives due to its grounding in an illegitimate and corrupt social order. This quandary is much the same as that raised by critical legal scholars regarding the use of the formal legal system by civil rights activists, or other oppressed persons, as a mechanism for social justice (Albiston 1999; Crenshaw 1995). To achieve change, actors often pursue individual victories by operating within the system of oppression, rather than rejecting this system, turning it on its head, and focusing on systemic change.

Although our participants primarily engaged in smaller acts of resistance rather than outright challenges or defiance of the law, these small acts of resistance were not pointless endeavors. As observed in prior legal consciousness studies (Chua 2012; Ewick and Silbey 1998; Sarat 1990), acts of resistance can be mechanisms to reclaim dignity, exact revenge, or to more directly avoid the law's costs for an individual. These forms of resistance, particularly upon the retelling of them, can act as incremental changes for the individual and those within the individual's social network. Further, when oppressed persons resist external definitions of their identities and their life experiences and make choices that reflect their self-definition, their "everyday life might be resistance" (Collins 1986). In this respect, the manner in which many of our participants resisted heteronormative family definitions in forming their families arguably rendered their everyday parenting a form of resistance.

Theory of LGBT Parents and Legal Consciousness

Our interviews with LGBT parents highlight a number of important factors in the construction of legal consciousness, or how individuals engage in the process of "doing law." Cultural discourse regarding the law is varied and conflicting, communicating notions of an immutable, legitimate, and objective authority; a malleable doctrine that is subject to human agency and that can be used by those with resources to achieve their ends; and an oppressive tool of those in power which must be resisted and, perhaps, altered (Silbey 2005; Ewick and Silbey 1998). LGBT parents, like most individuals in the United States, are recipients of all three of these types of messages about the law. They might accept, reject, or modify these ideas about law as part of the process of forming families or parenting.

As reflected in figure C.1, we found that LGBT parents take circulating cultural discourses and accept or modify them based upon (a) legal context (residing in a legally positive, neutral, or negative state);

(b) influences from mediating factors, including social networks, organizational or administrative resources, the media, and legal actors; and (c) individual factors, including individual parenting desires and demographic characteristics.

All three of these categories work in an interactive fashion. For example, the manner in which legal actors, such as attorneys and judges, affect LGBT parents' understandings of and interactions with the law is dependent on legal context. Accordingly, whether those interactions serve to reaffirm cultural ideas about the law as an objective definer of truths or as a tool of oppression is affected by legal context. Similarly, an individual's particular family desires are shaped by the existing legal environment within their state, as well as by mediating factors such as social networks (e.g., the routes to parenthood taken by friends or colleagues).

The manner in which dominant cultural schemas about the law are filtered and modified by legal context, mediating factors, and individual-level factors, constructs the legal consciousness of LGBT parents. In this respect, legal consciousness is a product of being acted upon by forces external to the individual, as well as something that is derived from the individual. Accordingly, LGBT parents are not simply powerless subjects of legality, but rather are participants in the construction of legality as it pertains to their family.

LGBT parents may apply differing weights to all of these categories, and these weights can be situational and vary for a single individual. As a result, the cultural discourse about legality that prevails at a particular moment or for a particular individual is adaptable. Much as prior legal scholars have observed, legal consciousness is not one size fits all (see, e.g., Ewick and Silbey 1998; Sarat 1990). Legal consciousness is affected by events and interactions, and thus it is "plural and variable across contexts" (Ewick and Silbey 1998, 50). In the following sections, we take a closer look at each of these categories to examine the manner in which they work in conjunction to produce legal consciousness.

Legal Context

Given the variability in laws and climate for LGBT parents across the United States, we were able to examine the manner in which legal

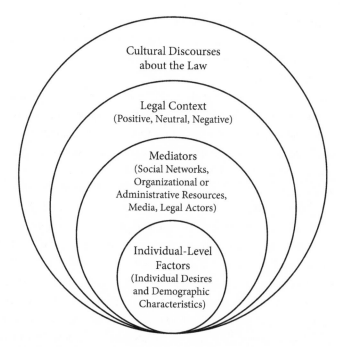

Figure C.1. Emergent theory regarding LGBT parents and legal consciousness

context plays a role in shaping legal consciousness for LGBT parents. In this section, we first trace the ways in which legal context produced differing outcomes for our participants across all three schemas (before, with, and against the law). We then explore, in greater detail, the manner in which our participants discussed the role that legal context played in shaping their interactions with the law with respect to their families.

LEGALLY POSITIVE STATES

Approximately 33 percent of our sample resides in a legally positive state. Our findings paint a picture of how a legally positive environment might shape legal consciousness for LGBT parents. Much as within legally negative or neutral contexts, participants located in legally positive states most commonly expressed sentiments aligned with viewing the law as a game or something that can be manipulated (see chapter 5). Approximately equal numbers of participants in legally positive states communicated acts of resistance related to the law (see chapter 6), or understanding the law as legitimate or a meaning-maker (see chapter 4). Participants in legally positive states, however, represented almost half of those individuals who viewed the law as legitimate or meaning-making (see chapter 4).

Marriage appeared to serve as an important shaper of legal conscious-ness for participants in legally positive states. This was likely attributable both to the availability of legal marriage in some legally positive states and to a friendly sociopolitical environment that perhaps encouraged partici-pants to marry elsewhere. Those who presented a "before the law" under-standing of legality often tied this belief strongly to the role of marriage in creating family identities or as a legitimator of families. In addition, participants located in legally positive states were most apt to articulate a feeling that the state cared about their families, or had their interests at heart. These feelings were intertwined with the measures that the states had taken to protect their families through overt legislation or positive legal decisions, but they extended beyond scenarios that involved direct interactions with formal law. Participants in legally positive states, overall, were most likely to feel that their families were protected and that they would be supported if they needed to challenge unfriendly practices.

These sentiments of the law or institutional structures being more "on their side" appeared to translate into the ways in which individuals in legally positive states played the legal game (see chapter 5). Partici-pants in these states seemed to feel more confident in their capacity to manipulate the legal system and emerge successful; this was seen in the ways in which they discussed the ability to use socioeconomic status or legal knowledge to garner positive outcomes for their families. Their nesting within an overall privileged environment (as compared to those LGBT parents in other legal contexts), fostered a sense of entitlement in some respects.

This sense of entitlement to a positive legal outcome was seen in some of the resistance tactics employed by individuals living in legally posi-tive states (see chapter 6). The majority of participants who made direct challenges to unfair practices were located in legally positive states, sug-gesting that their overall sense of security related to their families could lay the groundwork for challenging unequal treatment. Notably, such challenges were still rare within legally positive states. The precarious situation of LGBT families throughout the country was still frequently articulated by those within legally positive states. These individuals, however, were more likely to voice exercising legal options to try to offset some of these potential threats (e.g., second-parent adoption by those who are legally married as "extra security").

Many of the potential threats that concerned participants in legally positive states were those located outside of their legal context. For example, participants in legally positive states who reported masquerading as single were overwhelmingly doing so when engaged in adoption from less friendly states or internationally. Those who were legally married and also chose to engage in second-parent adoption frequently reported doing so out of fear that their marriages (and their claims to a parental relationship) would not be recognized when they crossed outside of their state. Accordingly, while participants living in legally positive states expressed elements of all three legal schemas, the manner in which their beliefs about the law translated into action were very much shaped by their relative sense of security within their state.

LEGALLY NEUTRAL STATES

Approximately 34 percent of our sample resides in legally neutral states. The greatest number of individuals living in legally neutral states treated the law like a game or something that could be manipulated (see chapter 5), but this was closely followed by those who engaged in everyday resistance tactics (see chapter 6). The fewest participants in legally neutral states articulated interactions with the law as a legitimate authority or a meaning-maker; however, participants from neutral states comprised the majority of those who *did* voice this particular viewpoint about the law (see chapter 4). Overall, participants in legally neutral states appeared to respond to the more ambiguous legal environment in which they were nested—where many family options were neither expressly permitted nor prohibited—by engaging in tactics to manipulate the law in their favor when possible, or to reject perceived legal limitations by engaging in resistance tactics. Unlike in legally positive or legally negative states, the uncertainty over legal outcomes generated more impetus to explore possible ways of working with or against the law in order to move the needle in our participants' favor.

Although the notion of the law as a legitimate source of authority was rare for our participants as a whole, participants from legally neutral states comprised over half of those in this group. They were particularly likely, compared to those in other states, to discuss the law as a source of commitment—either between partners or as a sign of commitment between parent and child. In addition, participants in a neutral legal context, as compared to those in other states, were more likely to talk about the law as something that they must adhere to because "it's the law," even in instances where the law was unfavorable to their families. This acknowledgment of the constraints of the law was articulated with a certain respect for the law as an authority source, rather than as simply a constraint that could not be bypassed (as voiced by those engaged in resistance practices).

The more uncertain nature of the legal environment in legally neutral states translated into participants recognizing the importance of manipulating legal outcomes in their favor. The use of creative approaches to interacting with the law was particularly emphasized by those living in these environments. For example, almost two-thirds of participants who engaged in forum shopping for friendly judges or jurisdictions were located in legally neutral states. In these legal environments, adoptions or second-parent adoptions were legally permissible but, due to the more negative sociopolitical environments, participants knew that their outcomes relied on finding a favorable forum. Relatedly, participants in legally neutral states comprised almost three-quarters of those who discussed the importance of having a "good attorney" as a resource in playing the legal game. This is very much linked to the notion of manipulating legal outcomes in an ambiguous environment, given that attorneys might either be able to identify a favorable forum or generate creative documents for their clients. In addition, participants in legally neutral states reflected this understanding of the law as uncertain and something that can be manipulated through their use of persistence to achieve legal victory. Although more common in legally negative states, participants in neutral states understood the importance of placing pressure on legal actors in order to bend outcomes in their favor.

Participants in legally neutral states were also disproportionately represented in the category of those who engaged in resistance tactics to achieve their family goals. Unlike legally negative states, where LGBT parents might expect to encounter backlash from acts of resistance, those in legally neutral states were more likely to test the legal waters via resistance. Participants in legally neutral states appeared to engage in resistance tactics that were designed to bypass legality, either by rejecting heteronormativity by engaging in creative approaches to family formation, or by masquerading as single or selecting social workers who would portray their family as single (e.g., portray the couple as roommates). In addition, three-quarters of participants who rejected legality in their family lives were located in legally neutral states. In all of these respects, participants who were engaged in resistance practices within legally neutral states were largely operating fairly quietly so as to avoid confronting the legal system and potentially learning that their family goals were impossible to attain.

Overall, those participants in legally neutral states expressed the most varied types of understandings and interactions with the law. Given the greater uncertainty about their legal environment, it is likely that their own demographics, social networks, or interactions with legal actors play a stronger role in shaping their ultimate understanding of the law in their family lives.

LEGALLY NEGATIVE STATES

Approximately 34 percent of our sample resides in legally negative states. Of those participants in legally negative states, the largest numbers treated the law as a game (see chapter 5); this pattern was similar to that of the other two legal contexts, where the "with the law" approach was also the most common. This, however, was closely followed by those engaging in everyday acts of resistance (see chapter 6). None of our participants in legally negative states articulated a view of the law as a legitimate authority or a meaning-maker (see chapter 4). This distinguishes participants in legally negative states from those in legally positive or neutral states, in that their expressed understandings of and interactions with the law are less varied and—predictably—less positive.

As compared to participants in other legal contexts, those in legally negative states were less likely to view the law as something that could be manipulated for one's benefit. At the same time, this understanding of the law was the most prevalent of the three articulated by those in legally negative states. In particular, participants in negative states were overrepresented among those who used heteronormative privilege (especially marriage) to access family goals. Further, over two-thirds of the transgender participants who discussed the use of heteronormative privilege resided in legally negative states. The manner in which these participants were able to call upon their marriages, even in a negative environment, to advance their family goals speaks to the power of heteronormative privilege across all contexts.

Participants in legally negative states were also overrepresented among those who used two particular resources to navigate legality with respect to their families: social networks and a persistent personality. Approximately two-thirds of participants who reported the use of social networks as a tool were located in legally negative states. This emphasizes the importance of access to individuals with the know-how or with powerful connections for those participants living in a legal environment in which their success is viewed as unlikely. Similarly, the majority of participants who reported using persistence as a legal tool were located in legally negative states. The understanding that they might be unlikely to achieve a family goal given their legal environment appeared to increase the likelihood that some participants in these states would apply pressure to achieve a desired outcome.

Although some participants in legally negative states reported using persistence to further their family goals, participants in legally negative states were overall less likely to engage in resistance practices or legal challenges than those in other legal contexts. Many participants in these states articulated concern regarding the potential backlash against their families if they were to participate in overt challenges to the law. Thus, while perhaps initially surprising that a negative legal environment does not produce more acts of resistance, it is understandable that these participants experience a greater sense of vulnerability regarding their families. Participants who engaged in "secret" second-parent adoptions were, however, overwhelmingly located in legally negative states. In contrast to those who forum shopped for friendly jurisdictions, these participants described second-parent adoption as an undercover operation and anticipated—and sometimes experienced—backlash if the adoptions were discovered. In addition, participants who masqueraded as single by overtly rejecting their sexuality (i.e., lying about their sexuality) were located in legally negative states. The secretive nature of resistance practices, then, in legally negative states was particularly salient.

Overall, those in legally negative states appeared to tread more carefully with respect to their relationship with the law. Their nesting in a negative legal and sociopolitical climate engendered a rejection of the notion that the law carries a moral legitimacy. This lack of respect for the law and for legal actors, however, created more caution than outright defiance. Concern for protecting one's children appeared to be the overarching deterrent for confrontation with the law.

LEGAL CONTEXT: A CLOSER LOOK

Elements of all three of the legal schemas were exhibited by LGBT parents across most legal contexts. In other words, residing in a legally positive state did not preclude individuals from enacting everyday resistance in a fashion reflecting an "against the law" consciousness. Nonetheless, our participants often linked legal context with rather distinct views of the law. This suggests that legal context tended to produce similar emotions regarding the law for LGBT families in each type of state, even while mediating and individual factors shaped the final interaction with the law. For example, Janet, a partnered, white lesbian in her thirties, described the way in which the negative environment in her state produced a sense of hopelessness and frustration with regard to the law:

> It just seems like things are going backward as a state, . . . as far as your rights. And it's really difficult now. Like I said, we don't have anything established with [my son] because, you know, there's nothing to establish. I could appoint [my partner as] guardian, but that could also be challenged by an outside party, like my mom. So yeah, it's very frustrating. . . . We've thought about the prospect of having to move someday just to make sure our family can stay intact. And I really don't see that changing. . . . The governor, he's going to override everything he can.

Janet's story communicates a common theme for those residing in legally negative states. LGBT parents in these environments often articulated feeling like their options were limited and that any attempt to create legal rights was subject to challenge. Similarly, for Katie, a married, white lesbian in her fifties, residing in a legally negative state determined whether she would even pursue greater information about her legal options. Although second-parent adoption would have been of benefit to her, when she was asked whether she investigated its availability, she responded: "We're in [this state]. I didn't have to investigate it." Where she lived was not simply a determinant of whether she in fact had available legal options. It also shaped whether she viewed the law as a potentially viable tool for her family, to the extent that she no longer felt that examining her legal options was worthwhile and assumed that the law was hostile to her family. In this respect, legal context can shape the ways in which LGBT parents choose to investigate, employ, or avoid the law in their family lives.

This feeling that the state was against one's family stood in contrast to sentiments articulated by those residing in legally positive states, who often voiced feelings of being insulated or protected due to their legal environments. For example, Laura, a married, white lesbian in her 40s who resides in a positive state explained: "We're so shielded here from kind of the culture wars. That's the main thing I feel about living here, is we just—We have health insurance coverage for our IVF, we had a gay lawyer who helped us navigate all the legal paperwork we needed before marriage became possible, then marriage became possible and we joined in. . . . So we don't feel super vulnerable, which is why these things don't matter to us so much." Residing in a legally positive state generated privilege for many LGBT parents like Laura. In particular, they often voiced a freedom from being at the mercy of the legal system (see chapter 5). This freedom allowed LGBT parents in these states to navigate legality with greater confidence of their success, pushing them towards a respect for the law or a sense that the law could be manipulated for their benefit.

While those residing in legally negative or legally positive states overwhelmingly articulated certainty regarding their legal situation, those living in legally neutral states instead faced ambiguity that often engendered anxiety regarding their family's future. For example, Hannah, a partnered, white lesbian in her forties, described her conflicted feelings regarding second-parent adoption in her legally neutral state:

> Honestly, I'm grateful that we live in a state that has second-parent adoption. . . . I feel, though, that if push kind of came to shove, whereby Beth and I separated or something happened, that I could very well lose [our child] or have reduced rights. . . . And this is just the perception that I feel like, even though I am legally the second parent, that because of the state

that we live in, the climate that we live in, that my rights could be easily undermined or challenged or extinguished. Because of us being in a same-sex relationship, I'm not 100 percent sure that the law would protect me as a same-sex partner with a child. . . . I don't trust the climate under which our judges operate.

This tension between the technical availability of legal rights and a negative sociopolitical environment generated uncertainty regarding the permanence of one's family situation for many participants in legally neutral states. Although Hannah was able to obtain second-parent adoption by forum shopping for a favorable jurisdiction, the overall climate in her state was such that these rights seemed fragile. This legal ambiguity served to formulate conflicting relationships with the law for many residents of legally neutral states.

Several of our participants had moved from a legally positive state to a legally negative state, or vice versa. These experiences of living in more than one legal environment crystalized the way in which LGBT parents' legal consciousness is shaped by legal context. For example, Tina, a partnered, white lesbian in her thirties, described the manner in which residing in two states with very different legal environments provided her with a more nuanced understanding of how the law affects LGBT parents. Tina currently resides in a legally positive state, but once lived in a legally negative state. She explained:

I think that I'm very fortunate to have lived in two states when it comes to gay and lesbian parenting and the ways they're viewed. I think that [my current state] affords certainly the same civil liberties for parenting that anyone is afforded. I think the standard is the same across the board and very fair. I think in [my prior state], it is not. I read recently that in [that state] you are not allowed to say the word *gay* in the classroom; the legislation just passed. It's a state where there is discrimination in the constitution about who can and can't get married. And I know people who have hidden their sexuality in their quest to become parents, or [portrayed] the status of their relationship as being a roommate versus partner because of the fear of people taking legal action to take their kids from them. And I think that's a shitty thing. So I think there is a big discrepancy state to state to state.

Having lived in very different legal environments, Tina was very aware of the patchwork nature of LGBT parenting environments. She described herself as "fortunate" for having been exposed to these different types of legal structures. To some degree, having previously lived in an unfriendly environment made her more appreciative and less likely to question legality within her more positive state of residence.

Similarly, Mary Ann and Tara, a married, white lesbian couple, described how their prior legal environments affected their perception of legality within their state. They currently reside in a legally negative state, but previously Mary Ann lived in a positive state and Tara lived in a neutral state. These prior experiences had an effect on how they viewed their current legal environment and, accordingly, their understanding of whether and how the law might work for their family:

> MARY ANN: I come from a state where there are statewide human rights and they have expansive domestic partnership and hopefully soon they're going to have marriage. So coming here feels much more restrictive and adversarial with the legal system. . . .
>
> TARA: And I've never lived anywhere but the Midwest, so this is not really that much more restrictive than in other places I've lived. And you know, when I was in [another state], we passed statewide human rights. Well, now [that state] is in the news because they have an amendment up, right? To the constitution [to ban same-sex marriage]. So, you know, I have always known and always experienced that my family's legal safety and my legal safety could change.

For Mary Ann, coming from a legally positive environment to a more restrictive environment was oppressive; her exposure to this prior, friendly environment made her more cognizant of the ways in which options were foreclosed to her family within their present state. Tara, by contrast, was more accustomed to a less-than-friendly legal atmosphere. Her experience with the shifting legal status of gay individuals in her prior state heightened her awareness that the law is contingent and that her family's legal status was tenuous. These stories emphasize that context plays a complicated role in shaping an individual's understanding of whether and how to use the law. It is not simply the legal context within one's current state of residence, but how the environment might compare with legality encountered in other states that serves to produce legal consciousness.

Similarly, understanding that the law is dependent on context raised anxieties for many participants, as they realized that their legal situation might easily shift within another state. For example, many participants living in legally positive states described how they adopted their children through second-parent adoption, even though they were married and both parents were listed on the birth certificate. In cases like these, participants were aware that the parental rights of a nonbiological parent were seemingly derived from their marriage—a marriage that is not recognized in many states, and which might or might not actually confer parental rights to the nonbiological parent. Thus, the notion of traveling or moving outside of their state of residence raised fears. As described in chapter 5, this led some participants to adoption as an added measure of securing a defensible parent-child relationship. Dana and Alexandra, a married, white lesbian couple in their thirties, indicated that they felt compelled to go through second-parent adoption in order to make their children "portable," saying:

> So we were both on the birth certificate for both kids. So, in [our state] we were both parents to both children, but that's not a fully portable right. So we went ahead and did a second-parent adoption which I think at this point is legal in all states. . . . So that felt really important to us that we could feel like that the kids were portable anywhere. So, for instance, we could go to Colorado, which doesn't recognize our marriage, and still be parents to both kids in a way that we are sure would be recognized.

This idea of parental rights transforming as one crosses state lines was very salient to our participants, shaping their understanding and use of the law. For this couple, as with many others, the recognition of the contingent nature of the law led them to further bolster their legal claim through second-parent adoption. In this respect, they used second-parent adoption as an additional weapon against those who might challenge their relationship to their child. They "played the game" in this fashion as a result of the legal environment in their own state, which afforded greater rights than elsewhere, and the legal environments in other states. This patchwork legality plays a significant role in shaping legal consciousness for LGBT parents in a way that is not readily apparent for many other populations. Its rarity provides additional insight into how context interacts with other environmental or individual factors to produce legal consciousness for individuals.

Mediating Factors

Although legal context played an important role in shaping participants' understandings of the law, context does not operate in isolation. Rather, legality is often mediated by factors such as social networks, legal actors, media, and organizational or administrative actors. Our participants frequently referenced the manner in which these factors guided them toward a particular path to parenthood (see chapter 2), served as a source for legal information (see chapter 3), or interacted with their legal context and individual desires in order to produce legal consciousness (see chapters 4–6).

Social networks, administrative and organizational resources, and information received from the media served to reinforce, challenge, or modify legality derived from legal context. For example, being embedded in a social network can shape LGBT individuals' perceptions of what their family formation options might be (see chapter 3), or can serve as a resource for directing individuals toward a particularly friendly judge or agency (see chapter 5), or revealing "secret" loopholes for LGBT parents (see chapter 6). Individuals with access to these networks are sometimes able to navigate an unfriendly legal environment in a manner that those without networks cannot. Indeed, we found that approximately two-thirds of those participants who reported using social networks as a tool to achieve legal ends were located in legally negative states. This finding emphasizes the importance of social networks for identifying strategies to achieve family goals.

On an even more fundamental level, participants reported that social networks affected their perception regarding the legitimacy of their familial relationships. For example, participants indicated that their relationships were afforded greater respect following legal marriage, including from their family and friends (see chapter 4). For some participants, the beliefs of their family and friends regarding the significance of marriage or having children played a role in shaping decisions regarding family formation or marriage. These findings emphasize how social networks can serve to bolster or modify individual desires or legal context in the construction of legality.

In addition to social networks, interactions with legal actors proved important in determining whether and how LGBT parents would engage with the law. For example, participants reported being powerfully affected by hearing judges or other legal actors sanction their relationships with their partners or with their children (see chapter 4). Legal actors, in this respect, were understood as an extension of the state and the law; their approval of LGBT families often appeared to be embraced as a sign of a greater, systemic approval. Similarly, participants who encountered unfriendly or resistant legal actors or administrative officials often were further deterred from engaging with formal law or were less willing to assert perceived rights. For some participants, therefore, interactions with legal actors played an important role in shaping their views on the utility of the law for their family.

Attorneys were also vital legal actors for LGBT parents. Although not all participants consulted an attorney as part of their family formation process (see chapter 3), they nonetheless viewed attorneys as an important resource when confronting potential challenges to their families from relatives or outsiders, identifying friendly jurisdictions for second-parent adoption, or designing creative documents or approaches to mimic other legal rights (see chapters 3, 5, and 6). Attorneys, when called upon as a source of legal information, were powerful players in determining what was possible with regard to one's family.

MEDIATING FACTORS: A CLOSER LOOK

To highlight the manner in which these mediating factors affect the construction of legal consciousness, we focus on examples derived from interactions with legal actors. Several of our participants discussed how a particular administrative worker, judge, or attorney influenced their understandings of, or interactions with, the law. Jenny and Joyce, for example, are married, white lesbians in their thirties who reside in a legally negative state. They described the way in which they encountered resistance and hostility from the staff when Joyce went to change her name on her driver's license following their marriage:

JOYCE: Even when we got married, I was able to change my social security to my new name. But when I went with my new social security card and my marriage certificate to get my license, they said you can't do this—that document means nothing to us. Not even the fact that there is a legal name change on that document, because the document it is on is trash. She actually told me it was trash.

JENNY: People were like really rude to her, it was in front of the manager and everybody else out there. They made a big scene in front of everybody.

JOYCE: Yeah they made it a big thing. Yeah, so my social security number doesn't match my driver's license, which makes things very difficult for banking or credit stuff. It is just very difficult.

Following this interaction, Joyce made two other unsuccessful attempts to change her license. At that point, she gave up and accepted this additional obstacle in her life. They explained that Jenny was unsurprised by Joyce's experience and had, in fact, tried to warn her of the likely outcome:

JOYCE: The first time, I left crying I was so upset. It was the first time I'd experienced it. Jenny has experienced it so many times in her life. I've never experienced it. . . . I'd been previously married to a man for a very long time, so I never ever experienced anything like this. . . .

JENNY: I stayed in the car.

JOYCE: I was like, "Just come with me, just come with me."

JENNY: And I was like, "Un-uh." I knew what was coming. I knew she wasn't coming out with it.

This exchange reveals the ways in which legal context acts upon legal actors, shaping their interactions with LGBT individuals; in turn, LGBT individuals' expectations regarding legal actors are shaped by their prior experiences within this context. Joyce was not only repeatedly denied a name change on her license due to a lack of recognition of her marriage, but was publicly shamed and told her license was trash. Joyce's expectation that her marriage would be honored originated from her understanding of their marriage license as a powerful document, embodying legitimacy derived from legality. By contrast, Jenny's experience within this legal context as an openly lesbian woman had removed any pretenses that the law or legal actors were acting on their behalf. Instead, her experience had produced an expectation of oppression. In this respect, their interaction with the driver's license office reflected the interactions of legal context, legal actors, and individual experiences in producing legal consciousness.

Interactions with legal actors affected understandings and use of the law for individuals residing in positive states, as well as for those in negative or legally neutral states. For example, Ellis, who identifies as a married, white female-to-male transgender individual, explained how he encountered obstacles in changing his sex on his birth certificate when he was living in a legally positive state:

> When I was changing my birth certificate, I had gone online to the [state] courthouse to get their form to change my birth certificate and I printed their form and filled it out and brought it to their county clerk's office. And the woman said, "I don't know what this form is. I don't know what this is." And I've got all my stuff and I'm like, this is your form! This isn't my fault. But of course she didn't know what to do, so I had to come back another day. And these are the kind of things that keep people from engaging with the law in general, right? Like, I did all the right things. I brought everything that your website tells me to bring.

Much like Joyce, Ellis was stymied in his legal goals by the response he received from an administrative worker. He adhered to the guidelines and anticipated a favorable outcome, yet he was nonetheless unsuccessful in his initial attempt to change his name. Unlike Joyce, however, his interaction was understood to be largely a byproduct of a lack of familiarity with the form rather than outright hostility from legal actors. Ellis was frustrated by the process, but not so frustrated that he gave up. Instead, he returned and was ultimately successful.

In both cases, responses from administrative workers acted to discourage LGBT individuals from achieving their legal goals. But the context in which the participants were situated also shaped their interpretation of, and response to, these obstacles. Joyce ultimately succumbed and reached the same understanding as Jenny—that legal context and legal actors worked against their interests and, accordingly, she must acquiesce to the constraints imposed by the law upon her life. Ellis, by contrast, was not permanently deterred by his experience. Living within a more positive legal environment at that time, Ellis had a different interpretation of the exchange and was able to anticipate being ultimately successful in his endeavor. Accordingly, his understanding of whether the law could be a useful tool, despite resistance from legal actors, differed from that of Joyce and Jenny.

Individual Factors

Individual desires with respect to family differ, as well as the demographic and socioeconomic characteristics that shape individuals' capacity and willingness to engage with the law. As emphasized throughout this study, the ability to access the law is affected in part by factors such as sex, gender, marital status, socioeconomic status, and race/ethnicity. In addition, one's own family desires serve to shape whether or how individuals interact with the law. Those who wish to parent a biological child, for example, will approach legality with respect to their family formation in a different manner than those who prefer adoption (see chapter 2). Further, individuals who expressed fear of biological parents or other family members making claims to their children, also pursued family formation and legal rights differently from those without such concerns. Legality, therefore, is not devoid of individual human agency, but discourses about the law are modified by contextual, mediating, and individual factors and their interrelationships.

In this section, we first summarize key patterns regarding the relationships between individual demographic factors and legal consciousness. We then provide an overview of the ways in which individual factors interact with contextual and mediating factors in the construction of legality for LGBT parents.

MARITAL STATUS

Marital status played a role in shaping the approach that participants took in interacting with the law. For example, marital status proved particularly important for those who viewed the law as important for creating family identities or relationships, legitimating families, or establishing commitments (see chapter 4). In all of these cases, many participants likely sought out marriage because of their beliefs regarding the transformative power of the law. In addition, participants who were married reported feeling the powerful effects of legal marriage in terms of social recognition or perceived legitimacy of their relationship, even when they had not expected to experience a change from marriage. Married individuals were also overrepresented in the group of participants who viewed law as a game or something to be manipulated (see chapter 5). This could suggest that individuals who have this view of the law understood legal marriage as part of the "game" to gain access to rights.

By contrast, individuals who were legally married were underrepresented in the group of participants who engaged in resistance practices or rejected legality (see chapter 6). These findings suggest that individuals who have sought out legal marriage are less likely to reject the law within their family lives. In addition, these individuals might be less likely to encounter conflicts that would require acts of resistance as compared to partnered or single individuals. For example, partnered participants were overrepresented in seeking out a social worker who will create a favorable picture of their family (such as describing a non-romantic relationship between partners) and were also more likely to masquerade as single when engaged in adoption. When individuals are married, hiding the relationship becomes more difficult; when individuals are single, there are fewer overt signs of sexuality that must be obscured.

SEX AND GENDER

Sex and gender also shaped the construction of legality for our participants. Sex played a role in affecting the options available for LGBT individuals who wished to have children (see chapter 2). Having biological children is both physically and financially more viable for women than for men. This has notable implications for LGBT individuals on a number of levels. Men are more constrained by the legal environment in which they are nested, as laws or a sociopolitical environment that render adoption an obstacle for gay individuals are more frequently encountered out of necessity. Women, by contrast, might bypass external legal forces through a more private route to parenthood via insemination. Inversely, women struggle with legal concerns connected with the rights of donors or the rights of the nonbiological parent over the child to a greater degree than do men (see chapters 2, 5, and 6). In these respects, men and women interact with their legal context and other mediating factors differently based upon issues related to their sex.

Of those participants who viewed the law as legitimate and a meaning-maker, women were the only ones who indicated that marriage serves to legitimate a family. As discussed in chapter 4, this could be attributed to the greater sanctions that women face from having children when unmarried. Men, by contrast, were overrepresented in adhering to the law because "it's the law" and one should respect its authority.

Men were only slightly overrepresented in the group of participants who viewed the law as something to be manipulated in their favor (see chapter 5). But the ways that male and female participants worked around the law differed in some respects. Men were overrepresented in the group of participants who forum shopped for children. This was largely attributable to the fact that the search for surrogates or more favorable surrogacy laws was one of the most common scenarios in which participants cited crossing jurisdictions in order to have children. For female participants, the ability to have biological children via insemination permitted many women to have children locally without engaging as directly with the law.

Women were much more likely than men to report exploring workarounds, such as alternative guardianships that could substitute for second-parent adoption. In addition, women were more likely to describe using self-taught knowledge or career-related legal knowledge in order to navigate legal forms or situations imbued with legality. Men, by contrast, were disproportionately more likely to describe the utility of having a "good attorney" in order to achieve legal goals. The gender difference between self-help and use of attorneys reflects in part the socioeconomic differences between men and women participants. Finally, approximately 80 percent of participants who described using persistence as a legal tool were gay men. This could reflect gender differences in both the use of aggressive tactics, as well as the ways in which men discuss their approaches to navigating family formation.

Sex also shaped the ways in which participants engaged in resistance tactics or rejecting legality (see chapter 6). In much the same way that women employed creative workarounds to generate legal protections, women were also overrepresented by those participants who reported modifying documents to resist laws or practices that were incompatible with their family. Due in large degree to insemination options for women, women were also overrepresented in taking advantage of unexpected health benefits (e.g., health insurance benefits for fertility treatment) and in engaging in family formation options that rejected heteronormative assumptions. Finally, men were disproportionately overrepresented in the group of participants who rejected legality, suggesting that men were more likely to engage in direct opposition to the law or to frame their discussion of legality in oppositional terms.

Given the relatively small number of transgender participants in our sample, it is difficult to draw conclusions as to whether and how their experiences in navigating legality differed from our other participants. We did observe, however, that transmen were sometimes able to traverse a negative legal environment more successfully due to their ability to gain access to heterosexual marriage. As described in chapter 5, the ability to "pass" as a straight couple carried both benefits and tensions for transgender participants and their partners when forming families.

RACE AND ETHNICITY

Given the limited racial and ethnic diversity within our sample, we did not observe a great deal of variation in approaches that we could attribute to racial and ethnic differences. However, a few differences emerged between white and nonwhite participants. With regard to manipulating the law or treating the law like a game, nonwhite participants were overrepresented in the group of individuals who reported having a "good attorney" as an important tool for achieving family goals (see chapter 5). By contrast, almost all participants who reported accessing social networks as a tool were non-Hispanic white. These findings could suggest that nonwhite LGBT parents experience a relative lack of access to social networks with ties to legal information or legal actors. This absence could result, for some nonwhite LGBT parents, in a greater belief in the importance or necessity of attorneys for achieving family goals.

We also found race and ethnicity distinctions among those participants who masqueraded as single in order to achieve adoption or other family goals (see chapter 6). Nonwhite participants were overrepresented in this group, with Hispanics being particularly overrepresented. We suggest that this finding could indicate that nonwhite LGBT parents feel more pressured to masquerade as single as a strategy to navigate multiple stigmatized identities during the adoption process.

SOCIOECONOMIC STATUS

Socioeconomic status served to shape available routes to parenthood for many individuals. This was most salient in the manner in which men were directed toward biological versus adopted children (see chapter 2). Surrogacy was an option primarily for men with very high incomes due to the extreme associated costs. Many men without a large income discussed selecting foster-to-adopt or other public adoption options due to the relatively low cost.

In addition, education often played a role in enabling individuals to navigate legal documents or the legal system successfully. As noted in chapter 5, for example, individuals with higher levels of education were sometimes able to engage in more self-help when interacting with the law. Socioeconomic status served as an additional layer of protection for LGBT parents, as well, in terms of providing them with a weapon against potential attacks. This notion was communicated aptly by Laura, who observed, "And obviously we're highly educated and wealthy, so we were shielded mainly by class from any kind of vulnerabilities."

A CLOSER LOOK: INDIVIDUAL CHARACTERISTICS

Demographic characteristics, such as sex, race, marital status, and socioeconomic status, interact with mediating and contextual factors in producing legal consciousness for LGBT parents. In this section, we highlight some of the ways in which our participants' stories reflected these interactions.

Several of our participants indicated that their prior marriages to a different-sex partner served to construct their understanding of legality within a very different framework. For individuals who were previously married to a different-sex partner, transitioning to a same-sex partnership was jarring in terms of the ways that their interactions with the legal system shifted. As noted in the earlier story about Mary Ann and Tara, their interactions with authority figures were differently affected by their relationship history. Mary Ann was previously married to a man, whereas Tara did not have this prior experience of privilege derived from her relationship status:

MARY ANN: I think there's a certain amount of heterosexual privilege that I got used to that I'm pretty pissed about not having at the moment. . . . Like when [Tara] started going to doctor's visits, it never occurred to her that I would come back with her. But I'm like, yeah, hello, when you go, the spouse comes back with you. They don't even ask. They're just like, come on, we're going.

TARA: And I had no idea. Because I've never been in a heterosexual relationship. . . . But she came back [with me] and I'm like, can you do this? She's like, uh-huh. So yeah, it's been very interesting. She often says it's like living with somebody who's spent a lot of time on another planet because I've never lived with a man, I've never been in a relationship with a man, and there are just a lot of things I was like, really? Really, that's how that goes?

The prior exposure to heterosexual privilege, in this instance, created expectations for Mary Ann in terms of her right to play a role in her wife's medical care. On the flip side, Tara's sense of what Mary Ann could or could not do was colored in part by having resided in a legally negative state and not having had access to heterosexual privilege. In this respect, their individual life histories intermingled with legal context to generate an understanding about rules and laws. We saw this play out in a similar fashion for couples in chapter 5, where the ability to access heteronormative privilege (particularly for trans individuals) affected the manner in which participants were able to navigate a tenuous legal landscape.

Participants also described ways in which gender interacted with legal context and mediating factors to shape legal consciousness. For Roger, a single, white gay man in his fifties who resides in a legally negative state, surrogacy presents a number of legal concerns for gay men, particularly those residing in a legally negative state. He explained:

For me personally, in thinking about that, there would be all sorts of legal issues that would just kind of throw up red flags for me. Like, having now been through a divorce and knowing we'd share custody, who's going to share custody in a surrogate situation? And would your sexuality come into play should a court have to step in and decide? Because in general, and particularly in [our state], courts tend to side with the mother. So, it could be a scary road for a guy that's wanting children by surrogacy. It could be in traditional ways too, but certainly a little bit easier to sort out. When the court has to step in and sort out a surrogacy issue, usually the person who is giving birth is going to get the child.

Roger's comments clearly highlight the intersection of individual factors, mediating factors, and legal context in generating legal consciousness. As a male, Roger believes he would be at a disadvantage in a surrogacy situation due to the privileging of motherhood by courts. Further, his prior interactions with legal actors generated knowledge regarding how custody battles might play out within families. And his nesting within a conservative, legally negative state made him more uncomfortable about the likelihood of success for a gay man in a custody battle.

Stories such as those of Mary Ann, Tara, and Roger highlight the ways in which individual characteristics interact with legal context and legal actors in the construction of legality for LGBT parents.

Concluding Thoughts

Overall, our findings illustrate that LGBT parenting culture is saturated by legality. Whether individuals are actually aware of the law's presence in their family formation and parenting, as well as the manner in which they interact with the law, varies depending on individual and contextual circumstances. But the role of the law in the family lives of LGBT individuals is virtually unavoidable, as they are much more likely than heterosexual individuals to encounter that moment when their family desires conflict with normative structures. By taking a closer look at LGBT parents specifically, we are able to make a contribution to the growing body of literature that examines the manner in which LGBT individuals understand and interact with the law (e.g., Richman 2008; Hull 2006; Connolly 2002). Prior studies have examined how LGBT individuals process legality pertaining to family-related issues such as marriage ceremonies (Hull 2006, 2003) or navigating second-parent adoption cases in the courtroom (Richman 2008). But less attention has been paid to parenthood, which is often more removed from formal laws due to the notion that family is a private matter (Mather, McEwen, and Maiman 2001; Jacob 1992; Ellickson 1991). In addition to the more overt interactions with formal law, such as those required by the act of marriage or the processing of second-parent adoptions, LGBT parents are surrounded by the law when making decisions about having children, how to have children, and parenting. This study contributes toward gaining an understanding of the more everyday interactions between LGBT individuals and the law with respect to their families.

Further, the rather unique position of LGBT individuals as situated within a patchwork of legality pertaining to their family presents the opportunity to see more directly the effects of legal context on the construction of legal consciousness for individuals. In this respect, our research contributes to legal consciousness studies by allowing the exploration of multilevel interactions in the construction of legality. Prior studies have examined the role of contextual factors in shaping legal consciousness, focusing primarily on the ways in which organizational culture or the location in which an organization is nested affects the construction of legality (see, e.g., Larson 2004; Hoffman 2003; Marshall 2005; Dellinger and Williams 2002). In addition, many studies have examined the manner in which the social identities of oppressed groups (e.g., Nielsen 2000; Merry 1990; Sarat 1990) play a role in shaping legal consciousness. The great degree of inconsistency in legal environments for LGBT parents in the United States provided the opportunity to more directly synthesize these two literatures by exploring the ways in which context affects how a group with a shared identity navigates the law.

Accordingly, rather than focus on individual characteristics or contextual characteristics, our research attempts to complicate the dichotomy by considering the multiplicative effects of individual and contextual characteristics and other moderating group-level factors. Throughout our work, we find that individual characteristics—including characteristics such as sexual orientation—do not work in isolation to produce legal consciousness. Rather, the manner in which being an LGBT individual affects one's outcomes is contextual, depending on the state in which individuals are nested, as well as their interactions with mediating factors within their state like legal actors and social networks. Thus, discussing the experience of LGBT parents with the law is complicated, as their experience is not a homogeneous one. Our findings emphasize the need to understand and study the legal consciousness of LGBT individuals—and any other population—not as a singular experience, but as varied and complex, paying particular attention to context.

Our research also has implications for the existing laws and policies surrounding LGBT families. Although awareness exists of the varied nature of legal environments for LGBT individuals, the implications of this patchwork legality are sometimes lost within broader movements for marriage equality. A recent legal decision by a state judge in New York highlights this disconnect between law and policy, and the actual experiences of LGBT parents who reside in a country with such great variation in legal contexts. The two parents in a second-parent adoption case, Amalia and Melissa, are a legally married couple in New York State (McKinley 2014). Melissa is the biological parent of their child but both of their names were listed on the birth certificate due to the presumption that a child born within a marriage (regardless of whether donor sperm or egg is used) is the child of the couple. Nonetheless, like so many of the participants in our own study, Amalia petitioned to adopt their child in order to secure legal rights given the spottiness in recognition of same-sex marriage.

In January 2014, a judge issued a decision denying the second-parent adoption. The rationale, articulated in her ruling, was that Amalia is already the parent as a result of the legal marriage (McKinley 2014). By granting a second-parent adoption, she argued, the marriages of same-sex couples would be treated differently than those of different-sex couples—as seemingly less authentic, requiring additional legal steps to shore them up. The response to this ruling has been an outcry from legal organizations, such as Lambda Legal, as well as from same-sex couples. The variation in recognition of same-sex marriage leaves nonbiological parents potentially vulnerable when traveling or moving throughout the country or abroad. If the presumption of parenthood derives from the marriage, and the marriage is not recognized in another state, then same-sex couples fear that parenthood rights are also illusory outside of friendly states.

Legally, a ruling such as this one appears facially beneficial for LGBT parents, given that it is derived from equal protection principles requiring the same treatment of different-sex and same-sex marriages. From a policy perspective, however, in terms of generating rights and security for LGBT parents and their children, decisions like these could be misguided. They fail to incorporate considerations of the contextual variation of legality for LGBT parents and, in doing so, can create vulnerabilities for families. As recounted in chapter 3, LGBT parents' understanding of their legal situation is strongly affected by media accounts of cases where parents have traveled or moved and have lost legal rights. From such media stories, fears regarding their tenuous grasp on legal rights—even for those parents living in legally positive states—become reality. Accordingly, as emphasized in chapters 5 and 6, LGBT individuals largely parent within an environment of uncertainty and worry—if not about the situation in their own neighborhood or state, than that within another locale that they might one day visit.

The New York case highlights the need to disentangle legal parenthood from marriage or biological ties. The situation of LGBT parents, with and without access to same-sex marriage, emphasizes the role that the state plays in constructing parent-child relationships and identities for all family types. From a queer theory perspective, we would assume that a greater focus on individuals whose families do not fit within the heteronormative framework of the law will contribute toward a critique of the ways in which the law privileges marriage and biology. In some states, there has been movement toward tying parenthood more to the intention to parent and the perceived benefit to the child, rather than to more traditional ties such as marriage and biology (Andersen 2009). Legalization of same-sex marriage and concerns about variation in recognition of parenthood could push the dialogue toward considering the ways in which similar changes might be needed to continue to address parenthood rights for LGBT individuals—both those who choose to marry and those who do not.

Relatedly, some individuals have raised questions regarding how the recognition of same-sex marriages might ultimately begin to transform the definition of family within the United States. Unlike some parts of Europe, where cohabitation has become a legitimate alternative to marriage (Badgett 2010; Kiernan 2000), marriage continues to serve as an important social institution for shaping identity and outcomes in the United States (Badgett 2010; Powell et al. 2010). Despite evolving definitions of family, legislators and judges privilege marriage through a variety of mechanisms such as decisions involving parenthood, taxes, social welfare programs, and access to health insurance. It remains unclear, therefore, whether LGBT individuals' increasing access to marriage will broaden conceptions of family within the United States, or whether

LGBT persons will gain entry into a legal union that is persistently heteronormative. Legal responses on issues such as parenthood identities will be one area that could provide evidence as to the way in which the battle over marriage might play a role in constructing family-related legalities for both LGBT and heterosexual individuals.

With the publicizing of each legal victory related to same-sex marriage and LGBT parenting, there likely also exists a greater awareness of the disparity in access to rights and privileges across the United States. The patchwork nature of the laws makes inequality more salient for LGBT individuals, as voiced by many of our participants. Most of those living in legally positive states articulated a reluctance to venture to any state with perceived lesser rights, and several also voiced a degree of judgment over LGBT individuals who would live in, or move to, legally negative states. By contrast, those in legally negative states who had experienced greater legal rights in another state or who were well-informed about legal variations indicated more resentment over their family's legal position. The increasing awareness of differential access to equality across legal context, then, becomes part of the discourse about the law which plays a role in shaping LGBT individuals' interactions with legality. In this respect, it is not just that being nested within a particular legal context has an effect on how LGBT individuals construct legality. Rather, the actual *conversation* about contextual variation in laws shapes LGBT individuals' legal consciousness. This results in a greater expectation that LGBT parents should be aware of the differences in laws across legal contexts, and that "good parents" will attempt to gravitate toward locations where the laws most benefit their families.

Overall, our results indicate that the constantly evolving legal landscape for LGBT families would benefit from incorporating an understanding of the ways in which interactions with the law are shaped by the interactive roles of legal context, individual characteristics, and moderating factors such as social networks and legal actors. These considerations will be important, even if same-sex marriage becomes accessible across the United States, as variations in formal law and its implementations will continue to produce conflicts between family needs and available legal rights for the foreseeable future. During that time, LGBT parents are likely to continue to encounter obstacles in providing security and rights for themselves and their children.

APPENDIX: METHODOLOGY

This project was largely derived from our prior demographic studies that drew on nationally representative US census data to explore the manner in which legal context might influence family formation for LGBT individuals. As described in chapter 1, findings based on this work raised questions for us regarding the degree to which LGBT individuals consider the law when forming families and how they understand and use the law as parents. These questions pushed us toward taking a more in-depth, qualitative look at the manner in which legal consciousness is constructed for LGBT parents. As such, we designed this project to address the experiences of LGBT parents with the law, in order to gain a more comprehensive picture of the manner in which legal considerations might play a role in parenthood paths and strategies.

Study Design and Sample Selection

To address our questions, it was important for us to gather a diverse set of parents across varied legal contexts. As described in the introduction, individuals must have been parents or in the process of becoming parents, and identified as LGBT, as being in an LGBT partnership, or previously parented within an LGBT partnership to be considered for the study. Our call specifically requested participants who identify as LGBTQ parents, or are in same-sex relationships. Since we were dealing with a "hidden" or "invisible" population, we recruited our sample via multiple referral chains, using affinity or social groups, formal organization leaders, individuals, and contact lists including social media such as Facebook and Twitter. Because LGBT parents are often subjected to scrutiny from researchers and the public, referrals were an important mechanism for gaining trust and rapport with participants.

We utilized the grounded theory approach, from which we employ the constant comparative method for our data collection and analysis

(Corbin and Strauss 1990; Glaser and Strauss 1967). Following initial interviews with LGBT parents located in two states, we analyzed our data and identified sex and legal context as two variables likely to produce differential outcomes in terms of how LGBT individuals form families and navigate legality. From our interviews with male and female parents, we came to consider how constructions of family might vary according to one's sex. For example, females can more readily have biological children via insemination; consequently, they face different legal considerations in their decision-making for parenthood paths. Drawing on the most recent American Community Survey (2008–2010) at the time of the study's start date, we then stratified based on sex and legal context. The 2008–2010 data included 82 percent female households and 18 percent male households containing children (Gates 2011), thus we sought to construct a sample with a similar sex composition.

In addition, we stratified across legal contexts. This enabled us to focus on a broader analysis of LGBT individuals compared to prior work on legal consciousness, as well as on individuals' interactions with the law in addition to their overall view of legality. A state's legal position on LGBT family issues was reflected by legislation and case law as of the start of our project in 2010. As detailed in chapter 1, states were identified as positive, negative, or legally neutral in terms of their LGBT family laws (adoption, second-parent adoption, fostering, and marriage) dependent on whether (a) the state had a clear (positive or negative) statute on the issue, or (b) the state had a court of appeals or higher judicial decision regarding a family law issue that was still good precedent (i.e., that had not been overturned by a higher court). If a state did not have a clear statute or legal precedent, the state was coded as "legally neutral," meaning that the law was neutral on its face. It was our goal to capture contextual and within-group variations in legal consciousness by sampling participants from all state types. The details regarding our coding process are contained in chapter 1 and, consequently, are not reiterated in the appendix.

Table A.1 depicts how each state, as well as Washington, DC, was coded based upon the legal status as of the start of our project. Legal statuses were derived from data compiled by the Human Rights Campaign (2010), Lambda Legal (2010), and UCLA's Williams Institute (2010). The last three columns of table A.1 indicate our coding of the state as legally

TABLE A.1. State laws based on status as of April 1, 2010

State	Marriage	Gay adoption		Second parent		Foster		State law coding		
		Pro	Anti	Pro	Anti	Pro	Anti	Pos-itive	Neg-ative	Neu-tral
AL										X
AK										X
AZ										X
AR			X		X		X		X	
CA	X	X		X				X		
CO				X				X		
CT	X			X				X		
DC	X	X		X				X		
DE				X				X		
FL			X		X				X	
GA										X
HI										X
ID		X		X				X		
IL		X		X				X		
IN				X				X		
IA	X							X		
KS										X
KY					X				X	
LA										X
ME		X						X		
MD										X
MA	X	X		X				X		
MI			X		X				X	
MN										X
MS			X		X				X	
MO										X
MT										X
NE					X		X		X	
NV										X
NH	X							X		
NJ		X		X				X		
NM										X

TABLE A.1. (*cont.*)

State	Marriage	Gay adoption		Second parent		Foster		State law coding		
		Pro	Anti	Pro	Anti	Pro	Anti	Pos-itive	Neg-ative	Neu-tral
NY		X		X				X		
NC			X		X				X	
ND										X
OH					X				X	
OK										X
OR		X		X				X		
PA				X				X		
RI										X
SC										X
SD										X
TN										X
TX										X
UT					X				X	
VT	X	X		X				X		
VA										X
WA										X
WV										X
WI					X				X	
WY										X
AL										X

positive, legally negative, or legally neutral. We coded a state as positive if it had one or more protective or positive laws that enabled family formation for LGBT individuals, negative for one or more laws that created obstacles to family formation, and legally neutral if there were no relevant laws in place. In selecting our interview sites, we focused on states with more than one positive law for legally positive states, and more than one negative law for legally negative states.

The iterative sampling procedure involved continually reevaluating our sample characteristics in order to bring our final sample in line with these theoretically relevant characteristics (see, e.g., Glaser and Strauss 1967). Data collection continued until saturation had been reached

(Corbin and Strauss 1990; Glaser and Strauss 1967), at which time no new themes were emerging.

Data were collected through semistructured interviews with 137 LGBTQ parents interviewed in 97 interview sessions (some interviews were conducted with couples) across the United States between 2010 to 2012. Approximately 61 percent of participants were interviewed with their partners, of which 40 percent resided in legally negative states, 35 percent in legally neutral states, and 25 percent in legally positive states. We were cognizant of the potential effects of interviewing in couples rather than individually, but no clear differences emerged across interview structures. Couples were more likely to call upon each other to refresh recollections regarding dates or details of events.

All participants went through the informed consent process. Further, participants were provided the opportunity to review any quotes used within the final book manuscript. A flexible interview structure allowed us to focus conversations around participants' experiences and interests. The interviews covered topics including basic demographic information for all family members, factors influencing the decision to become a parent, method of becoming a parent, and everyday parenting decisions. In addition to asking probing questions about the role of the law at each of these stages of the parenting process, we also included questions designed to probe whether and how parenting outcomes were affected by interactions with legal actors, social networks, organizations, media, and legal context. The full interview schedule is available upon request.

The interviews were conducted in person (85 percent) and by phone (15 percent); in-person interviews were conducted at a location chosen by the subject. Both authors were present for 75 percent of the interviews, while 25 percent were conducted by only one of the authors. We are both Caucasian females, with one of us identifying as heterosexual and one identifying as nonheterosexual, and one of us being a parent and the other a nonparent at the time of the interviews. On average, interviews were about an hour and a half long and ranged in length from just under an hour to three hours.

Additional details regarding our interview process are discussed in the introduction.

Data Analysis

Coding categories were formulated inductively, as part of the ongoing data collection process as well as after the completion of data collection (Charmaz 2001; Glaser and Strauss 1967). Our primary coding involved identifying routes to parenthood and identifying categories of legal consciousness—drawing on Ewick and Silbey's three schemas of legal consciousness. We then developed secondary codes related to sources of legality. Finally, we coded across categories of explanations for parents' ultimate decision-making regarding parenthood paths and the employment of attorneys or the law, along with mediating factors such as social networks, interactions with legal actors, and the media; and individual factors, including familial desires and demographic and socioeconomic characteristics.

Both researchers participated in the coding process. Approximately, 10 percent of the interviews were coded by both researchers; the remainder were divided equally between the authors and coded independently across the agreed-upon categories. Further, we continually consulted with each other throughout the coding process to ensure a high level of agreement.

As part of our data analysis, we included approximate percentages of participants falling into our coding categories, as well as the approximate breakdown by legal context and demographic characteristics (see chapters 3–6). We appreciate the way in which delineating breakdowns across contexts, groups, and demographic characteristics allowed us to demonstrate more directly the interactions that comprise the construction of legality. In particular, we believe that these breakdowns allowed us to identify patterns, which led to the development of our theory regarding the legal consciousness of LGBT parents. Nonetheless, we would like to emphasize that categories overlap, participants often fall into more than one category, and some themes might not have emerged as clearly as others (resulting in not being fully captured in these breakdowns). Thus, these percentages are estimates calculated to reflect patterns rather than an attempt to categorize participants into mutually exclusive boxes, and to then quantify those behaviors and beliefs related to the law. We believe, ultimately, that what we are measuring is too complex to fully quantify—a belief that directed us from an assessment of census data and toward an interview-based project.

Sample Characteristics

This study reports on results from a sample of 137 LGBT parents. Sample characteristics are summarized in tables I.1 and I.2 in the introduction. In this section, we provide a summary of how our sample characteristics compare with those of same-sex partners captured by the US Census Bureau's American Community Survey (ACS) data, a nationally representative survey. According to the ACS, women are much more likely to be same-sex parents, with only 20 percent of parents in the ACS being male, while 80 percent are female (Gates 2013). Our participants mirrored the composition of the ACS, with 78 percent of our participants identifying as female, 17 percent male, and 5 percent as transgender. In terms of self-identified sexual orientation, 80 percent of our sample identified as gay or lesbian or homosexual, while 5 percent identified as bisexual, and 15 percent as queer. Regarding marital status, 43 percent identified as legally married, 43 percent identified as partnered, and 14 percent as single. The average age of our participants is thirty-nine, with the youngest parent being twenty-three and the eldest parent at seventy years old.

The ACS data further indicate same-sex parents are more racially and ethnically diverse than same-sex partners as a whole (Gates 2013), and also compared to our participants. Gates (2013) found that 39 percent of same-sex parents living with children under eighteen were racial and ethnic minorities. While our participants are mostly non-Hispanic white (84 percent), their households are fairly diverse with 37 percent living in transracial households. Thus, at the household-level our participants are more racially aligned with the ACS data due to the presence of partners or children of a different race than the participant.

Our participants, on average, had some college education, which is comparable to the ACS data on same-sex partners (Gates 2013). Economically, ACS data indicate that same-sex couples raising children have a median income of $64,000 and those that report biological children have a median income of $86,000 (Gates 2013; Krivickas and Lofquist 2011). The household income for the participants in our sample ranged from $9,000 to $800,000 annually, with a median household income of $100,000. The higher median income for our sample is largely driven by our participants who have undergone adoption or surrogacy. The median income of our participants who identified their children as biological via heterosexual relationships was the lowest of all parenthood routes at $77,000 (see table 2.1), and likely reflected the inclusion of single parents within our study whereas the ACS data only include partnered individuals. Many of these differences between our sample and the ACS data are attributable in part to our study focus (in seeking out diversity among routes to parenthood), and to our sample being derived partially from linked social networks and participation in LGBT organizations, which are disproportionately white and higher income.

We have also included a summary of sample characteristics at the household level. As reflected in table A.2, we interviewed participants located in ninety-seven households. In terms of geographic variation, 39 percent of our households came from legally positive states, 30 percent from legally neutral states, and 31 percent from legally negative states. The median household income was $100,000, with the highest median household income reported in legally neutral states, followed by legally positive states, and legally negative states with the lowest median household income. Although 84 percent of our participants were non-Hispanic white (see table I.2), approximately 37 percent were from transracial households, meaning that they contained partners or children who were of different races or ethnicities or both. Approximately 20 percent of the households were single-headed, with a disproportionate number of these located in legally neutral states.

Table A.3 reflects the characteristics of our participants' children, by legal context. In total, our participants were parents to 114 children; some of these children were shared across partnered participants, thus there are fewer children than total participants in the study. The average age of participants' children was 8.5 years, and 56 percent are male. Children reflected greater racial diversity, with 71 percent being non-Hispanic white; greater racial and ethnic diversity was reflected in legally neutral states (58 percent white) and legally negative states (71 percent white) than in legally positive states (84 percent white). Approximately 79 percent of children lived in the home with participants; this varied across legal contexts, with 91 percent of children living in the home in legally positive states, 81 percent in legally negative states, and only 65 percent in legally neutral states.

TABLE A.2. Household characteristics, by legal context

Demographic characteristics	All		Positive state		Neutral state		Negative state	
	N	%	n	%	n	%	n	%
Number of households	97	100	38	39.2	29	29.9	30	31.0
Median household income ($)	100,000		105,000		110,000		97,000	
Transracial household	36	37	14	37.0	13	45.0	9	30.0
Female household	72	74	31	82.0	18	62.0	23	77.0
Single-headed household	19	20	5	13.0	9	31.0	5	17.0
Routes to parenthood								
Heterosexual intercourse	25	26	4	11.0	11	38.0	10	33.0
Insemination	68	70	25	66.0	17	59.0	26	87.0
Adoption	37	38	12	32.0	17	59.0	8	27.0
State	22	23	7	18.0	10	34.0	5	17.0
Private	7	7	3	8.0	3	10.0	1	3.0
International	8	8	3	8.0	3	10.0	2	7.0
Foster	7	7	2	5.0	5	17.0	0	0.0
Surrogacy	5	5	1	3.0	3	10.0	1	3.0
Other	8	8	2	5.0	3	10.0	3	10.0
Legally heterosexual household	3	3	1	3.0	0	0.0	2	7.0

TABLE A.3. Characteristics of participants' children

Demographic characteristics	All		Positive state		Neutral state		Negative state	
	N	%	n	%	n	%	n	%
Number of children	114	100	43	38	40	35	31	27
Average age	8.5		6.6		8.6		10.9	
Female	50	44	19	44	18	45	13	42
Race and ethnicity								
White	81	71	36	84	23	58	22	71
Black	7	6	1	2	6	15	0	0
Other	2	2	0	0	0	0	2	6
Multiracial	15	13	3	7	6	15	1	3
Hispanic	9	8	3	7	5	13	6	19
In home	90	79	39	91	26	65	25	81
Shared custody	9	8	2	5	6	15	2	6

A Note on Terminology

We recognize the complexity of, and diversity within, the LGBT community, especially as related to individual identities and the labels by which individuals are most comfortable referring to their selves and their families. Covering issues related to the LGBT community often involves a "rhetorically charged climate" (GLAAD 2010, 2). It is important to us that we both acknowledge and reflect the range of diversity of our respondents, their families, and their experiences. As such, we have opted to follow the Gay and Lesbian Alliance Against Defamation (GLAAD) Media Reference Guide (2010) regarding our language and terminology, referring to our participants as LGBT. We select this particular terminology because it is in line with what are both common and accepted labels in the gay and lesbian communities, as well as in the academic literature (Baumle, Compton, and Poston 2009; Badgett 2001; Boswell 1980). Further, these terms communicate a largely shared understanding of sexual orientation and gender.

We predominantly use LGBT to refer to the greater community in order to be more inclusive of varying identifications of sexual orientation, sex, and gender. When referring to our respondents specifically, we will use the identity and terms in which they self-identified in their interview. For example, a number of respondents identified as queer. The term *queer* is used by some scholars and laypersons to describe an inclusive gay, lesbian, bisexual, and transgender community and in reference to queer theory to denote culturally marginal sexual self-identifications (Jagose 1996). In speaking specifically of our respondents who identify as queer and of their experience, we refer to them by their chosen identity. Given, however, that this term has not been completely reclaimed and is largely considered to be a derogatory term by mainstream American culture and by many of those within the LGBT community (GLAAD 2010), we do not use *queer* as a general descriptor. The same holds for the term *homosexual* (GLAAD 2010; Baumle, Compton, and Poston 2009; Risman and Schwartz 1988; Boswell 1980; Foucault 1978), which possesses negative connotations particularly as related to the labeling of gay individuals as psychologically deviant and is largely considered out-of-date.

The category of *LGBT families* does apply to the majority of our families and we use it to reference them, especially those parents in same-sex relationships, unless they otherwise specifically identify. For example, we had a few families indicate that one parent was bisexual while the other was not. In this case, we still refer to their family as an LGBT family reflecting that the partners are of the same sex, however the individual is referred to as bisexual. Further, we use *gay families* and *lesbian families* when making points related to gender differences. *Families* also refers to any family with an LGBT parent and child, irrespective of the parent's partnered or marital status. Thus, our usage of LGBT families is also inclusive of single parents.

When drawing on the census data, we refer to *same-sex partners*, as these data are only able to speak to persons who are in self-identified same-sex partnered relationships. Consequently, our analysis of census data excludes LGBT individuals who are single or couples that do not live in the same primary residences. Nor does the census data allow us to capture those who would not identify as being in a "marriage-like" relationship with a same-sex partner or who might be in such relationships, but choose not to identify their relationships on the census form. Census data also do not permit a direct examination of the demographics of individuals who are bisexual or transgender, although some of these persons might have identified themselves as same-sex unmarried partners and therefore be participants in the analyses (Baumle et al. 2009). Thus, at all times when we reference census data in this work, we are discussing the demographic outcomes of partnered individuals and will reference them as such.

Lastly, due to the absence of negative connotations associated with the term, we use *heterosexual* as both noun and adjective to refer to and describe individuals and their communities (GLAAD 2010; Baumle, Compton, and Poston 2009; Katz 1995).

Prior Studies and Census Data Analyses

The addition of the same-sex unmarried partner category to the US census in 1990 opened the door for demographers to pay greater attention to the ways in which variables of sexual orientation might be incorporated within demographic research. Since these data became available for studying same-sex unmarried partners, we have drawn upon the data to examine demographic patterns and issues of sexual orientation.

In work that we refer to as "the demography of sexual orientation," two of our studies examined the manner in which individual contextual characteristics affected family outcomes for same-sex partners. We introduce these studies in chapter 1, with special focus on the manner in which legal context affects family outcomes for same-sex families. For details regarding the methods, coding of variables, and the full outcomes of the analyses of these studies, refer to Baumle and Compton (2011) and Baumle and Compton (2013).

NOTES

CHAPTER 1. THE STATE OF THE LAW FOR LGBT PARENTS

1 California, Connecticut, Delaware, Illinois, Iowa, Maine, Maryland, Massachusetts, Minnesota, New Hampshire, New Jersey, New Mexico, New York, Rhode Island, Washington.

2 Michigan second-parent adoptions were ceased as a result of a guiding memorandum from Judge Archie Brown (2002) and a position statement from the Michigan Attorney General (2004).

3 California, Colorado, Connecticut, Delaware, District of Columbia, Hawaii, Idaho, Illinois, Indiana, Iowa, Maine, Maryland, Massachusetts, Minnesota, Montana, Nevada, New Hampshire, New Jersey, New Mexico, New York, Oregon, Pennsylvania, Rhode Island, Vermont, and Washington.

4 This approach allowed us to simultaneously examine the role of individual-level predictors of having children (such as age, education, race, etc.) and state-level contextual factors (such as sociopolitical climate, economic climate, and—most importantly—state-level laws).

5 Twelve states (Arizona, Arkansas, Colorado, Connecticut, Florida, Michigan, Nebraska, Nevada, New York, Ohio, Tennessee, and Wisconsin) had statutes or judicial decisions that could be classified as being negative gay family laws (Lambda Legal 2006; National Gay and Lesbian Task Force Organization 2006a; National Gay and Lesbian Task Force Organization 2006b; Soulforce 2006; Blanks, Dockwell, and Wallance 2004).

6 As of the 2000 census, only five states (Illinois, Massachusetts, New Jersey, New York, and Vermont) and Washington, DC, had any sort of positive family parenting laws or case law (Lambda Legal 2006; National Gay and Lesbian Task Force Organization 2006a; National Gay and Lesbian Task Force Organization 2006b; Soulforce 2006; Blanks, Dockwell, and Wallance 2004).

7 Due to the limited number of prosurrogacy or fostering laws, we could not consider the effect of these laws separately.

8 Legal statuses were derived from data compiled by the Human Rights Campaign (2010), Lambda Legal (2010), and UCLA's Williams Institute (2010).

9 We focused on courts of appeals or higher decisions, given that such decisions tend to serve as persuasive precedent for peer courts or district courts in other geographic jurisdictions, and as binding precedent for district courts in their jurisdiction. A decision by a single district court, on the other hand, would be af-

forded less weight by other courts and serves as less of a signal of the state of the law.

10 Information regarding legislation and caselaw was derived from data compiled by the Human Rights Campaign (2010), Lambda Legal (2010), and UCLA's Williams Institute (2010).

CHAPTER 2. ROUTES TO PARENTHOOD

1 Our sample included one man who coparents with a lesbian couple categorized under insemination, and five transmen who were included in the insemination category.

2 The NSFG does not ask a similar question of men.

REFERENCES

Albiston, Catherine. 1999. "The Rule of Law and the Litigation Process: The Paradox of Losing by Winning." *Law and Society Review* 33 (4): 869–910.

Appell, A. R. 2001. "Legal Intersections: Lesbian and Gay Adoption." *Adoption Quarterly* 4 (3): 75–86.

Baca Zinn, Maxine, and D. Stanley Eitzen. 2008. *Diversity in Families*. 5th ed. New York: Longman.

Badgett, M. V. Lee. 2001. *Money, Myths, and Change: The Economic Lives of Lesbian and Gay Men*. Chicago: University of Chicago Press.

———. 2010. *When Gay People Get Married: What Happens When Societies Legalize Same-Sex Marriage*. New York: New York University Press.

———. 2013. "Demographics of Same-Sex Marriages." In *International Handbook on the Demography of Sexuality*, edited by Amanda K. Baumle. Dordrecht, NL: Springer Press.

Baer, Judith. 1999. *Our Lives before the Law: Constructing a Feminist Jurisprudence*. Princeton, NJ: Princeton University Press.

Baker v. State of Vermont, 744 A.2d 864 (Vt. 1999).

Baumle, Amanda K., and D'Lane R. Compton. 2011. "Legislating the Family: The Effect of State Family Laws on the Presence of Children in Same-Sex Households." *Law and Policy* 33 (1): 82–115.

———. 2013. "Heterogeneity of Parent-Child Relationships in Same-Sex Households." Paper presented at American Sociological Association's Annual Meeting, New York.

———. 2014. "Identity versus Identification: How LGBTQ Parents Identify their Children on Census Surveys." *Journal of Marriage and Family* 76 (1): 94–104.

Baumle, Amanda K., D'Lane R. Compton, and Dudley L. Poston Jr. 2009. *Same-Sex Partners: The Demography of Sexual Orientation*. Albany: State University of New York Press.

Baumle, Amanda K., and Dudley L. Poston. 2011. "The Economic Cost of Being Homosexual: A Multilevel Analysis." *Social Forces* 89 (3): 1005–1031.

Biblarz, Timothy, and Evren Savci. 2010. "Lesbian, Gay, Bisexual, and Transgender Families." *Journal of Marriage and Family* 72 (3): 480–497.

Boot v. Boot, 2001 Mich. App. LEXIS 607 (Mich. Ct. App. 2001).

Boswell, John. 1980. *Christianity, Social Tolerance, and Homosexuality*. Chicago: University of Chicago Press.

Brown, S., and W. Manning. 2009. "Family Boundary Ambiguity and the Measurement of Family Structure: The Significance of Cohabitation." *Demography* 46 (1): 85–101.

Cahill, Sean, Mitra Ellen, and Sarah Tobias. 2002. *Family Policy: Issues Affecting Gay, Lesbian, Bisexual, and Transgender Families*. New York: National Gay and Lesbian Task Force Policy Institute.

Charmaz, Kathy. 2001. "Grounded Theory." In *Contemporary Field Research: Perspectives and Formulations*, edited by Robert M. Emerson, 335–352. Prospect Heights, IL: Waveland.

Chua, Lynette J. 2012. "Pragmatic Resistance, Law, and Social Movements in Authoritarian States: The Case of Gay Collective Action in Singapore." *Law and Society Review* 46 (4): 714–748.

Cochran, J. K., and M. B. Chamlin. 2000. "Deterrence and Brutalization: The Dual Effects of Executions." *Justice Quarterly* 17 (4): 685–706.

Collins, Patricia Hill. 1986. "Learning from the Outsider Within: The Sociological Significance of Black Feminist Thought." *Social Problems* 33 (6): S14–S32.

Connolly, Catherine. 2002. "The Voice of the Petitioner: The Experiences of Gay and Lesbian Parents in Successful Second-Parent Adoption Proceedings." *Law and Society Review* 36 (2): 325–346.

Coontz, Stephanie. 2000. *The Way We Never Were: American Families and the Nostalgia Trap*. New York: Basic Books.

Corbin, Juliet, and Anselm Strauss. 1990. "Grounded Theory Method: Procedures, Canons, and Evaluative Criteria." *Qualitative Sociology* 13 (1): 3–21.

Crenshaw, Kimberlé. 1995. "Race, Reform, and Retrenchment: Transformation and Legitimation in Antidiscrimination Law." In *Critical Race Theory: The Key Readings that Formed the Movement*, edited by Kimberlé Crenshaw, Neil Gotanda, Gary Peller, and Kendall Thomas, 103–122. New York: New Press.

Davis, Mary Ann. 2011. *Children for Families or Families for Children: The Demography of Adoption Behavior in the US*. New York: Springer.

Dellinger, Kirsten, and Christine L. Williams. 2002. "The Locker Room and the Dorm Room: Workplace Norms and the Boundaries of Sexual Harassment in Magazine Editing." *Social Problems* 49 (2): 242–257.

Demo, David H., Katherine R. Allen, Mark A. Fine. 2000. "An Overview of Family Diversity: Controversies, Questions, and Values." *Handbook of Family Diversity*. New York: Oxford University Press.

Dorf, Michael C., and Sidney Tarrow. 2013. "Strange Bedfellows: How an Anticipatory Countermovement Brought Same-Sex Marriage into the Public Arena." *Law and Social Inquiry* 39 (2): 449–473.

Ellickson, Robert C. 1991. *Order without Law: How Neighbors Settle Disputes*. Cambridge, MA: Harvard University Press.

Ewick, Patricia, and Susan Silbey. 1998. *The Common Place of Law: Stories from Everyday Life*. Chicago: University of Chicago Press.

Florida Adoption Act, Fla. Stat. § 63-042-3 (2003).

Foucault, Michel. 1978. *The History of Sexuality*. Vol. 1. New York: Pantheon Books.

Fritsvold, Erik D. 2009. "Under the Law: Legal Consciousness and Radical Environmental Activism." *Law and Society Review* 34 (4): 799–824.

Garner, Abigail. 2005. *Families Like Mine: Children of Gay Parents Tell It Like It Is.* New York: HarperCollins.

Gates, Gary J. 2007. *Geographic Trends among Same-Sex Couples in the US Census and the American Community Survey.* Los Angeles: Williams Institute, UCLA.

———. 2011. "Family Formation and Raising Children among Same-Sex Couples." *National Council on Family Relations.* Issue FF51. http://williamsinstitute.law.ucla.edu/wp-content/uploads/Gates-Badgett-NCFR-LGBT-Families-December-2011.pdf.

———. 2013. *Same Sex and Different Sex Couples in the American Community Survey: 2005–2011.* Los Angeles: Williams Institute, UCLA. http://williamsinstitute.law.ucla.edu/research/census-LGBT-demographics-studies/ss-and-ds-couples-in-acs-2005-2011/.

Gates, Gary, and Lee Badgett. 2007. *Adoption and Foster Care by Gay and Lesbian Parents in the United States.* Los Angeles: Williams Institute, UCLA.

Gay and Lesbian Alliance Against Defamation (GLAAD). 2010. *Media Reference Guide.* 8th ed. New York: Gay and Lesbian Alliance Against Defamation. http://www.glaad.org/files/MediaReferenceGuide2010.pdf.

Glaser, Barney G., and Anselm L. Strauss. 1967. *The Discovery of Grounded Theory: Strategies for Qualitative Research.* Chicago: Aldine.

Goldberg, Abbie. 2012. *Gay Dads: Transitions to Adoptive Fatherhood.* New York: New York University Press.

Halberstam, Judith, and Jacob C. Hale. 1998. "Butch/FTM Border Wars: A Note on Collaboration." *GLQ: A Journal of Lesbian and Gay Studies* 4 (2): 283–285.

Henehan, D., E. D. Rothblum, S. E. Solomon, and K. F. Balsam. 2007. "Social and Demographic Characteristics of Gay, Lesbian, and Heterosexual Adults with and without Children." *GLBT Family Studies* 3 (2–3): 35–79.

Hastings, Chris, and Susan Bissett. 2002. "Councils Encourage Gay Adoption." *Telegraph*, November 3. http://www.telegraph.co.uk/news/uknews/1412032/Councils-encourage-gay-adoption.html.

Hoffman, Elizabeth A. 2003. "Legal Consciousness and Dispute Resolution: Different Disputing Behavior at Two Similar Taxicab Companies." *Law and Social Inquiry* 28 (3): 691–716.

Hull, Kathleen. 2003. "The Cultural Power of Law and the Cultural Enactment of Legality: The Case of Same-Sex Marriage." *Law and Social Inquiry* 28 (3): 629–657.

———. 2006. *Same-Sex Marriage: The Cultural Politics of Love and Law.* New York: Cambridge University Press.

Human Rights Campaign. 2010. "Maps of State Laws and Policies." http://www.hrc.org/resources/entry/maps-of-state-laws-policies.

———. 2014. "Second Parent Adoption." http://hrc-assets.s3-website-us-east-1.amazonaws.com//files/assets/resources/second_parent_adoption_6-10-2014.pdf.

Irish v. Irish, 300 N.W.2d 739, 741 (Mich. Ct. App. 1980).

Jacob, Herbert. 1992. "The Elusive Shadow of the Law." *Law and Society Review* 26 (3): 565–590.

Jagose, Annamarie. 1996. *Queer Theory: An Introduction*. New York: New York University Press.

Katz, Johnathan. 1995. *The Invention of Heterosexuality*. New York: Penguin Books.

Kiernan, K. 2000. "European Perspectives on Union Formation." In *Ties That Bind: Perspectives on Marriage and Cohabitation*, edited by Linda Waite, C. Bachrach, M. Hindin, E. Thomson, and A. Thornton, 40–58. New York: Aldine de Gruyter.

Krivickas, K. M., and D. Lofquist. 2011. "Demographics of Same-Sex Couple Households with Children." Washington DC: US Bureau of the Census. http://www.census.gov/hhes/samesex/files/Krivickas-Lofquist%20PAA%202011.pdf.

Lambda Legal. N.d. "In Your State." New York: Lambda Legal. http://www.lambdalegal.org/states-regions.

———. 2010. "Overview of State Adoption Laws." New York: Lambda Legal. http://www.lambdalegal.org/cgi-bin/iowa/documents/record2.html?record=1923 (no longer available online).

Lareau, Annette. 2003. *Unequal Childhoods: Class, Race, and Family Life*. Berkeley: University of California Press.

Larson, Erik. 2004. "Institutionalizing Legal Consciousness: Regulation and the Embedding of Market Participants in the Securities Industry in Ghana and Fiji." *Law and Society Review* 38 (4): 737–767.

Lewin, Ellen. 2009. *Gay Fatherhood: Narratives of Family and Citizenship in America*. Chicago: University of Chicago Press.

Louisiana Adoption Act, La. Ch. C. § 1198 (2004), 1221 (2004).

Macaulay, Stewart. 1979. "Lawyers and Consumer Protection Laws." *Law and Society Review* 14 (1): 115–171.

Marshall, Anna-Maria. 2005. "Idle Rights: Employees' Rights Consciousness and the Construction of Sexual Harassment Policies." *Law and Society Review* 39 (1): 83–124.

Marshall, Anna-Maria, and Scott Barclay. 2003. "In Their Own Words: How Ordinary People Construct the Legal World." *Law and Social Inquiry* 28 (3): 617–628.

Mather, Lynn, Craig A. McEwen, and Richard J. Maiman. 2001. *Divorce Lawyers at Work: Varieties of Professionalism in Practice*. New York: Oxford University Press.

McKinely, James C. 2014. "N.Y. Judge Alarms Gay Parents by Finding Marriage Law Negates Need for Adoption." *New York Times*, January 28. http://www.nytimes.com/2014/01/29/nyregion/ny-judge-alarms-gay-parents-by-finding-marriage-law-negates-need-for-adoption.html?_r=0.

Meadow, Tey. 2013. "Queer Numbers: Social Science as Cultural Heterosexism." Paper presented at American Sociological Association's Annual Meeting, New York City. August 12. http://socialinqueery.com/2013/08/14/queer-numbers-social-science-as-cultural-heterosexism/.

Merry, Sally Engle. 1990. *Getting Justice and Getting Even: Legal Consciousness Among Working-Class Americans*. Chicago: University of Chicago Press.

Moore, Mignon. 2011. *Invisible Families: Gay Identities, Relationships, and Motherhood among Black Women*. Berkeley: University of California Press.

National Gay and Lesbian Task Force Organization. 2006a. "Adoption Laws in the US." New York: National Gay and Lesbian Task Force. http://www.thetaskforce.org/downloads/AdoptionLaws.pdf.

———. 2006b. "Foster Care Regulations in the US." New York: National Gay and Lesbian Task Force. http://www.thetaskforce.org/downloads/FosteringMap.pdf.

Nielsen, Laura Beth. 2000. "Situating Legal Consciousness: Experiences and Attitudes of Ordinary Citizens about Law and Street Harassment." *Law and Society Review* 34 (4): 1055–1090.

Polikoff, Nancy. 2008. *Beyond (Straight and Gay) Marriage: Valuing All Families under the Law.* Boston, MA: Beacon Press.

Powell, Brian, Catherine Bolzendahl, Claudia Geis, and Lala Carr Steelman. 2010. *Counted Out: Same-Sex Relations and Americans' Definitions of Family.* New York: Russell Sage Foundation.

Richman, Kimberly. 2008. *Courting Change: Queer Parents, Judges, and the Transformation of American Family Law.* New York: New York University Press.

———. 2013. *License to Wed: What Legal Marriage Means to Same-Sex Couples.* New York: New York University Press.

Riggs, Diane. 1999. "Two Steps Forward, One Step Back: Single and Gay Adoption in North America." North American Council on Adoptable Children. http://www.nacac.org/adoptalk_articles/two_steps.html (no longer available online).

Risman, Barbara. 2009. *Families as They Really Are.* New York: W. W. Norton.

Risman, Barbara, and Pepper Schwartz. 1988. "Sociological Research on Male and Female Homosexuality." *Annual Review of Sociology* 14: 125–147.

Rousseau, Jean-Jacques. (1762) 1997. "Of the Social Contract." In *"The Social Contract" and Other Later Political Writings,* edited by V. Gourevitch, 39–152. Cambridge: Cambridge University Press.

Sarat, Austin D. 1990. "'The Law Is All Over': Power, Resistance, and the Legal Consciousness of the Welfare Poor." *Yale Journal of Law and the Humanities* 2 (2): 343–378.

Silbey, Susan. 2005. "After Legal Consciousness." *Annual Review of Law and Social Science* no. 1: 323–368.

Soulforce. 2006. "Discrimination in Adoption and Foster Care of Children." Lynchburg, VA: Soulforce. http://www.archives.soulforce.org/1998/01/01/discrimination-in-adoption-and-foster-care-of-children/.

Stacey, Judith. 2011. *Unhitched: Love, Marriage, and Family Values from West Hollywood to Western China.* New York: New York University Press.

Stacey, Judith, and Timothy J. Biblarz. 2001. "(How) Does the Sexual Orientation of Parents Matter?" *American Sociological Review* 66 (2): 159–183.

Stolzenberg, Ross M., and Linda J. Waite. 2005. "Effects of Marriage, Divorce, and Widowhood on Health." In *Work, Family, Health and Well-Being,* edited by Suzanne M. Bianchi, Lynne M. Casper, and Rosalind B. King, 36–77. Mahwah, NJ: Lawrence Erlbaum Associates.

Thornton, Arland, and Linda Young-Demarco. 2004. "Four Decades of Trends in Attitudes toward Family Issues in the United States: The 1960s through the 1990s." *Journal of Marriage and Family* 63 (4): 1009–1037.

Vermont Adoption Act, Vt. Stat. Ann. tit. 15, § 1-102(b) (2003).

Waite, Linda J. 2005. "Marriage and Family." In *Handbook of Population*, edited by Dudley L. Poston and Michael Micklin, 87–108. New York: Kluwer Academic/Plenum Press.

Wardle, Lynn, and Travis Robertson. 2013. "Adoption: Upside Down and Sideways? Some Causes of and Remedies for Declining Domestic and International Adoptions." *Regent University Law Review* 26 (1): 209–270.

William's Institute. 2010. "Research by State." Los Angeles: Williams Institute, UCLA. http://williamsinstitute.law.ucla.edu/#mapwrap.

Wilson, Joshua C. 2011. "Sustaining the State: Legal Consciousness and the Construction of Legality in Competing Abortion Activists' Narratives." *Law and Social Inquiry* 36 (2): 455–483.

Weston, Kath. 1991. *Families We Choose: Lesbians, Gays, Kinship*. New York: Columbia University Press.

Yngvesson, Barbara. 1997. "Negotiating Motherhood: Identity and Difference in 'Open' Adoptions." *Law and Society Review* 31 (1): 31–80.

INDEX

ACLU. *See* American Civil Liberties
Union
ACS. *See* American Community Survey
administrative/organizational resources,
5, 18, 31, 53, 55–56, 72, 108, 112–14, 118,
123, 125, 127, 134, 163–66, 173–74, 181–82,
189–90, 204–5, 210–14, 217–18, 220,
224, 227, 233, 240–41, 252–55
   as "affirming," 112–14
   and legal constraints, 127
   "legitimates" family, 118
   and persistence, 182. *See also* persistence
   personal relationship with, 72, 182,
212, 233, 253–55
   and transgender, 163–66
   See also birth certificates; passports;
social security cards
administrative workers, 72, 182, 212, 233,
253–55
adoption, ix, 2, 4, 7, 11–12, 14, 16, 19, 21–23,
25–32, 35–41, 44–46, 48–56, 58–60, 62–
67, 72–78, 80–85, 87–88, 90, 93–96, 98–
99, 101–2, 105–6, 108–12, 115, 118–20,
123, 125, 131, 133–34, 136–45, 148–59, 170,
190–95, 243–44, 251, 257–64, 268–70,
273, 275, 279n2
   as "affirming," 111–12
   and affordability, 52
   and assumptions of legality, 98–99
   and attorneys, 63–77
   and bans on gay adoption, ix
   and fostering, 49–56. *See also* foster-
to-adopt programs; fostering

   and a "good attorney," 170
   and Internet knowledge, 74–75
   and law "makes them a parent," 109.
See also legitimacy
   by legal context (table), 50–56
   and legal paperwork, 65
   and masquerading. *See* masquerading
   and self-readings of the law, 77–78
   See also international adoption;
private adoption; second-parent
adoption; "secret" adoptions
Adoption and Foster Care Reporting
System, 49
"against the law," 6, 8, 17, 189–233
   and challenging unfair practices,
220–24
   defined, 6
   and demographics, 228–29
   and disrupting recorded documents,
210–15
   and "following the rules," 190–200
   and masquerading as single, 200–
210. *See also* masquerading
   and rejecting legal heteronormativity, 215–19
   and rejecting the law, 224–26
   See also resistance
agency, 5, 7, 10, 15, 17–18, 23, 125, 133, 168,
177, 239, 256
American Civil Liberties Union (ACLU),
88
American Community Survey (ACS), 13–
14, 27–28, 30, 273–74

ABOUT THE AUTHORS

Amanda K. Baumle is Associate Professor of Sociology at the University of Houston. She is the co-author of *Same-Sex Partners: The Demography of Sexual Orientation* and the author of *Sex Discrimination and Law Firm Culture on the Internet.*

D'Lane R. Compton is Associate Professor of Sociology at the University of New Orleans. She is the co-author of *Same-Sex Partners: The Demography of Sexual Orientation.*